ALTERED EARTH

Altered Earth aims to get the Anthropocene right in three senses. With essays by leading scientists, it highlights the growing consensus that our planet entered a dangerous new state in the mid-twentieth century. Second, it tries to get the Anthropocene right in human terms, bringing together a range of leading authors to explore, in fiction and non-fiction, our deep past, global conquest, inequality, nuclear disasters, and space travel. Finally, this landmark collection presents what hope might look like in this seemingly hopeless situation, proposing new political forms and mutualistic cities. "Right" in this book means being as *accurate* as possible in describing the physical phenomenon of the Anthropocene; as *balanced* as possible in weighing the complex human developments, some willed and some unintended, that led to this predicament; and as *just* as possible in envisioning potential futures.

JULIA ADENEY THOMAS is an intellectual historian of Japan and the Anthropocene, and Associate Professor of History at the University of Notre Dame, Indiana.

T0381668

ALTERED EARTH

Getting the Anthropocene Right

Edited by

Julia Adeney Thomas

CAMBRIDGE
UNIVERSITY PRESS

CAMBRIDGE
UNIVERSITY PRESS

University Printing House, Cambridge CB2 8BS, United Kingdom

One Liberty Plaza, 20th Floor, New York, NY 10006, USA

477 Williamstown Road, Port Melbourne, VIC 3207, Australia

314–321, 3rd Floor, Plot 3, Splendor Forum, Jasola District Centre,
New Delhi – 110025, India

103 Penang Road, #05-06/07, Visioncrest Commercial, Singapore 238467

Cambridge University Press is part of the University of Cambridge.

It furthers the University's mission by disseminating knowledge in the pursuit of
education, learning, and research at the highest international levels of excellence.

www.cambridge.org
Information on this title: www.cambridge.org/9781316517475
DOI: 10.1017/9781009042369

© Julia Adeney Thomas 2022

First published 2022

A catalogue record for this publication is available from the British Library.

ISBN 978-1-316-51747-5 Hardback
ISBN 978-1-009-04553-7 Paperback

In memory of Paul Crutzen (1933–2021)
and in honor of Christof Mauch and Helmuth Trischler

Contents

PART THREE FUTURE HABITATIONS

Figures

Foreword

What makes this collection of powerful and imaginative writings on the Anthropocene a timely, critical, and much-needed intervention in contemporary debates on the topic is its overall intellectual ambition. Taken together, the essays assembled here seek to situate these debates on a shared understanding of our planetary challenge while taking care at the same time to nurture a democracy of voices by sustaining multiple approaches to "the Anthropocene." They represent different genres of writing, ranging from the fictive to the scientific. The authorial strategies they deploy are visibly different. Radically different kinds of sources undergird the propositions they put forward. "Not even our citation styles are same," remarks the editor, pointing out that that is indeed something the volume does not even "try to mask." But there is a "common denominator" the essays share, and that is their "shared respect for scientific evidence." All contributions to this volume accept as foundational the basic findings of Earth System science and those of the Anthropocene Working Group of the International Commission on Stratigraphy.

I cannot overemphasize the importance of this stance. A generalized suspicion of science has dogged the idea of the Anthropocene from its very inception, especially in the interpretive human sciences. Some have expressed the fear, for example, that allowing scientists to define the physical parameters of the problem will lead inevitably to techno-fixes, undermining the possibility of democratic action involving citizenly and popular participation. Still others have famously taken exception to the use of the term "anthropos" in naming the new geological epoch, "the Anthropocene." Their claim, familiar by now, is that it projects an undifferentiated picture of humanity ("anthropos") that is oblivious of all the anthropological inequalities of race, class, gender, caste, sexuality, and thus the name "Anthropocene" diverts attention away from the "real" cause of our problem, which they define not as the Anthropocene but as global warming. The single cause of this crisis, they say, is the rapacious and extractive capitalist economy that catches us all in its web. While this criticism was first voiced about ten years ago, it has an enduring appeal to scholars in the social sciences, as may be seen in a 2021 call for papers issued by the respected American journal, *Radical History Review*, for a special edition to be called, significantly, "Alternatives to the Anthropocene." A "technocratic, scientific definition of our current epoch," argue the editors of this special issue, has "limits" when it comes to "periodizing" and understanding "the last 500 years [and] the social movements that have challenged the extractive capitalism essential to this epoch." They seek contributions that would "contest dominant readings of the Anthropocene as a post-1800 phenomenon and ... [center] environmental history that examines the beginning of the era of European colonial expansion." While this is but a single example, it demonstrates the reluctance of many humanistic and social scientists to even consider whether a transformed planet might transform our questions and narratives about the human past.

The debates on the Anthropocene have been ideological, partisan, and sometimes acrimonious and divisive. This volume strikes a very different note. It does not deny the role of capitalism and inequality in our current environmental crisis. But it does not see the sciences and the humanities as engaged in a mortal combat over the meanings and power of truth. The editor and contributors here visualize and stage generative conversations across disciplines in a spirit of mutual respect. They may disagree on how to make human sense of the Anthropocene, but they take stratigraphy and Earth System science as providing them with their various starting points. They see the Anthropocene as a much larger phenomenon than either climate change or loss of species, though the latter two are included in their understanding of the Anthropocene. But they all concede that the planetary problem of the Anthropocene owes its first formulation to the work of Earth System scientists. The Earth has seen warming events and biodiversity loss at various points in its history, even when there were no humans around to either experience or explain the phenomenon. One can also imagine cultures today where experiences of extreme "natural" events receive explanations that are not rooted in the physical or life sciences. But clearly, we would not have the framework of the Anthropocene to think with if we did not already have the markers (such as the Holocene) that scientists use in dividing up the inhuman stretches of geological time.

The multidimensional and planetary environmental crises that the world faces today call for conversations across different branches of human knowledge and imagination. That is what this volume sets out to achieve. I very much hope that this brave and timely book will meet with the positive reception that it so richly deserves.

Dipesh Chakrabarty
University of Chicago

Acknowledgments

Writing acknowledgments is my favorite part of any project. Casting an eye back on all the helping hands, false starts, brilliant disagreements, and energies behind a book is always a delight, but because this volume is unusually multidisciplinary and multicultural, the thanks are more manifold than usual.

The *primum movens* of this project was the Rachel Carson Center for Environment and Society, piloted by its remarkable directors, Christof Mauch and Helmuth Trischler. In the fall of 2019, Christof and Helmuth invited Jan Zalasiewicz and myself to Munich to speak as part of the celebration of the RCC's tenth anniversary, along with the remarkable environmental historian Jane Carruthers. Afterward, editor Harriet Windley skillfully ushered our lectures into print as *Strata and Three Stories*, with the able assistance of Kristy Henderson. Our tandem perspective on the Anthropocene became the final volume in the *RCC Perspectives: Transformations in Environment and Society* series. It built on earlier work in that series, including Christof Mauch's *Slow Hope: Rethinking Ecologies of Crisis and Fear* and Helmuth Trischler's *Anthropocene: Exploring the Future of the Age of Humans*. This book is dedicated to them for their institutional vision and intellectual contributions to the field of environmental history.

Shortly after the RCC celebration, I met with Lucy Rhymer, editor extraordinaire at Cambridge University Press. Over coffee, our conversation first plunged into darkness about our environmental future, but then resurfaced into light with the hope of this book. This hope is that a shared understanding of the Anthropocene can form the basis for the new ways of mutualistic living envisioned in the final collaborative chapter, spearheaded by paleobiologist Mark Williams. With Lucy's encouragement, I set out to bring together the many sciences and stories of our damaged Earth System and to find contributors willing to cross disciplinary lines and speak generously with one another and to our readers. Another star Cambridge editor, Rachel Blaifeder, shouldered some of the work of moving the book forward while Lucy was on leave. Natasha Whelan guided the production process with elegant firmness. Jo Tyszka did an extraordinary job with the copyediting. My heartfelt thanks go to Lucy, Rachel, Natasha, Jo, Michael Watson, and the whole Cambridge team. I also had a lot of fun working with freelance editor Maren Meinhardt whose wit, skill, and friendship kept me buoyant throughout. Publishers and editors don't get nearly the credit they deserve for shaping our intellectual landscape.

Many other shapers of the Anthropocene's intellectual landscape have profoundly influenced this book. They include, but are hardly limited to, Ian Angus, Maria Antonaccio, Marco Armiero, Gareth Austin, Alison Bashford, Ian Baucom, Christophe Bonneuil, Jane Carruthers, Elizabeth Chatterjee, Peter Coates, Meehan Crist, Giacomo Dalisa, Lorraine Daston, Elizabeth DeLoughrey, Bathsheba Demuth, Danny Dorling, John S. Dryzek, Rohan d'Souza, Marianna Dudley, Martin Dusinberre, Mike Ellis, Thomas Hylland Erikson, Kata Fodor, Jean-Baptiste Fressoz, Debjani Ganguli, Brad Gregory, Gabrielle Hecht, Toshihiro Higuchi, Eva Horn, Mike Hulme, Faisal Husain, Sheila Jasanoff, Alison Frank Johnson, Giorgio Kallis, Olaf Kaltmeier, Duncan Kelly, Jason Kelly, Thomas Lekan, Tim Lenton, Eugenio Luciano, Terada Masahiro, Peter Matanle, Franz Mauelshagen, John R. McNeill, Tobias Menely, Ian J. Miller, Ruth Morgan, Micah Muscolino, Debbie Nelson, Buhm Soon Park, Geoffrey Parker, Prasannan Parthasarathi, Jonathan Pickering, Ken Pomeranz, Amanda Power, Giulia Rispoli, Libby Robin, Eleonora Rohland, John Sabapathy, Jordan Sand, Matthias Schemmel, Juliet Schor, Roy Scranton, Emily Sekine, Lisa Sideris, John Sitter, Zoltán Boldizsár Simon, Dan Smail, Greg Smits, Sverker Sörlin, Meera Subramanian, Kaoru Sugihara, Ying Jia Tan, Zev Trachtenberg, Davor Vidas, Brett Walker, Paul Warde, Colin Waters, and Andy Yang. To all of them, my thanks.

Friends including Susan Bielstein, Mandy Burton, Kristel Clayville, Terry Evans, Sam Evans, Ted Fishman, Karen Reimer, Brenda Shapiro,

Sara Stern, Jim Welch, and Marianne Welch have been subjected to more conversations about the Anthropocene than is humane. Mark Ravina and Fabian Drixler call me "the Queen of the Anthropocene," but is this a compliment? Alan Thomas, publisher of several instant classics on the Anthropocene, often wonders aloud at dinner if we might discuss *something else*.

While we were finishing this work, Paul Crutzen died on January 28, 2021. Many of the contributors here knew Paul, the atmospheric chemist who famously coined the term "Anthropocene" in 2000. They celebrate his life and mourn his death. Even those of us who never got the chance to meet him are profoundly grateful for his research on the dangers of the ozone hole (for which he won the Nobel Prize) and for instigating the vital way of understanding Earth that we explore here.

This volume was supported by the Liu Institute, the Institute for Scholarship in the Liberal Arts, College of Arts and Letters, and a Recovery and Resilience Grant, all at the University of Notre Dame, and I owe special thanks to my colleagues there, Michel Hockx and Patrick Deegan. My greatest thanks of all goes to the contributors whose spirit of adventure and goodwill matches their insights in this book. They are good company on a troubled planet.

Introduction: The Growing Anthropocene Consensus

Julia Adeney Thomas

This book aims to get the Anthropocene right in three senses. First, it conveys the scientific evidence of our altered Earth, showcasing how the concept of the Anthropocene captures the magnitude and complexity of the planet's dangerous transformation. Second, we try to get the Anthropocene right in human terms, exploring the kaleidoscope of experiences, contingencies, and decisions that led to the Anthropocene, from the deep history of our relationship with infectious diseases to recent nuclear disasters. These histories are echoed and expanded through fiction with two short stories bringing the vast scales of geology and Earth System science "to earth" in emotional and ethical terms, especially around the issues of colonialism and inequality. Finally, we talk about what hope might look like in this pretty hopeless situation, proposing mutualistic cities, greater equity, and new political forms. "Right" in this book means being as *accurate* as possible in describing the physical phenomenon of the Anthropocene; as *balanced* as possible in weighing the complex human developments, some willed and some unintended, that led to this predicament; and as *just* as possible in envisioning potential futures.

In other words, this book brings together many stories about our singular situation. Deep-time narratives plunge us back to Earth's origins and trace our species' long struggle with dangerous microbes. Narratives on shorter timescales unfold the way Earth System scientists have come to see our planet; the way the indigenous people see the winds sweeping over a Mexican isthmus; and how different modern political systems shape the natural world. The nuclear disaster at Chernobyl and tiny Crawford Lake in Canada make star appearances. Imaginative tales of a

1

fleeing spaceship, a living mountain, and flourishing futuristic cities also figure here. We even get a hands-on account of reorienting a cultural institution to absorb the startling truth that global cultures and planetary change have converged. What holds all these tales together? In a nutshell, the *reality* of the Anthropocene. Recent discoveries show that in the mid-twentieth century, Earth entered a different – and, for human beings, difficult – new stage due to things people have done and in all too many cases are still doing. To try to make sense of this human-altered Earth, the contributors here – scientists, humanists, social scientists, writers, and institution builders – have joined together to tell stories of our transformed world. We represent a democracy of voices, all responding to a single, shared, complex danger.

But what is the "Anthropocene"? In some ways it is an accidental concept, a high-profile improvisation made in 2000 by the Nobel Laureate and atmospheric chemist Paul Crutzen (though the term and concept had been used independently, in a more low-key manner, by biologist Eugene Stoermer). Accidental or not, this concept crystallized the growing perception of global change, set in train by human activities. So great is this change that Crutzen suggested a new geological epoch. Just two decades on, overwhelming evidence has been assembled to show that around 1950 our planet entered another distinct chapter in its approximately 4.54-billion-year history. The complex, integrated Earth System has moved away from the relative stability of the Holocene epoch to a less stable, less benign, and still evolving phase with, in many ways, no precedent in Earth's long history.[1]

Humans will not find it easy to live in the Anthropocene. It now seems clear that life as we have experienced it for the last ~12 millennia (known

---

[1] Earth System science approaches Earth as a single, integrated system in which the atmosphere, hydrosphere, cryosphere, lithosphere, pedosphere, and biosphere – and now the human sphere – mutually impact one another in complex ways. See Will Steffen, Katherine Richardson, Johan Rockström, et al., "The emergence and evolution of Earth System science," *Nature Reviews Earth & Environment* 2020; 1, 54–63. https://doi.org/10 .1038/s43017-019-0005-6. In this book, we follow the convention of capitalizing both "Earth" and "System" to make it a proper noun, as explained by Will Steffen in "The evolution of Earth System science," blog post, *Future Earth* (December 14, 2015): https:// futureearth.org/2015/12/14/the-evolution-of-earth-system-science/

as the Holocene) is going to be changing very rapidly, and largely for the worse. The air carries a third more carbon dioxide and so the climate will, almost certainly, soon be hotter than it has ever been in the history of *Homo sapiens*. The seas are rising. Global biodiversity is shrinking rapidly, thinning our life support system. People weren't around 65 million years ago when the last great extinction event occurred, but now our numbers and needs leave little habitat for other species. Fresh water is becoming scarce. Topsoil is being lost at the rate of at least 36 billion tons every year, endangering food supplies.[2] The pressure on the systems that nurture, shelter, and fuel us will become ever more intense in the years to come as human populations and demands rise. These intensifying pressures will impact our societies unevenly and unfairly, but no part of the globe will be unchanged.

The Anthropocene, with these novel ingredients, is a very new part of Earth's history, but to make sense of it, we need to look at more than the last few decades. We need to place it in the context of our planet's past, beginning roughly 4.54 billion years ago. We also need to place it in relation to the deep past of human history, in which *Homo sapiens* evolved some 300,000 years ago, to emerge slowly as a dominant force and then to explode into a planet-changing species in the mid-twentieth century. The extraordinary transformations of the Earth System that we are seeing today have taken place, effectively, within a single human lifetime. In terms of speed of change, the nearest comparison in the last half-billion years of Earth history is the meteorite impact that brought the Mesozoic Era to an abrupt close. Suddenly the age of dinosaurs was at an end. Now *we* are the meteorite, and it seems just as difficult to alter our trajectory as it would be to alter the course of a ten-kilometer-wide rock hurtling through space.

Understanding this very recent, massive human impact means explaining how the long course of human history formed a platform for the recent rise of the powerful anthropogenic forces that accelerated Earth's transformation in the twentieth century. As we examine the

---

[2] Pasquale Borrelli, David A. Robinson, Larissa R. Fleischer, et al., "An assessment of the global impact of 21st century land use change on soil erosion," *Nature Communications* 2017; 8 (1) DOI: 10.1038/s41467-017-02142-7

narrative leading from the earliest patterns of humankind to the vertiginous growth of economies, inequality, and human populations, we also seek stories that resist this destructive trajectory. Not all individual actions nor all social systems pushed the Earth System beyond Holocene norms. Some were mutualistic with their environment. These counterpoints to the dominant trajectory are also Anthropocene stories. They suggest that our arrival at this new epoch was not foreordained. Further, they provide political and cultural resources for imagining how we might, with a bit of luck and much determination, reshape our societies to mitigate the Anthropocene's harshest effects. If human activities are the equivalent of that ten-kilometer-wide rock hurtling through space, renarrating our human stories to account for pathways not taken is one means of cushioning the impact. To have any hope of understanding this new reality and transforming our societies, we need to span the enormity of geological time and deep human history, while also delving into the intimate and immediate exchanges between organic and inorganic systems and human behavior, values, ideas, and institutions. In the collective experiment in these pages, we wobble a course toward the kind of multidisciplinary understanding that is needed to grasp – and perhaps to cope with – our collective predicament.[3]

In short, the aim of this book is to give readers a handle on the Anthropocene both as a scientific concept and as a human dilemma. We assume no specialist knowledge. Instead these essays are gestures of inclusion from an array of people who care, as almost everyone does, about a habitable Earth. We aim to be generous. Our goal is not to impress readers with erudition or righteousness, but to open vistas on our common planetary dilemma. The very term "Anthropocene" implies that Earth's story and human stories can no longer be told without reference to one another. Earth's story and ours have converged in an

---

[3] For expanded discussions of this approach, see Julia Adeney Thomas, Mark Williams, and Jan Zalasiewicz, *The Anthropocene: A Multidisciplinary Approach,* (Cambridge: Polity Press, 2020) and Jan Zalasiewicz, Colin N. Waters, Erle C. Ellis, et al., "The Anthropocene: comparing its meaning in geology (chronostratigraphy) with conceptual approaches arising in other disciplines," *Earth's Future* March 2021; 9(3) https://doi.org/10.1029/2020EF001896

unprecedented way as human activities relentlessly alter biogeochemical systems and etch themselves into Earth's surface.

But stitching Earth's story and human stories together is no easy task. We speak and write from different perspectives and in different ways. Not even our citation styles are the same, something that this book doesn't try to mask. Each chapter uses the conventions most familiar to that particular author or set of authors. This is a deliberate choice. We want to make evident the scratchy textured way in which this new knowledge is being cobbled together. We also want to be as clear as we can, explaining terms, using metaphors, examples, and anecdotes to make larger points. These pieces are meant to intrigue, even as they show the bleak enormity of our collective destructiveness.

Facing this new world is tough. It doesn't require a history degree to know that in bad situations, the hydra-headed monster of fear, distrust, and contentiousness often rears its head, sowing dissent in a seemingly zero-sum game. Shouting past one another (or worse) is a common human reaction. But many studies have shown that trust brings better results.[4] That is what we've attempted here, recognizing that trust needs a shared foundation. As the contributors to this book try to explain to one another – and to our friends, students, and colleagues – what the Anthropocene looks like from where each of us stands, we all reference a common denominator. That common denominator is a shared respect for the scientific evidence – emerging from geology, Earth System science, and allied fields – that supports the Anthropocene concept. This reality is the foundation of our work. I think each of us has wished, privately and sadly, that the evidence was less compelling and that the science deniers were right. It would be a wonderful thing if Earth's resources were infinite and the stability of the Earth System assured. It would be glorious if our numbers and desires could grow forever, if all people on Earth now and in the future could live lives of increasing, heedless bounty, equitably shared. Many modern histories and theories

---

[4] Elinor Ostrom, the first woman economist to win a Nobel Prize, is one of among the many possible citations here. See, for instance, Elinor Ostrom, Joanna Burger, Christopher B. Field, Richard B. Norgaard and David Policansky, "Revisiting the commons: local lessons, global challenges," *Science* Apr. 9, 1999; 284(5412), 278–282.

of human society promised as much, but the discovery of the Anthropocene has ruptured that hopeful human trajectory.[5] Now, realistically, the sky *is* our limit; the thinning stratosphere, biosphere, pedosphere and much else constrain human possibilities. Even where our essays describe different aspects of how we got here, all take the physical reality of the Anthropocene and its difficult, complex challenges as our starting point – even though we'd happily wish them away if that were possible.

In short, the distinctive quality of all true Anthropocene stories is that they respond to geologists' evidence of the recent, global, near-synchronous, durable, human-made layer in the Earth's crust and to the corresponding findings in Earth System science showing that the old Holocene Earth System has been destabilized, and is now lurching toward dangerous thresholds and state shifts. The aim of each contributor here is to recount a story of the Anthropocene that is both true to the science as currently understood and true to that contributor's particular concerns. While sociologists, for instance, needn't become stratigraphers, they need to understand how stratigraphy's findings alter our view of societies. Conversely, stratigraphy, which once paid little attention to, say, economic systems, now must consider global capitalism's impact on the formation of strata. Our stories are rightly plural, rich, and nuanced, but on our altered planet they can no longer be rendered as soliloquies.[6]

Perhaps it goes without saying that there are other helpful ways of approaching the world. Certainly this book doesn't claim that the Anthropocene is the *only* useful concept. "Ecological crisis," "global warming," "pollution," and a host of other terms frame our challenges differently. Rubrics such as "early human migration and land use change," "the invention of agriculture and the rise of states," "climate

---

[5] Clive Hamilton introduced the helpful concept of "rupture" in "The Anthropocene as rupture," *The Anthropocene Review* 2016; 1–14, https://doi.org/10.1177/2053019616634741

[6] For an interesting exploration of this issue, see Roberta Biasillo and Claudio de Majo, eds. "Storytelling and environmental history: experiences from Germany and Italy," *RCC Perspectives: Transformations in Environment and Society* 2020, (2). doi.org/10.5282/rcc/9116.

change and capitalism," "species transfer and imperialism," or, simply, "modernity" provide other angles of understanding. What we *do* claim, however, is that the Anthropocene is a specific and distinctive framework, particularly helpful in connecting the local with the planetary and deep history with the future, and most particularly in orchestrating knowledge of the whole of the Earth System and its stratigraphic markers with all human activities from myth-making to microchip manufacture. The concept of the Anthropocene directs our attention to the magnitude of the many changes on Earth, and to their integration and interrelatedness, beginning with the minutely local and extending to the planetary across eons. It pushes us away from siloed-thinking to systems-thinking. Along with South Asian environmentalist and scholar Sharachchandra Lele, we see the need to move beyond a "narrowed framing of the problem: one value (sustaining future generations), one problem (climate change), one goal (reduce carbon emissions), and one solution (renewables)."[7] And that calls for a full understanding of the range of pressures we are putting on the planet, long- and short-term timescales, and of our interdependence with nature and one another. In short, this volume sees the Anthropocene as requiring new ways of systems-thinking from all disciplines, governments, and civic institutions: new knowledge for a new planet.

THE OCCASION FOR OUR BOOK: GROWING CONSENSUS

Altered Earth: Getting the Anthropocene Right appears at an important moment. Born in 2000, the concept of the Anthropocene has "grown up" on a human timescale of a little more than two decades. This book marks its maturity. It coincides with the growing consensus that the Anthropocene is an evidenced, accurate, and useful framework for understanding our planetary predicament.

The year 2022 sees the culmination of the Anthropocene Working Group's efforts. This group, known as the AWG, was created in 2009 to investigate the geological plausibility of Paul Crutzen's intuition. By 2019,

---

[7] Sharachchandra Lele, "Environment and well-being: a perspective from the global south." *New Left Review* 2020; 123, 41–63.

after a decade of evidence-gathering and debate, a binding vote by 88 percent of the AWG confirmed its consensus that Earth has entered a new phase marked by a distinctive, near-global stratal unit, reflecting the sudden rise in human population, globalization, and industrialization over the last 70 years or so. In December 2022, the AWG plans to meet to finalize its formal proposal. The proposal will rely on mounds of evidence, including the core samples collected by geologist Francine McCarthy and her team, as described in Chapter 9 and on display at Berlin's Haus der Kulturen der Welt (the HKW or House of World Culture) as described in Chapter 10. If committees higher up the geostratigraphic feeding chain approve, the Anthropocene would officially join the Eocene, the Pleistocene, and other such units on the great canvas of the Geological Time Scale charting the Earth's lifespan.

Other international organizations are also embracing the concept, shifting their frameworks away from "climate change" to "the Anthropocene." In 2018, the United Nation's Intergovernmental Panel on Climate Change (IPCC) acknowledged the Anthropocene as the overarching framework for understanding planetary change. Just as our book appears, the IPCC, currently in its sixth assessment cycle, will release its 2022 "Synthesis Report" for policy makers, drawing together the massive efforts of three working groups and three special reports.[8] Other United Nations organizations have adopted the Anthropocene as well. The 2020 UN Human Development Report was titled *The Next Frontier: Human Development and the Anthropocene*, explicitly recognizing that we face not a solvable problem, but a complex, many-faceted predicament that needs to be navigated.[9]

Important academic and civic institutions are taking this new description of our planetary reality as their point of departure. For instance,

[8] Intergovernmental Panel on Climate Change (IPCC) "AR6 Synthesis Report: Climate Change 2022." www.ipcc.ch/report/sixth-assessment-report-cycle/ (accessed September 2021).

[9] UN Human Development report: The Next Frontier: Human Development and the Anthropocene (http://hdr.undp.org/en/content/human-development-report-2020; accessed September 2021). See Julia Adeney Thomas, "Why the 'Anthropocene' is not 'climate change' and why it matters." *AsiaGlobal Online* 10 January 2019. www.asiaglobalonline.hku.hk/anthropocene-climate-change/ (accessed September 2021).

historian of science Buhm Soon Park persuaded the South Korean government to fund the Center for Anthropocene Studies at KAIST (Korea Advanced Institute of Science and Technology), one of the country's premier universities. In these pages, you will read how Bernd Scherer, Director-General of the HKW, decided to reorient his institution to confront the Anthropocene, gaining support from the German government. In May 2022, the HKW hosts a meeting of the AWG and exhibits the core samples supporting its conclusions. As Scherer notes, these core samples are artifacts of both culture and nature or, more precisely, the culture–nature conjunction that is the Anthropocene.

Likewise, the social sciences, humanities, and literature are reconsidering their narratives in relation to Earth's transformation. Recently, political theorists Duncan Kelly, Mark Beeson, John S. Dryzek, Jonathan Pickering, and Manuel Arias-Maldonado have laid the groundwork for a politics of the Anthropocene.[10] Anthropologists too are alert to the challenge. In *Overheating*, for instance, anthropologist Thomas Hylland Eriksen deploys the lens of accelerating change to show how current environmental, economic, and identity crises have converged.[11] Studies of specific communities by anthropologists Marisol de la Cadena, Anna Lowenhaupt Tsing, Cymene Howe and Dominic Boyer, among others, remind us that we live in "a world of many worlds."[12] Historians have also pivoted to the Anthropocene. In 2000, the same year that Paul Crutzen coined "Anthropocene," historian John R. McNeill published *Something New Under the Sun*, grappling with how planetary and human history have

---

[10] Manuel Arias-Maldonado, "Bedrock or social construction? What Anthropocene science means for political theory," *The Anthropocene Review* 2020, 7(2), 97–112. doi:10.1177/2053019619899536; *Antropoceno: La política en la era humana* (Madrid: Taurus, 2018); and Manuel Arias-Maldonado and Zev Trachtenberg, eds., *Rethinking the Environment for the Anthropocene: Political Theory and Socionatural Relations in the New Geological Epoch* (Abingdon: Routledge, 2019). See also Duncan Kelly, *Politics and the Anthropocene* (Cambridge: Polity, 2019) and John S. Dryzek and Jonathan Pickering, *The Politics of the Anthropocene* (Oxford: Oxford University Press, 2019). Nigel Clark and Bronislaw Szerszynski provide an overview in *Planetary Social Thought: The Anthropocene Challenge to the Social Sciences* (Cambridge: Polity, 2021).

[11] Thomas Hylland Eriksen, *Overheating: An Anthropology of Accelerated Change* (London: Pluto Press, 2016).

[12] This lovely phrase is the title of Marisol de la Cadena and Mario Blaser, eds. *A World of Many Worlds* (Durham, NC: Duke University Press, 2018).

come together.[13] Since then, this discipline has puzzled over why, when, and how humans came to overwhelm the great forces of nature, questions engaged here by Dipesh Chakrabarty, Kyle Harper, Kate Brown, and myself. All of these approaches to the Anthropocene are helpful but insufficient without works of imagination. This is where the volume's short stories told by Clive Hamilton and Amitav Ghosh come in.

None of these perspectives individually is the complete story. Indeed, there can be no complete story. The Anthropocene is still unfolding conceptually and physically. For our communities, its instigations and effects are uneven and heterogeneous – and will continue to be so. No totalizing vision, no single cause, no easy solution is possible.

ORGANIZATION

Altered Earth is divided into three parts. In the first part, Jan Zalasiewicz and I lay out the stakes for the physical sciences and the human sciences respectively. Part II consists of eight "stories" from different scientific and humanistic points of view. Part III, the final section, looks to the future.

In the first part, stories of human beings (the *anthropos*) and stories of planetary time (*cene*) are brought together. From the most official vantage, the Anthropocene story belongs to stratigraphers, the men and women strangely fascinated by layers of rock and what they tell us about time. These geologists explore the Anthropocene as part of Earth's vast history and as a very recent layer of the planet's crust, one that attests to humanity's sudden, brutish imprint with the twentieth-century "Great Acceleration."[14] As told by geologist Jan Zalasiewicz, former chair of the AWG, the central protagonist in this long story is the Earth System itself,

---

[13] John R. McNeill, *Something New Under the Sun: An Environmental History of the Twentieth-Century World* (New York: Norton, 2000).

[14] The Great Acceleration refers to the evidence produced by the International Geosphere Biosphere Program (IGBP) charting the abrupt, synchronous social and physical impacts on the planetary system in the twentieth century. See Will Steffen, Angelina Sanderson, Peter Tyson, et al., *Global Change and the Earth System: A Planet Under Pressure*, The IGBP Book Series (Berlin, Heidelberg, New York: Springer-Verlag, 2004), and Will Steffen, Wendy Broadgate, Lisa Deutsch, et al., "The trajectory of the Anthropocene: The Great Acceleration," *Anthropocene Review* 2015; 2:1, 81–98.

with its dramatic changes over eons and the swift, recent rupture of Holocene norms. But, the Anthropocene also nominates human beings as players in the planetary drama. Depending on how that human story is framed in relation to Earth's history, various people, societies, or our species as a whole can be seen as lucky primates, blind fools, greedy sods, despicable culprits, innocent casualties, and sometimes all these at once. The activities that laid the foundation for the twentieth-century Anthropocene can be said to begin when our ancestral species mastered fire, even before *Homo sapiens* emerged, or at any number of times thereafter. Humanity's story can be told collectively, incorporating us all across time and space, or as a multitude of stories emphasizing the differences among cultures, politics, technologies, ideas, and much else. What is no longer possible in the Anthropocene is a human story unconstrained by planetary limits.

The next eight contributions tell more particular stories. In Chapter 3, scientist Will Steffen takes us far into outer space to see not just Earth, the blue, vibrant, tangible sphere we inhabit, but the Earth System, the intangible, evolving, integrated complex that is our planetary home. This relatively new idea – Earth System in the singular – guided Crutzen's initial recognition of the Anthropocene and remains a conceptual twin-star to the geological understanding of our planet's abrupt alteration. Originally, Crutzen had thought that the late-eighteenth-century Industrial Revolution in England might serve as the starting point of the Anthropocene, but data from Steffen's Great Acceleration graphs in 2004 changed his mind. Only in the mid-twentieth century did human pressures on the Earth System swoop upward. There had been, in other words, a long gestation for anthropogenic Anthropocene forces. Just how long is the question of the next chapter.

In Chapter 4, historian Kyle Harper does a deep dive into human history to find the antecedents of our ascendency. We are, he finds, a mucky bunch, ridden with many more disease-causing pathogens than our nearest relatives, the chimpanzees. It might seem unlikely that such germ-ridden creatures would ever thrive, but thrive we have, despite – or perhaps because of – our complex relationship with pathogens. One way to tell human history is to see it as a long, slow struggle against these evolving, invisible agents of misery until, finally, we managed to disinfect much of the planet and sent our numbers soaring. However, as Harper warns and recent history shows, no victory in the evolutionary arms race between pathogens and hosts is ever permanent.

In Chapter 5, anthropologists Cymene Howe and Dominic Boyer take on the triumphal story of "green" energy. The winds of the Mexican Isthmus of Tehuantepec have attracted high-tech investors bent on "solving" climate change by building turbines across indigenous lands. These entrepreneurs speak the linear language of climate change: a single problem, a single solution, and off we go. Their top-down, siloed approach mimics the relations of power that gave rise to the Anthropocene in the first place and ignores the way indigenous people understand the wind. Once the reductive picture of climate change is expanded to include biodiversity, land use, competing ideas of a good life, and the symbolic, community-creating capacity of winds, we begin to grasp the irresolvable conundrums of the Anthropocene.

In Chapter 6, one of the world's leading novelists, Amitav Ghosh, tells something of the same story, but as dark parable: the terrible assault of the Anthropoi on the sacred Living Mountain and those who once flourished in its shadow. Into the Valley come strangers, the Anthropoi with their armies and their savants who justify their actions. Desecration follows. Worst of all, the Valley-dwellers come to desire the life of the Anthropoi. They join in waves, climbing, digging, and exploiting the Living Mountain they once revered, even as its snows melt, crevasses widen, and avalanches destroy the Valley floor. The lone exception is one old woman who can still feel the Mountain's heartbeat with the soles of her feet and knows no one can master it. "The Ascent of the Anthropoi" lays bare modernity's consoling lie that growth is the key to justice and that instrumental knowledge trumps the sensuous acceptance of life.

In Chapter 7, political scientist Manuel Arias-Maldonado picks up on Ghosh's dark vision: in the Anthropocene, whether we will or no, we have all become Anthropoi. Few remember the old way of life. A new collective political actor has been born: humanity as a whole. The political challenge for this new actor is nothing less than stabilizing the Earth System. Given this urgent task, Arias-Maldonado makes the case for pivoting away from past recriminations and directing our energies toward creating international institutions able to cope with the unprecedented emergency. By mapping the ways liberal democracy, ecoauthoritarianism, and green communitarianism currently address Anthropocene challenges, he shows that each offers some mitigation strategies, but none is entirely satisfactory. The situation calls for creativity, forbearance, and clear-eyed recognition that, in the sliver of time remaining to us, we can, if we pull together, build better societies in keeping with planetary limits.

The next two chapters deal in different ways with the sharpest and most globally synchronous of the Anthropocene's many geological proxy signals: artificial radionuclides. Nuclear detonations and nuclear reactor accidents have left their mark in the stratigraphic record. Historian Kate Brown takes us into the dark world of state secrets, widespread suffering, and heroic doctors, local officials, and scientists in the USSR and Russia after the Chernobyl nuclear plant meltdown of 1986. She shows that from a ground-level view this disaster engulfed – and still engulfs – human and non-human communities in different ways and at different speeds. The greatest harm is done not by the immediate fallout from a nuclear accident, but by the persistent low-level radiation in soil, food, and infrastructure. Despite the nuclear industry's insistence, backed by the UN, that the death-toll of Chernobyl was low, her research shows how radiation continues its deadly work. Nor is the Chernobyl meltdown the only nuclear problem in Ukraine. In an old bombing range nearby, a deformed and blighted pine tree signals the disturbing fact that a decade before the Chernobyl plant was even built, nuclear fallout contaminated these forests. Nuclear radiation's lingering effects preclude narrative closure for Brown's story just as the continuing impact of the Great Acceleration precludes forecasting the Anthropocene's trajectory. Today, fracking for oil and natural gas, as a recent investigation shows, sloshes radioactive brine in the name of "clean" energy.[15]

---

[15] Justin Noble, "America's radioactive secret: Oil-and-gas wells produce nearly a trillion gallons of toxic waste a year. An investigation shows how it could be making workers sick and contaminating communities across America," *Rolling Stone* (21 January 2020) www.rollingstone.com/politics/politics-features/oil-gas-fracking-radioactive-investigation-937389/ (accessed September 2021).

Geologist Francine McCarthy uses a different archive to tell her Anthropocene story in Chapter 9. She and her research team have been studying the sediment beneath the waters of Crawford Lake in southern Ontario, Canada. Due to the lake's great depth and lack of strong currents, delicate layers of light and dark sediment are laid down each year like tree rings. Each pair is called a varve. These varves tell a thousand years of history. Some stories are local, such as the ecosystem disruptions by Iroquoian farmers beginning in the late thirteenth century and by a lumber mill that began operating in the late nineteenth century. The most recent layers, however, tell a new story of human activities on a global scale. These recent varves are evidence of the Anthropocene and the Great Acceleration's abrupt and world-wide impact, even on this small lake in rural southern Ontario. Along with other teams searching for an appropriate stratigraphic marker, known as the Global Boundary Stratotype Section and Point (GSSP) or "Golden Spike," the Crawford Lake team will present its evidence to the AWG in 2022. Their core sample will figure in the Berlin exhibition at the HKW, a testament to the power of the *anthropos* on the planet.

Part II closes with the story of the transformation of Berlin's House of World Culture, the HKW. Established to showcase international art in 1989, the HKW had been dedicated to human creativity. But more than a decade ago, director Bernd Scherer questioned the implied separation of culture from nature. As he recognized, world culture's biggest creation now is our altered Earth System. As described above, his work reaches a culmination in 2022, when the HKW hosts a meeting of the AWG and exhibits the ice cores and other evidence of our human-altered world.

The Anthropocene is like nothing that's happened before. Human beings have always been biological, chemical, physical, and geological agents altering the world around us. Never has humanity placed its stamp on the planet in ways comparable to a meteorite. People, by our sheer numbers, productivity, and consumption, are now Earth System agents. No place escapes human influence; gyres of plastic swirl in the oceans; remote patches of rainforest and desert, never having felt the tread of human feet, now feel the impact of our predation as biodiversity dwindles and the climate changes. Forests burn to provide for impoverished swidden farmers; vast underground reservoirs are drained by parched cities and needy farmers. Rising nitrogen and phosphate production, concrete-intensive building, energy use, mobility, communications, urbanization, and global flows of toxins are at the heart of our ever-escalating pressure on the Earth System. The mass of human-made things outweighs the living biomass.[16] On the planetary scale, the Anthropocene's narrative arc hurtles toward Hothouse Earth where human habitation may be impossible. Yet the pace is not the same everywhere. More locally, human life-worlds are changing at different speeds. Understanding the disjunctures between quickness and slowness, change and continuity, top-down developments and particular local values are important to the task of figuring out how we might, with ingenuity, flexibility, and a bit of luck, turn this humiliating tragedy into a tale of fortitude and resilience with decency. Is there a guaranteed – or even a likely – happy ending? Sadly, no.

The last section of *Altered Earth* turns to the future. In his fictional contribution, Clive Hamilton imagines a mission to Mars speeding away from an uninhabitable Earth. Among the chosen few on board are Pearl and Denis, two young people at odds with the captain's decision to leave the vast majority behind to die. With clear-eyed honesty, this sympathetic pair recognize the ethic of what might be termed "shared life," the intricate web of mutually nurturing living beings. In other words, without us all, we are nothing. Trapped in a metal tube flying through space, what can they do with their yearning? Such a scenario is not beyond the realms of possibility; anyone watching the news can see that the ambition to settle another planet is no longer a science fiction fantasy – although the more aggressive term "colonize" is a better word than "settle." If we could build on Pearl and Denis's understanding of our shared predicament, we might be able to create an alternative story, one that does not end with a privileged few monopolizing all hope of refuge.

It is to that end that our book concludes with a vision of mutualistic cities put forward by Mark Williams and colleagues. Most of Earth's

---

[16] Emily Elhacham, Liad Ben-Uri, Jonathan Grozovski, Yinon M. Bar-On, and Ron Milo "Global human-made mass exceeds all living biomass," *Nature* 2020; 588, 442–444. https://doi.org/10.1038/s41586-020-3010-5

human population are urban dwellers. Today, there are 33 megacities with more than 10 million inhabitants, 10 million being the total worldwide human population at the beginning of the Holocene. Our hope lies in turning these dense communities from net-consumers to net-producers of biodiversity, clean air, better soils, and fresh water. If such regenerative processes can be established, we'll be a lot closer to stabilizing the Earth System. Williams' chapter, co-authored with a multidisciplinary group of scholars, makes a distinction between mutualistic cities and other approaches. Unlike "smart cities" that rely on sophisticated technology to monitor and respond to environmental conditions, and unlike "sustainable cities" that stress reduction and reuse, the concept of a "mutualistic city" is modeled on the biological systems where all organisms benefit one another. The focus is on regenerative cycles and virtuous feedback loops. If we could begin to develop such mutualistic cities, the anthroposphere would begin to meld back into Earth's biosphere, lithosphere, hydrosphere, and atmosphere; and, human beings might, as Williams says, be drawn to new roles redefining "success" not as "high-paying jobs, let alone massive wealth" but as "dense circles of friendship and honour within communities." If the basis of hope is action, this vision maps our next steps.

STORIES

Our collective effort might be compared with the old parable of the blind men and the elephant.[17] Each contributor responds truly and perceptively to the bit in their hands. The person stroking the ivory tusk says that "elephant" is a hard, sharp-pointed cylinder, but the man with his hands on the creature's side describes "elephant" as a large, rough wall. Their friend holding the tail laughs at his fellows, and declares "elephant" to be just like a tasseled cord for drawing heavy curtains. This surprises the man with the trunk, who declares that there's nothing

---

[17] One of the earliest written versions of this story is found in the Buddhist text *Ud 6:4 Sectarians (1) (Tittha Sutta)* discussing the limits of perception. The blind men describing the elephant to the Buddha use different metaphors than the ones I use here. www.dhammatalks.org/suttas/KN/Ud/ud6_4.html (accessed September 2021).

tasseled about this strong, snake-like being. And on and on. All these people have their hands on part of the same "elephant," but to understand what they confront, they must come together and share what they know. Our Anthropocene, like their elephant, is what we hold in common. While our stories are rightly plural, rich, and nuanced, they can no longer be soliloquies on our altered planet. We all speak to this new reality of the Anthropocene and with one another. We want to step up, and say "Well, it's an elephant alright," and we hope you'll join us in trying to grasp our common predicament.[18]

---

[18] I thank Clive Hamilton for suggestions on this final line.

PART ONE

STRATA AND STORIES

CHAPTER 1

Science: Old and New Patterns of the Anthropocene

Jan Zalasiewicz

In 2000, on that fateful day in Mexico, when Paul Crutzen gave in to a moment of irritation among a crowd of fellow scientists assembled to discuss the growing symptoms of a troubled Earth, he surely could not have foreseen the repercussions of his brusque intervention. What had got on his nerves was the constant reference to the Holocene Epoch, the interval of post-glacial geological time (in which we still, formally, live) and the new trends developing within it. These trends – of deforestation, of fundamental change to the chemistry of the atmosphere and the oceans, of accelerating biodiversity loss, of the onset of climate change – to him did not chime at all with the general concept of the Holocene. The Holocene, after all, is an epoch of relative stability, the latest of 50-odd interglacial phases of the 2.6 million years of the Quaternary Period (the Ice Age of common parlance); its conditions enabled humanity to burgeon. Here, one can see the growth of communities, towns and cities, and then empires, and all the marks of peace such as trade and farming, and of war, with destruction and despoliation, alternating in seemingly endless cycles. All this is preserved in a rich archaeological record, extending through – and indeed before – the 11.7-thousand-year span of the epoch.

Underlying all this feverish human activity, though, the signals of the Earth as a planet were ones of dependability: of climate, of sea level – once the mighty polar ice-sheets had finished their prodigious melt phase after the last Ice Age, some 7000 years ago – of geography, and of animals (bar mostly the large land animals beginning to suffer the effects of hunting) and plants. This was a planet as bedrock, a backcloth so reassuringly stable and supportive for human activities, of such seeming permanence, that it could be assumed to be always there. And, whatever the destruction wrought by the latest war, or by the spread of patches of nature tamed as farms and towns, this stable Earth would heal, would recover, and would endure to support the next human adventure. Only – as Paul Crutzen then felt so acutely – at some recent time in history, around the time when large-scale industrialization started, the human-wrought changes began to take on a quite different scale and order: of such a scale, indeed, as to threaten the planetary stability that supported both human civilization and the complex web of nonhuman life. Hence that outburst, that moment of inspiration and that on-the-spot improvised new word: the Anthropocene.[1]

That word, as we now know, was to catalyze many things in a surprisingly short space of time (the catalysis, indeed, continues, and at breakneck speed). One was simply the wider use of the term among the scientific community that Paul was part of, the Earth System science (ESS) community associated with the International Geosphere-Biosphere Programme. They simply voted with their feet, using the term matter-of-factly, as a vivid and useful conceptual addition to their discourse and their wider communication.[2] These were for the most part chemists, physicists, ecologists, oceanographers, and so on, dealing with the present world. Aware of the Geological Time Scale – of which the Holocene is the latest (and remains the latest) rung – they had, however, few dealings with the particular geological community that oversees the Geological Time Scale; no more so than most scientists have day-to-day dealings with the kinds of committees that decide, ponderously and with infinite meticulousness, the precise length of the meter or exact weight of the kilogram.

---

[1] Paul J. Crutzen and Eugene F. Stoermer, "The 'Anthropocene'," *Global Change IGBP Newsletter*, no. 41 (2000): 17. This journal issue includes several intimations, direct and indirect, of this new concept, which was later more widely broadcast in a vivid, one-page article: Paul J. Crutzen, "Geology of mankind," *Nature* 415 (2002): 23.

[2] This early adoption may be seen in, for instance: Michel Meybeck, "Global analysis of river systems: from Earth System controls to Anthropocene syndromes," *Philosophical Transactions of the Royal Society. Series B, Biological Sciences* 358, no. 1440 (2003): 1935–55; and W. Steffen, A. Sanderson, P.D. Tyson, et al., *Global Change and the Earth System: A Planet Under Pressure* (Berlin: Springer, 2004).

Nevertheless, a few years after the Anthropocene began its spread through the scientific literature, this particular community of geologists became aware of this new word, which was being used just as if it was a standard geological time term. But, of course, it was not: it had not gone through the exhaustive, lengthy, detailed analyses and scrutiny – one would say ordeal, if we were dealing with a human – that a term must go through before it is finally, after passage through several increasingly powerful committees, agreed upon (at all stages) by supermajority vote. The Geological Time Scale is meant to be stable, to provide a common grammar for the discipline across both national boundaries and generations. It is only modified rarely and grudgingly, for real purpose; and quite a few proposed terms have never made it into formal use, having fallen at one or other of these hurdles. The Anthropocene is now being prepared for just such a trial, in the next few years. There is no guarantee it will survive, formally.

While the formal lens provides only one perspective on the Anthropocene, there is also the question of the *reality* – the physical, chemical, and biological rationale that lay behind Paul Crutzen's intuition. These are all of course geological too, in that the Earth comprises all of these dimensions – that one may term respectively lithostratigraphical, chemostratigraphical, and biostratigraphical, in the jargon of the trade. Through these prisms, one may process an almost infinite amount of data – the Earth is a large and complex phenomenon, after all.[3] But many of the various patterns of the Anthropocene betray a striking simplicity. This new concept is not subtle, and does not need sophisticated statistical analysis to reveal some vague hidden trend in a sea of variability. It is terribly straightforward.

FUNDAMENTAL PATTERN OF THE ANTHROPOCENE

Take, for instance, the pattern that last year was calculated by Clément Poirier, one of the Anthropocene Working Group (AWG) members, and

---

[3] A good deal of the evidence is very tightly summarized in C. N. Waters, J. Zalasiewicz, C. P. Summerhayes, et al., "The Anthropocene is functionally and stratigraphically distinct from the Holocene," *Science* 351, no. 6269 (2016): 137.

1.1. The Anthropocene Working Group logo (right), based on the rate of change of atmospheric CO_2, over 20,000 years, as worked out by Clément Poirier, and (left) its relation to geological time units. The AWG logo image was devised by the Max Planck Institute for Chemistry, Mainz, and is reproduced with permission.

then worked into the new logo of the AWG, courtesy of Astrid Kaltenbach and the Max Planck Institute for Chemistry in Mainz. It is an almost-horizontal line that, at its right-hand end, turns into an almost vertical line. It represents the rate of rise of carbon dioxide into the atmosphere from the earth/ocean system over the past 15,000 years (Figure 1.1).

For most of these 15 millennia, this rate held almost steady: there are some slight wobbles in the first third of the line at its left-hand end, representing the standard glacial-to-interglacial rise in atmospheric carbon dioxide levels from 180 to around 265 parts per million (ppm), largely by outgassing from the ocean. This is quite a large rise, but it did take several millennia from start to finish, so the line does not depart much from the horizontal trend, which then persists *almost* until the present. The sharp inflection towards the vertical is humanity's contribution, mostly from the burning of gargantuan amounts of fossil fuels. The near-vertical line is not quite straight: the first part is a little less steep, and represents the time from about 1850 CE, the beginning of what is sometimes called the "thermo-industrial" revolution, and the second, steeper part represents the time from around 1950 CE, the time of the "Great Acceleration" of population, industrialization, and globalization, since which point more than 87 percent of the fossil fuels exploited have been consumed.[4] This is a large part of the

[4] The diagrams that form the basis for the AWG logo are shown and described in Fig. 1 in the 2019 response piece by J. Zalasiewicz, C. N. Waters, M. J. Head, C. Poirier, et al., "A formal Anthropocene is compatible with but distinct from its diachronous anthropogenic counterparts: a response to W.F. Ruddiman's 'Three Flaws in Defining a Formal Anthropocene'," *Progress in Physical Geography* 43, no. 3 (2019): 319–33.

reason why the human consumption of energy in the seven decades since 1950 CE is estimated to be greater than that in all of the previous 11.7 millennia of the Holocene.[5]

Carbon dioxide is just one parameter. A very similar pattern, though, can be made from an analysis of human population growth, of atmospheric methane levels, and much else. The notorious "hockey stick" of Earth's temperature proposed by Michael Mann[6] and his colleagues is part of this suite, albeit a (so far) blurred and relatively poorly developed one, as Earth's surface temperature has yet to catch up with the effects of climate drivers such as increased atmospheric carbon dioxide (the Earth is a big object, and so it will take some centuries for the increased heat to work its way back through to the atmosphere; at the moment, for instance, most of the extra heat is being absorbed by the oceans). This fundamental pattern, therefore, divides the old epoch and the (proposed) new one. As a first approximation, the Holocene is horizontal, and the Anthropocene is vertical.

CLIMATE CONTEXT OF THE ICE AGE

Is this striking pattern *geology*, though, or just a few millennia of environmental history? In other words, is the Anthropocene a blip, a minor fluctuation destined to be lost within the noise of Earth time, or is it something larger and more serious? Here, context is everything. The current CO_2 rise can be grafted onto the record of carbon dioxide fluctuations over the last 800,000 years – an astonishing archive that is perhaps the most valuable treasure yielded to us by the great Antarctic ice-sheet, as fossilized air bubbles trapped in the annual ice-layers. Without this natural archive, we really would be groping in the dark to

---

[5] This analysis, which ranges wider than energy consumption, is in J. Syvitski, C. N. Waters, J. Day, et al., "Extraordinary human energy consumption and resultant geological impacts beginning around 1950 CE initiated the proposed Anthropocene Epoch", *Communications Earth & Environment* 1 (2020):32.

[6] Michael Mann is a climatologist at Penn State University, who has pioneered techniques of reconstructing the climate history of the past 1000 years. The pattern he obtained, of a sharp twentieth-century rise, is also shown by many other parameters of the Anthropocene.

understand the significance of the modern rise, given how difficult it is to divine ancient atmospheric carbon dioxide levels from "normal" strata made of sand, mud, and lime.

The ice-layers clearly show the extraordinarily metronomic oscillations of CO_2 levels that took place during the Ice Ages, and their exceedingly close correspondence with the temperature record deduced from other chemical properties of the ice archive: thus, CO_2 levels regularly fluctuated between around 180 ppm in cold phases of the Ice Ages, to around 280 ppm in warm interglacial phases (of which the Holocene is the latest). On this scale, the modern CO_2 outburst is clear as a near-vertical line, extending high above the upper limit boundary of these oscillations. Hence, since 1850 CE, more carbon dioxide (approximately 130 ppm) has been added to the atmosphere than is exchanged in normal glacial-to-interglacial transitions in the Ice Ages – and this has taken place more than a hundred times more quickly. It is, of course, still rising near-vertically. It may be the most rapid major change in atmospheric carbon dioxide levels in the Earth's history.[7]

The amount of "our" carbon dioxide is enormous, when we try to think of it in real terms. Although we intuitively think of gases as weightless – of being, indeed, "as light as air" – they do possess mass. That "extra" human-produced carbon dioxide weighs about a trillion metric tons, or about the same as 150,000 Great Pyramids of Khufu, hanging in the air above us. Considered as a layer of pure gas around the Earth, it is about a meter thick, and so waist-high to an adult, but already over the head of a small child. As it is now thickening at about a millimeter a

---

[7] The grafting of the Anthropocene carbon dioxide (and methane) trend onto the almost million-year Quaternary pattern preserved in Antarctic ice-layers is nicely shown in Fig. 2. in E. W. Wolff, "Ice sheets and the Anthropocene," in *A Stratigraphical Basis for the Anthropocene*, ed. C. N. Waters, J. A. Zalasiewicz, M. Williams, et al. (London: Geological Society London Special Publication 395, 2014), 255–63 (except that the diagram now needs to be perceptibly amended after another half-decade's worth of growth in atmospheric carbon dioxide and methane). In more detail, the shockingly abrupt rise that (in effect) terminates Holocene air, can be seen in Fig. 2 in J. Zalasiewicz, C. N. Waters, M. J. Head, C. Poirier, et al., "A formal Anthropocene is compatible with but distinct from its diachronous anthropogenic counterparts: a response to W.F. Ruddiman's 'Three Flaws in Defining a Formal Anthropocene'," *Progress in Physical Geography* 43, no. 3 (2019): 323.

1.2. *The Exhaust* by Anne-Sophie Milon. The illustration portrays rising levels of carbon dioxide that surround us all, invisibly, as we go about our daily lives. Image reproduced here with permission.

fortnight, it will, at current rates, keep up with – or outpace – the growth of that child (Figure 1.2).[8]

Some gases have only brief life-spans in the atmosphere. Methane, for instance, although a much stronger greenhouse gas than carbon dioxide, is oxidized in the atmosphere (to be converted into carbon dioxide) in a matter of a few years to decades. Carbon dioxide, though, has a relatively long residence time. It stays in the atmosphere for many millennia, until it is finally removed by the growth (and burial) of extra plant life, and by slowly reacting with rocks in what is termed "silicate weathering" – the latter probably being the most important (if slow-acting) thermostat-type control of Earth's temperature over geological timescales. The extra carbon dioxide added by humans so far has been estimated to be enough, already, to postpone the next Ice Age by some

---

[8] These calculations, and other equally extraordinary ones relating to the Anthropocene, may be found in J. Zalasiewicz, M. Williams, C. N. Waters, et al., "Scale and diversity of the physical technosphere: a geological perspective," *The Anthropocene Review* 4, no. 1 (2017): 9–22.

50,000 years (with only modest further emissions being needed to prolong that to 100,000 years). This kind of timescale is already taking the Anthropocene beyond the scale of a "blip," even a geological one.[9] As we shall see, some aspects of the Anthropocene will have a longevity far in excess even of this.

That current carbon dioxide rise is largely responsible for the temperature rise the Earth has experienced over the last century, now a little over 1 °C above pre-Industrial levels. The rise has been irregular, with pauses, largely because of the irregular way that heat is exchanged between oceans and atmosphere during natural climatic fluctuations such as that of the El Niño-Southern Oscillation (ENSO). Overall, the Earth is still – just – within the "normal" interglacial temperature limits of the Ice Age, though overall both oceans and atmosphere are on a clear heating trend. If continued, this will see the Earth break through, later this century, into the kind of temperature regime last seen in the Pliocene Epoch some three million years ago, when the Earth was a couple of degrees warmer, yet was, albeit, still an "icehouse" world with a substantial Antarctic ice-sheet. If business-as-usual carbon dioxide emissions are continued for somewhat longer, then the world will be taken into the kind of world the dinosaurs enjoyed: a hothouse Earth *without* major polar ice-caps. That would be a fundamentally different kind of planet from today's.[10]

As the Earth slowly warms in response to increased greenhouse gas levels, sea level responds yet more slowly to increasing warmth,[11] partly by thermal expansion of seawater, and partly through the melting of ice masses on land. So far, the total sea level rise above the remarkably stable

---

[9] This forward projection – or at least a succession of alternative projections, depending how much carbon dioxide we ultimately emit – is clearly illustrated in P. U. Clark, J. D. Shakun, S. A. Marcott, et al., "Consequences of twenty-first-century policy for multi-millennial climate and sea-level change," *Nature Climate Change* 6, no. 4 (2016) 360–69.

[10] This perspective, in the sixty-plus million-year record of the Cenozoic, is shown in Fig. 1 of K. D. Burke, J. W. Williams, M. A. Chandler, et al., "Pliocene and Eocene provide best analogs for near-future climates," *PNAS* 115, no. 52 (2018): 13288–293.

[11] The amount of extra heat entering the oceans from the greenhouse effect of carbon dioxide far exceeds the direct energy we gain from burning fossils fuels; estimates include those by L. Zanna, S. Khatiwala, J. M. Gregory, et al., "Global reconstruction of historical ocean heat storage and transport" *PNAS* 116, no. 4 (2019): 1126.

level of the last few millennia has been of the order of 20 centimeters, which is trivial (almost invisible) on the scale of deep geological time, but nevertheless enough to give some perceptible change on contemporary coastlines. The rate of sea level rise, though, has accelerated from some 1 millimeter per year in the mid-twentieth century to around 3 millimeters per year early in this millennium to approximately 4 millimeters per year in the last decade. The recent acceleration is due largely to the onset of major melting of Antarctica's and Greenland's ice-caps since about 2000 CE (each has lost about 5 trillion tons of ice in that time) while some 10 trillion tons of ice have been lost from mountain glaciers over a somewhat longer time interval, stretching back to the last century.[12]

There is a telling geological context here, too. In the last warm interglacial phase, about 125,000 years ago, when CO_2 levels were about 270 ppm and global temperatures were only slightly higher than today, sea level rose to somewhere between 6 and 9 meters above today's level, probably because of substantial melting of ice on Antarctica as waters warmed around it (sea levels during the third-from-last interglacial, about 400,000 years ago, may have reached yet higher levels[13]). When considering overall interglacial oscillations in sea level over a period of approximately 130 million years, 5–10 meters clearly represents a small fluctuation – one that might take place (or not) depending on relatively subtle differences in the configuration of Earth's "climate machine" at different peak interglacial times. As already noted, human impact on this system has now moved, via emission of greenhouse gases, well beyond the "subtle."

---

[12] There have been a number of recent assessments of the accelerating ice melt, including J. Mouginot, E. Rignot, A. A. Bjørk, et al., "Forty-six years of Greenland ice sheet mass balance from 1972 to 2018," *PNAS* 116, no. 19 (2019): 9239; E. Rignot, J. Mouginot, B. Scheuchl, et al., "Four decades of Antarctic ice sheet mass balance from 1979–2017," *PNAS* 116, no. 4 (2019): 1095; and M. Zemp, M. Huss, E. Thibert, et al., "Global glacier mass changes and their contributions to sea-level rise from 1961 to 2016," *Nature* 568, no. 3 (2019): 382–86.

[13] It seems that even parts of the "stable" East Antarctica ice-sheet may be lost at such times when, as was pointedly noted, carbon dioxide levels were not anywhere near as high as today's: T. Blackburn, G.H. Edwards, S. Tulaczyk, et al., "Ice retreat in Wilkes Basin of East Antarctica during a warm interglacial," *Nature* 583, no. 7817 (2020): 554–59.

Today, trends in sea level are clearly pointing upwards, and projections suggest anything from a rise of some 65 centimeters to a couple of meters by the end of this century, while beyond this, the amount of further sea level rise will reflect whether CO_2 emissions are held back tightly (to allow preservation of most of the Greenland and Antarctica ice-sheets) or whether they let rip in continued business-as-usual trends (to bringing about loss over centuries/millennia of much or most of this ice, triggering sea level rise of several tens of meters[14]). Given that many coastlines and deltas have been built out to extend to the approximately stable sea level of the mid to late Holocene, even a 1–2 meter scale (still geologically very small) sea level rise will inundate much densely populated land. The difficulties encountered in such a case will therefore not represent extreme Earth System change (in this respect at least), but will reflect how eagerly human populations have congregated around – and hardwired their enormous urban constructions into – the world's coastlines. These human communities have often made their positions more precarious, too, by causing meter-scale local subsidence of the ground by land drainage and the pumping of groundwater, oil, and gas.[15] So, while the provocation (thus far) remains small in relative geological terms, the human vulnerability is large. This is a manufactured vulnerability, and a natural part of an Anthropocene process.

A MINERAL EPOCH

While the processes behind Anthropocene climate change and sea level rise are pretty much as old as the Earth itself, other aspects are quite novel. The minerals that form our planet are its fundamental building blocks. Although intuitively one might think that Earth's mineral assemblage has been more or less constant through its history, our planet has in fact undergone a profound and distinctive form of mineral evolution, the course of which has been elegantly described by the mineralogist

---

[14] These scenarios and the feedbacks involved are discussed in J. Garbe, T. Albrecht, A. Levermann et al., "The hysteresis of the Antarctic ice sheet," *Nature* 585 (2020): 538–44.

[15] J. P. M. Syvitski, A. J. Kettner, I. Overeem, et al., "Sinking deltas due to human activities," *Nature Geoscience* 2 (2009): 681–89.

Robert Hazen and his colleagues.[16] They demonstrated a succession of mineral eras and epochs that have essentially showed increased mineral diversity through time.

The process begins in interstellar space, where primordial minerals condense as dust grains following supernova explosions; about a dozen of these have been identified, including diamond and a few carbides and nitrides. As dust clouds gathered to build our solar system, these dust grains were heated and aggregated into the building blocks of planets: asteroids and planetesimals, where new minerals formed, including various silicates and oxides. About 250 minerals were present in this phase, and these can be identified in meteorites that land on Earth, which represent the debris from this planet-building phase. As the Earth grew, and processes such as plate tectonics with volcanism and metamorphism began, planetary chemistry was further stretched out to give about 1,500 minerals, the natural complement of a dead rocky planet. As life appeared, more than 3.5 billion years ago, it initially made little major difference to the Earth's mineralogy. But, when photosynthesis evolved to oxygenate the Earth's oceans and atmosphere about 2.5 billion years ago, a large suite of oxide and hydroxide minerals formed, taking the total towards approximately 5,000 minerals. Since that time, this composition has stayed more or less stable – until now.

When humans entered the picture and began to manipulate the Earth's surface environment, they made new minerals, too, or at least new inorganic crystalline compounds, which are minerals in everything but formal classification. The International Mineralogical Association, which sets the standards for such things, recently *excluded* synthetic, human-made minerals from their classification. This exclusion is in itself wholly artificial, but there is a practical kind of logic to it, for otherwise mineralogists might have been overwhelmed by the flood of new materials for them to study.

What kind of "minerals" do humans make? Metals are one of the first examples. Pure "native" metals are rare in nature, with gold as the best-known exception, while native copper is occasionally found, and iron yet

---

[16] R. M. Hazen, D. Papineau, W. Bleeker, et al., "Mineral evolution," *American Mineralogist* 93 (2008): 1639–720.

more rarely as meteorites (such iron was prized in ancient times, meteoritic iron implements being found within Tutankhamen's tomb, for instance). Most metals in nature, though, are bound within chemical compounds – and it is humans that have become adept at separating them, firstly with copper, tin, and then iron in ancient times, and much more recently with others such as aluminium and titanium, that only exceedingly rarely occur as metal in nature, and molybdenum, vanadium, magnesium, and so on, which do not. Some metals are now separated in gargantuan amounts; the total amount of aluminum produced globally, which now exceeds 500 million tons (almost all since 1950 CE), is enough to cover the USA land surface and part of Canada in standard, kitchen aluminum foil. The amount of iron produced is well over an order of magnitude greater still. These novelties are therefore present in *geological* amounts – sufficient to help characterize Anthropocene strata, particularly in urban settings.

The phenomenon goes well beyond metals, to include many inorganic crystalline compounds synthesized in materials science laboratories worldwide for a wide diversity of purposes: novel synthetic garnets for lasers, tungsten carbide for ballpoint pens, semiconductor materials, the abrasive boron carbide ("borazon"), harder than diamond, and many others. How many? An early 2014 study hazarded that the number of minerals *sensu lato* may perhaps have been doubled by the synthesizing activities of humans.[17] That was way off the mark. In a thorough 2016 assessment of "Anthropocene mineralogy," Hazen and colleagues[18] noted the existence of a Karlsruhe-based Inorganic Crystal Structure Database, which then had records of more than 180,000 such inorganic compounds! (As of November 2019, there were more than 216,000 listed). Human ingenuity, therefore, has multiplied the number of "minerals" on Earth more than 40-fold, mostly over the last 100 years or so. In a commentary on this paper, the mineralogist Peter Heaney

---

[17] J. Zalasiewicz, R. Kryza, and M. Williams, "The mineral signature of the Anthropocene," in *A Stratigraphical Basis for the Anthropocene*, ed. C. N. Waters, J. A. Zalasiewicz, M. Williams, et al. (London: Geological Society of London Special Publication 395, 2014), 109–17.

[18] R. M. Hazen, E. S. Grew, M. J. Origlieri, and R. T. Downs, "On the mineralogy of the 'Anthropocene Epoch'," *American Mineralogist* 102 (2017): 595–611.

noted that while in most aspects, the story of the Anthropocene was one of destruction and reduction in diversity, in this respect the Anthropocene represented a huge, extraordinary *increase* in diversity, one with no parallels on any other planet in the Solar System – and perhaps with any planet in the cosmos.[19]

Among the materials that we synthesize are the plastics. These are not quite minerals as such, because they are organic compounds, with chemical compositions that can vary within fixed limits (nevertheless, there are organic "minerals" recognized in geology with which comparison may be made, such as amber). But this family of modern "mineraloids" is rapidly growing to become a part of – or even overwhelm, some might say – the Anthropocene, with a capacity to become a part of global geology that is in some ways greater than that of minerals *sensu stricto*. Plastics have a growth curve that closely resembles that of aluminum, with negligible pre–World War II production, growing to roughly 1 million tons per year by 1950, and then rapidly to more than 300 million tons per year today.

Plastics are so useful to us for a variety of reasons: they are light, strong, and resistant to abrasion, breakage, and decay, which is what makes them so geologically important. Once discarded (and much plastic is designed to be discarded immediately after a single use) plastic debris is easily transported by wind and water across landscapes and, with rivers as major conduits, to coastlines. From there it is carried by currents onto distant coastlines and into the deep ocean. A major component recognized only relatively recently is microplastics, especially textile-derived fibers, which have been shown to contaminate sediment almost universally in the ocean – even sea-floor sediments in the very deep ocean, thousands of miles from land.

It is such a recent, and recently recognized, global phenomenon that scientists are scrambling to get to grips with it. As a topic, it was barely on the radar when the Anthropocene Working Group began its analysis in 2009; by 2015, it had become a major issue in environmental studies generally, and as one spin-off, plastics were emerging as a major

[19] P. J. Heaney, "Defining minerals in the age of humans," *American Mineralogist* 102 (2017): 925–26.

characterizing element of Anthropocene strata.[20] There are still many unknowns – for instance, paradoxically, the distribution of plastics on land is far more complex, and therefore difficult to assess, than it is in the oceans. The land is still by far the greatest store of plastics, and so will continue to leak plastics into the oceans for centuries, and likely millennia, to come. Those plastics are clearly becoming a (indigestible, damaging, and often lethal) part of the biological food chain, too, and hence the enormous public concern about them.

The incorporation of plastics into the sedimentary record – that is, into far-future rock strata – is significant in demonstrating the geological character of this modern material. Contemplating the plethora of distinctive far-future fossils that will be produced – something that may intrigue some far-future paleontologist – may seem abstract. But there is a more immediate and practical significance here too, working in the short term. When plastics are at the surface, it is clear that they can interact with the local ecosystem, almost always to its detriment. Once they are buried deeply enough to become part of some future stratum, they are removed from biological interactions, and may be thought to be safely and permanently sequestered. But it is the intervening stage – when plastics are buried out of sight for easy study but interacting with soil ecosystems on land and benthic ecosystems on the sea floor, and yet are still capable of being reworked back to the surface – that is critical, biologically significant, and currently largely mysterious. This transitional phase, when plastics are *becoming* geology – but have not yet become so – is now ripe for study.

BULK MATERIALS

Plastics are one kind of newly created material that have been produced on a geological scale; the approximately 9 billion tons produced so far since the mid-twentieth century would allow the whole globe to be wrapped in somewhere between one and two layers of standard kitchen food wrap. But other materials have been extracted and dispersed by

[20] J. Zalasiewicz, C. N. Waters, J. Ivar do Sul, et al., "The geological cycle of plastics and their use as a stratigraphic indicator of the Anthropocene," *Anthropocene* 13 (2016): 4–17.

humans in far greater bulk – if perhaps not yet dispersed quite as widely as plastics.

Currently something like 316 *billion* tons of material are moved and reworked annually by humans[21] – of which, therefore, plastics are a one-thousandth part. Something approaching a tenth part is made up by concrete: a material that, although made (after a fashion) by the Romans, has become the signature synthetic rock of the Anthropocene, the graph of its seemingly inexorable rise in production[22] being remarkably similar to that of plastics, carbon dioxide emissions, "mineral" species, and many other of the aspects that Will Steffen, John McNeill, and their colleagues have demonstrated as showing the "Great Acceleration" of population growth, industrialization, and globalization in the mid-twentieth century.[23]

A large part of this crescendo of earth and rock movement is in the digging for such things as coal, where one needs to consider not only the mass of the material itself (with coal currently nearing 8 billion tons, or roughly double the mass of the annual production of cement) but also the mass of the earth and rock "overburden" that needs to be shifted in order to get to the hydrocarbon mineral itself. For coal, this can currently be up to 20 times the amount of the mineral itself; for a high-value mineral like diamond, up to ten tons of rock might be processed to obtain a single gram of diamond. And then, more prosaically, there is the scale of landscape movement, as towns and cities are built and rebuilt – which is much harder to assess globally (and even locally). In the study that produced the 316-billion-ton estimate, the arbitrary figure factored in for such landscape reshaping was twice that of the concrete involved, likely a large underestimate, while such forms of earth movement as

[21] A. H. Cooper, T. J. Brown, S. J. Price, et al., "Humans are the most significant global geological driving force of the 21st century," *The Anthropocene Review* 5 (2018): 222–29.
[22] See Fig. 1 in C. N. Waters, J. Zalasiewicz, C. P. Summerhayes, et al., "The Anthropocene is functionally and stratigraphically distinct from the Holocene," *Science* 351, no. 6269 (2016): 137.
[23] The original classic paper is: W. Steffen, P. J. Crutzen, and J. R. McNeill "The Anthropocene: are humans now overwhelming the great forces of nature?," *Ambio* 36 (2007): 614–21. It was later updated: W. Steffen, W. Broadgate, L. Deutsch, et al., "The trajectory of the Anthropocene: the Great Acceleration," *Anthropocene Review* 2, no. 1 (2015): 81–98.

ploughing, deep sea trawling, and mountain road construction were omitted altogether, to prevent the study, already gigantic in scope, from becoming endless and unfinishable. Hence the annual 316 billion tons calculated (the figure for 2015 CE, and now probably larger by a few billion tons) is likely to be a significant underestimate.

Nevertheless, the 316 billion tons comfortably exceeds – by some 24 times – the amount of sediment annually transported by rivers into the sea. Even this comparison has been skewed by the forces of the Anthropocene, for humans have interfered mightily with the world's fluvial plumbing in the construction of dams across most of the world's major rivers and a good proportion of the minor ones, with much sediment now being held back behind these dams, rather than reaching the sea.

Add all of this up, as another research group did – and this time to include the ploughlands, the trawled sea floor, and so on, all as part of what one might call the "physical technosphere" (more on the technosphere anon) – and a back-of-an-envelope calculation indicated that humans use, have used, and have discarded, some 30 trillion tons of Earth material, most of it since the mid-twentieth century.[24] This is equivalent to a layer of rubble and soil averaging 50 kilograms on each square meter of the Earth's surface – land and sea. As a species, therefore we are almost literally trudging ankle-deep though the debris of the Anthropocene, with progress becoming almost perceptibly harder each year.

THE SCALE OF ABSENT LIFE

While dealing with these multiples of billions of tons of mainly inorganic matter, we can note the comparison with the mass of life on Earth. This has recently been calculated – an extraordinary task! – with the error bars for some categories being very great. We know, for instance, that there is a "deep buried biosphere" of microbes with extremely slow metabolic rates living within fractures and pore spaces in rocks a

[24] J. Zalasiewicz, M. Williams, C. N. Waters, et al., "Scale and diversity of the physical technosphere: a geological perspective," *The Anthropocene Review* 4, no. 1 (2017): 9–22.

kilometer and more below the Earth's surface – but how much of such cryptic, subterranean life is there? Estimates have ranged from amounts comparable with visible surface life to only a small fraction of it. Even weighing a forest that can be imaged precisely with a satellite and also walked through in "ground-truthing," is not a trivial task. Nevertheless, a figure was arrived at for the mass of all life on Earth, totalling 550 billion tons of carbon-equivalent.[25] Add in the other elements of which life is composed, and the water content too, and life on Earth weighs in at some 2.5 trillion tons (or, about a trillion tons on a dry-mass basis, leaving out the water); a large figure, but dwarfed by the combination of our constructions and abundant cast-offs.

Much of this mass of Earthly life is made up of those forests – and here there is a clear human impact too. The authors of the study suggest, in a throwaway remark, that humans have roughly halved this living mass, largely by replacing forests with biotas that, while more immediately useful to us – such as pastures and cornfields – possess much less living *avoirdupois*. This trend, of course, has been in progress throughout much of the Holocene, if intensifying in the Anthropocene.

Within this overall decline, there have been some substantial winners and a rather larger number of losers. The major winners show up clearly on mass estimates of medium- to large-sized terrestrial vertebrates. These are humans, who collectively now make up about a third of the entire total of this category of body mass – a remarkable ascendency for one species. Most of the remaining two-thirds is made of the animals we keep to eat: the cows, pigs, goats, chickens, and others, though here the numerical abundance can only be regarded, for the animals concerned, as the most heavily qualified of victories.

The geological baseline clearly shows just how large this skewing of the terrestrial fauna has been. The paleontologist Anthony Barnosky in 2008 reviewed the number of species of terrestrial megafauna (those weighing more than 44 kilograms) in the Pleistocene, before humans

---

[25] Y. M. Bar-On, R. Phillips, and R. Milo, "The biomass distribution on Earth," *PNAS* 115, no. 25 (2018): 6506–511.

began to make an impact on their numbers.[26] Then, this terrestrial biomass was divided among some 350 species, including such iconic forms as the mastodon, mammoth, and woolly rhinoceros. Hunting by humans (largely) then roughly halved this number between about 50,000 and 7,000 years ago in what has come to be called the Quaternary Megafaunal Extinction, with the peak losses being clustered about 10,000 years ago.

This reduction in wild terrestrial vertebrates, though, was later balanced and then outweighed by the growing stocks of domestic animals, a trend that was also caught up in the steep upswing of the Great Acceleration, notably when the synthesis of nitrogen-based fertilizers allowed the supercharged production of grain and increased pasture growth that allowed animals to be fed efficiently, before they were fed to us. By this means, the total bulk of large vertebrates globally has increased perhaps tenfold over long-term baseline values, and continues to increase, while populations of wild mammals continue to fall.

One animal that symbolizes this ecological metamorphosis is the chicken, and specifically the broiler chicken. Grown for meat, it is now a staple of supermarkets and ready-made sandwiches globally. The chicken has a long history of domestication, reaching back perhaps 8,000 years in tropical south and south-east Asia, where its free-running, long-lived ancestor, the red jungle fowl *Gallus gallus*, still lives. The domesticated version, bred for fighting as well as meat, was taken to the Mediterranean region and Europe (its bones being common at Roman archeological sites, for instance) and to the New World in the sixteenth century. Through all of this time, the bird did not differ greatly from its wild ancestor, at least as far as its basic skeletal infrastructure was concerned.

This changed in the early post-WWII years. A series of Chicken-of-Tomorrow contests among chicken breeders in the USA morphed into a program that led to genetic modification through intense breeding and industrial-scale "vertical integration systems". These new systems put

---

[26] A. D. Barnosky, "Megafauna biomass tradeoff as a driver of Quaternary and future extinctions," *Proceedings of the National Academy of Sciences (USA)* 105, no. 1 (2008): 11543–48.

breeding units, farms, slaughterhouses and marketing together into gargantuan combines that now dominate production in the United States and in many other parts of the world. As a result, the chicken is now bigger-boned, much heavier, with hypertrophied breast meat, and far shorter-lived (<2 months). It has become by far the most numerous bird globally, with a standing stock of some 23 billion (by contrast, the population of sparrows is about half a billion, and of pigeons about 400 million), and indeed it outweighs all the other birds in the world *combined*, more than twofold.

Since the mid-twentieth century, it has also become a different bird, some three to four times larger in bulk than its wild ancestor: its bones are super-sized to match, and are now clearly distinct from those of both the wild ancestor and of the chicken remains recovered from pre-1950 archaeological sites. Paleontologists would call it a new morphospecies – and one of extraordinary abundance, for its hyperabundance at any one time is combined with a life-cycle, from egg to abattoir, of little more than six weeks. There is a correspondingly huge flux of these hypertrophied bones, therefore, going from dinner plates to rubbish tips and landfill sites, where, buried, they are protected from immediate scavenging and decay, enhancing the prospects for long-term fossilization. Amid all of the complexity of biological change across the Holocene–Anthropocene interval, the sudden appearance worldwide of this monstrously overgrown chicken skeleton is one clear paleontological marker of the Anthropocene. To add to its distinctiveness, the bones are chemically recognizable too – the carbon and nitrogen isotope ratios are clearly distinct, reflecting the change from scratching around in farmyards and back gardens to a factory-controlled diet via multinational animal-feed suppliers.[27] It is yet one more consequence (a planned and earnestly desired one, this time) of the steep rise in fertilizer use, which fuels the new food chain designed for humans (Figure 1.3).

As one food chain grows, another one diminishes. This is not a preordained rule, but at least for some parts of Earth's biology it is now empirical observation. The steep decline in large wild animals

---

[27] C. E. Bennett, R. Thomas, M. Williams, et al., "The broiler chicken as a signal of a human reconfigured biosphere," *Royal Society Open Science* 5 (2018): 180325.

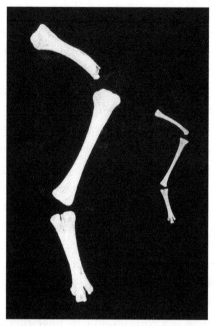

1.3. Comparison of the limb bones of a modern broiler chicken (left) and its ancestor, the red jungle fowl of Asia (right) at the same age of ~6 weeks. The jungle fowl can go on to live a decade or more, while the broiler chicken has reached slaughter age (and would not live much longer in any case). Image copyright of the Trustees of the Natural History Museum, London. The two specimens are held by the Natural History Museum and the University of London. Image reproduced here with permission.

worldwide, the contemporary continuation of the megafaunal extinctions, is at least obvious; these are large targets. But the extraordinary decline in flying insects is less obviously intuitive, as one thinks of flies, wasps, mosquitoes, and midges as the ultimate survivors, organisms that can survive and flourish in any circumstances. Hence, the palpable sense of shock that followed the beautifully conducted if deeply sobering study of the Krefeld Entomological Society, that showed these age-old pests of humans to be sensitive and indeed acutely vulnerable to changes in the world around them.[28] The study is a classic example of painstaking, systematic, methodical – and, to be sure, highly tedious – data collection, with no guarantee that any striking scientific result will

[28] A. Hallmann, A. Sorg, E. Jongejans, et al., "More than 75% decline over 27 years in total flying insect biomass in protected areas," *PLOS One* 12, no. 10 (2017): e0 185809.

emerge. Indeed, it would have been much better in hindsight if the results had been as tedious and mundane as the research behind it.

The study was carried out annually from 1986, trapping flying insects in nature reserves in Germany, collecting them, and weighing them. Obtaining meaningful results in such a study is a decidedly non-trivial exercise. The insects were logged on average every 11 days at 63 different locations, giving a haul of 53.54 kilograms of insects (equivalent to, say, the body mass of a small adult human) from a "total trap exposure period" of 16,908 days (or just over 46 years). Cleaning out the Augean Stables, that legendary task of Hercules, seems to represent a light spring-clean by comparison. The weighing alone was a fraught exercise, as the insects were stored in alcohol: a full half-page of text is taken up outlining the careful protocol needed to weigh alcohol-sodden dead insects and extract a representative mass value from the results. And as for looking in more detail – trying to identify the insects taxonomically instead of treating them all together in their *en masse* laboratory grave – the researchers merely said that that was another task for another (yet longer) day.

As it happens, there was probably not quite the need for such hair-splitting exactitude: the results are not in the least bit subtle. Over that 27-year period, the mass of flying insects in *nature protected* areas (not farms, not towns or cities) declined by three-quarters – and in summer by over 80 percent. It is a striking reduction in organisms near the base of the food chain. Was it just a regional phenomenon, in a central European country that is highly urbanized, and with modern agriculture? No – similar patterns and similar levels of insect decline were reported elsewhere,[29] in the tropical forests of Puerto Rico, as well as in Denmark and the UK. The precise reasons remain unclear. In Europe, factors such as pesticides, habitat loss, and light and noise pollution are quoted; in Puerto Rico, it's suggested that a warming climate is mainly to blame.

Something big is clearly going on – indeed, of a geological scale, with reverberations beyond the insect world, as concomitant declines in insectivorous birds are being reported too. *But*, most of these extraordinary studies, like those of the Krefeld community, began towards the end

---

[29] For example: P. Cardoso, P. S. Barton, K. Birkhofer, et al., "Scientists' warning to humanity on insect extinctions," *Biological Conservation* 242 (2020): 108426.

of the twentieth century, well after the phenomena of the "Great Acceleration" were underway, and so insects were likely already in considerable decline even at the start of these studies. Indeed, as landscape changes from agriculture and urbanization date back well into the Holocene, it is likely that insect communities were beginning to change thousands of years ago.

The trouble comes when trying to get any sensible idea of the scale of these changes. For this, one would need to have a *long-term* baseline measure of flying insect abundance, in the way that ice cores provide a marvellous record of atmospheric carbon dioxide measurements, and the way that cores of lake sediment can show when long-lived pesticides such as DDT, dieldrin, and aldrin began to become widely dispersed, even in remote environments, in the mid-twentieth century.[30] Insects and paleontology, though, do not go together as easily as do, say, molluscs (or even dinosaurs) and paleontology; the insect exoskeleton is marvellously adapted to serve these organisms in life, but many are too small and frail to help transfer into the fossil record after death. And so this particular kind of biological change is not easily inscribed into the usual geological archives.

That is not to say that insects do not fossilize at all. There is that almost fabled record of fossilized dragonflies with half-meter wingspans from the coal forest swamp strata of Carboniferous times, for instance (the fable turns out to be true in this case – albeit very rarely encountered). And there are some well-established paleontological cottage industries among the many forms of science done on the deposits of the Ice Age: the fossilized wing-cases of beetles and head-capsules of midges are among the kinds of biological proxy used to help reconstruct the scale and speed of climate change in the past. But it is one thing to do this kind of science where the discovery of just one fossil specimen can provide a clue to past climate, and quite another to use these patchy finds to work out the total biomass of all flying insects in the region at

---

[30] Scotland's Lochnagar is a nicely studied example: D. C. G. Muir, and N. L. Rose, "Persistent organic pollutants in the sediments of Lochnagar," in *Lochnagar: The Natural History of a Mountain Lake, Developments in Paleoenvironmental Research*, ed. N. L. Rose (Dordrecht: Springer, 2007), 375–402.

some prehistoric time. The power of the Anthropocene concept in providing deep-time baselines can therefore vary markedly, depending on the "fossilization" potential of each component phenomenon within the Earth System. Will some ingenious paleo-entomologist ever manage to work out a technique to provide a plausible baseline against which the modern insect decline can be placed? That would be a fascinating, and indeed important, development in paleontology.

THE RISE OF TECHNOLOGY

The driver of all of these changes is of course in one sense the ingenuity, social nature, and manipulativeness of the growing number of humans on this planet, as the term "Anthropocene" implies. But, for all of the extraordinary powers of the human brain, individually and collectively, and of the opposable thumb, there is much more to it than that. To take over a planet, one needs the proper tools. Given the potential of those two human organs, these tools came to be.

Technology is clearly a means to ratchet up human ability to win and use resources for our species' benefit. This has been the case from the Stone Age times of the late Pleistocene onwards, with the ubiquity of flint arrowheads and axe heads and the progressive developments through the use of metals, textiles, and other materials through the Holocene. But as technology has vastly diversified and become more powerful, sophisticated, and pervasive since the Industrial Revolution, one might say that it is now arguably the key driver of Anthropocene change.

The geologist Peter Haff speaks of it in terms of the *technosphere*,[31] and makes several points about this new "sphere" on Earth. One is that it is not just the sum total of all our technological objects, interpreted widely to be not just machines but also buildings, roads, dams, reservoirs, and

---

[31] P. K. Haff, "Technology as a geological phenomenon: implications for human well-being," in *A Stratigraphical Basis for the Anthropocene*, ed. C. N. Waters, J. Zalasiewicz, and M. Williams (London: Geological Society of London, Special Publication 395, 2014), 301–9. See also: P. Haff, "The technosphere and its physical stratigraphic record," in *The Anthropocene as a Geological Time Unit: A Guide to the Scientific Evidence and Current Debate*, ed. J. Zalasiewicz, C. N. Waters, M. Williams, and C. P. Summerhayes (Cambridge, UK: Cambridge University Press, 2019), 137–55.

farms (part of the farm machinery is now the supermarket chicken, a technological construct, quite unable to survive in the wild and fated to endure its short existence within a still-biological and sentient frame). Humans, in this view, individually and collectively, are also components of the technosphere: utterly dependent upon it – for without our various technological aids the Earth could not support more than a few tens of millions of people, living as in the Pleistocene as hunter-gatherers. Much human effort is now directed to maintain and ever further develop the already gigantic, and growing, technological construct on this planet. And the technosphere is taking on – perhaps not quite a life (yet) – but at least a momentum and dynamic of its own.

The technosphere is greater than the sum of its parts. In the same way that the biosphere is not just the total tally of all the animals, plants, and microbes on Earth, but includes all of the fluxes and interactions of matter and energy between them – and also between it and the rocks of the lithosphere, and the water and air of the hydrosphere and the atmosphere. The technosphere includes all of these interactions and is now large and powerful enough to change the nature of these other spheres. It unfolded from the biosphere, and is now growing rapidly at the expense of it.

The rate of growth and evolution of this planetary novelty is extraordinary. The biosphere can change and show major innovations too, of course, and the nature and rate of this change can be tracked in the geological record. Of famously rapid transitions, the most iconic is the development of a complex ecosystem of multicellular animals, following the billions of years of microbial domination of Earth. This half-billion-year-old transition, the "Cambrian explosion," that so puzzled Charles Darwin, is indeed a step change in the Earth System. And yet, anatomized in real time as generations of geologists have pored over the critical intervals of strata, this "explosion" turns out to have taken some 30 million years, encompassing, as stages within it, the emergence of burrowing animals, the development of hard skeletons, and the appearance of those poster-child fossils, the trilobites, that went on to dominate the sea floors of the Paleozoic Era. As Preston Cloud, that noted savant of Precambrian times, observed, it was more like a "Cambrian eruption."

The development of a technosphere, now becoming comparable in mass and energy consumption to the whole of the biosphere, took, by contrast, a matter of a few millennia (if one wants to include its early, locally dispersed stages) or a few centuries if one considers it as an interconnected planetary system. Most of its growth and diversification has happened since the mid-twentieth century Great Acceleration. How can one appreciate its scale and scope? Considering it in terms of human technological history puts it in a category that is *sui generis* – phenomenal, but isolated, with nothing to compare with in the natural world. But considering it as something that lies within the reach of paleontology does provide a certain kind of context.

The manufactured objects of the technosphere are artifacts to an archaeologist or historian, putting them firmly within the human realm. But thinking of them as biologically constructed, potentially fossilizeable objects – technofossils[32] – brings them into the realm of ichnofossils, also known as trace fossils, where they share conceptual space with fossilized burrows and footprints. Perhaps more particularly, technofossils may be compared to some of the more elaborate constructs of the animal world. Among the million-year-old volcanic strata of Tenerife, for instance, there are fossil soils among which can be found hundreds of acorn-sized and -shaped nests made by burrowing wasps, constructed of carefully selected pumice fragments as precisely and neatly assembled as any of the stone huts made by our ancestors. And on a larger, more collective scale, there are the mega-skyscrapers of the insect world: the termite nests that entomologists marvel at, with their myriad internal passages and heat regulation and air conditioning systems, which can be up to 10 meters high and a thousand cubic meters in volume. These intricate structures can be fossilized too – fine examples have been found in Africa and South America, ranging back to Jurassic antiquity. Such structures yield little to the Empire State Building in sophistication – and suggest that thinking of the technological constructions of humanity through a paleontological lens may not be completely outlandish as an exercise.

---

[32] J. Zalasiewicz, M. Williams, C. N. Waters, et al., "The technofossil record of humans," *The Anthropocene Review* 1 (2014): 34–43.

The petrified early Jurassic termite nests of South Africa show "advanced" construction, according to their discoverers.[33] Hence this iconic kind of animal architecture has existed on Earth for some 150 million years – having evolved from simpler constructions that have been found amongst the strata of the Triassic Period, some 50 million years previously. The hardware manufactured by these organisms is therefore evolving at rates comparable to biological evolution, where individual species spans are typically a few million years, and more fundamental changes in biological ground plan – the appearance of plankton communities with calcium carbonate skeletons, for instance (also an invention of Jurassic times) – take place every few tens or hundreds of millions of years. The "technology" of nonhuman animals is thoroughly a part of the biology of those organisms, and the complex behaviors that allow such constructions are as much under direct genetic control as are the biochemical processes that make their tissues and skeletons – and have also been integrated over geological timescales into the ecological webs of the Earth's biosphere.

Human technology, though, has departed from this long-established pattern. The earliest human technologies – indeed, pre-dating our own species – remained much the same over many millennia. Technology and the nature of artifacts evolved, in fits and starts, more quickly over the Holocene. But, an eighteenth-century human, even one living, say, in the heart of Paris, Berlin, or London, could not have foreseen the speeding – the *zoom*, as the science journalist Andrew Revkin has put it – of the rate of this kind of evolution, nor the rate of increase in the diversity and sophistication of the technological objects that were to come. Now, one human lifetime can encompass the change from typewriters and fountain pens to computers and the internet; little more than one human decade can see the introduction of a novelty like the mobile phone, and see it spread across the entire world and undergo several generations, each more sophisticated than the last. Technological evolution is now completely decoupled from the biological evolution of the

---

[33] E. M. Bordy, A. J. Bumby, O. Catuneanu, et al., "Advanced early Jurassic termite (Insecta: Isoptera) nests: evidence from the Clarens Formation in the Tuli Basin, Southern Africa," *Palaios* 19 (2004): 68–78.

humans that make the technology. It might even be argued that it is at least partly detached from the cultural evolution of humans (while technological evolution may be, rather, to a greater extent, driving cultural evolution).

Whatever the social and technological processes at the heart of this, the *paleontological* record will be one of the sudden appearance of an almost surreal hyper-diversity of fossilizeable objects. There are now likely hundreds of millions of distinct "technospecies," many of which are built for robustness and durability[34] – and hence, fossilizeability. This far exceeds a standing stock of biological species; of the order of ten million biological species exist today, many, if not most, soft-bodied and therefore not easily fossilizeable. And, these novel technospecies are now evolving several orders of magnitude more quickly than organisms have evolved at any time in Earth's previous history. The rate of evolution, indeed, is so great that few strata, natural or human-made, will be capable of preserving its precise pattern into the far future. Even a single landfill site may span all of humanity's electronic revolution. Any paleo-archaeologist of the far future[35] will see a transition as abrupt as the Cretaceous–Tertiary boundary, but expressed as an evolutionary radiation – at least of technofossils (and minerals too) – rather than as a mass extinction.

POSSIBILITIES

The possibilities here – of what our far-future paleo-archaeologist might see in the strata that will come to overlie the ones we know – seem too various now to project, perhaps even to enumerate. The trajectory of global warming, of sea-level rise, of ocean acidification, even of mass biological extinction, can be modeled and projected, based in part on solid physico-chemical principles and in part on the many examples we

---

[34] See discussion in J. Zalasiewicz, M. Williams, C. N. Waters, et al., "Scale and diversity of the physical technosphere: a geological perspective," *The Anthropocene Review* 4, no. 1 (2017): 9–22.

[35] The perplexities of a far-future paleontologist are explored in J. Zalasiewicz, *The Earth After Us: The Legacy That Humans Will Leave in The Rocks* (Oxford: Oxford University Press, 2008), 272.

can read from ancient strata, reflecting the times when the Earth has gone through comparable crises. But, dealing with one of the true novelties of the Anthropocene, the global spread and intensification of the technosphere, we have nothing to go on.

Will the technosphere's evolution be brought to a rapid halt, overwhelmed as its waste products destabilize Earth's heat balance and stifle the capabilities of its human intermediaries to maintain it? Will it undergo a succession of boom–bust cycles before attaining some kind of stable relationship with the biosphere, instead of (as at present) parasitizing and weakening it? Can it become independent of humans – and indeed come to behave as if the biosphere was expendable? Silicon intelligence (that does not necessarily have to be sentient) coupled with technological agency is a wild card in Earth history that makes narrative options alarmingly open.

What will determine which, if any, of these planetary options, which seem more like more lurid sci-fi brought alive than respectable Earth System science, will emerge? And so how different will the emerging Anthropocene be from the Holocene – and from all the preceding geological epochs too? The pathways, at least for now, still largely seem to depend on the interplay of human forces (that in turn determine these physical *forcings* affecting the planet), within familiar political, economic, and social arenas. These are the forces that will be discussed next, as Julia Adeney Thomas takes this narrative further and deeper. *Much* further and deeper, indeed, into realms that are far more complex and mysterious than anything that this simple narrative has produced.

Part of this leap in what one might call the scale of perplexity is the difference between tackling problems of cause and effect. It is a difference that is seen in geology, too. For instance, the end-Cretaceous mass extinction is now pretty well tied down to a giant asteroid impact on Mexico, 66 million years ago. The effects are uncomplicated enough: a whole lot of fossil species disappear at that stratal level, and new ones slowly begin to appear in the younger levels above; a thin layer at the disappearance level appears with more iridium than is seemly, with tiny particles of physically shocked mineral, and so on. It took a lot of steady work to pin down this physical succession (impatient scientists need not apply for this kind of task), but the techniques are generally straightforward, and the resulting patterns are as simple as you please – just as sharp and simple as are the Anthropocene patterns of a sudden flood of plastic particles, of a sharp jump in atmospheric levels, and so on. The resulting picture is clearly defined, and about as subtle as a brick.

Ah, but, working out quite *why* the Mexico impact was so lethal is quite another matter. There were other large impacts in the geological record that did not generate anything like so much mayhem within the biosphere – so what particular combination of blast forces, chemical fallout, climate feedbacks, ecosystem responses, and so on (one can carry on adding potentially significant factors for quite some time) were responsible for the scale of the mass kill, and how did they work? This conundrum is still a work in progress.

There are many such riddles in geology, where one has to try to puzzle through the workings of physical, chemical, and biological processes. But none so far, where one has to also factor in investment decisions by brokers, political ambitions, military strategy, religious ideals, community traditions, football team allegiances, tax policy, advertising revenues, agricultural subsidies, women's rights, levels of economic inequality (and here one can go on for *much* longer than in considering the workings of Cretaceous times). All these socio-economic and political factors are in the process of producing geology, some on a huge scale. This is something quite new and quite bewildering for geologists, who are not so much fish out of water here, as fish tipped into outer space on the far side of some distant asteroid.

This is where the kind of narratives developed by Julia Adeney Thomas in the following pages are so important, in beginning the task of making sensible and useful patterns out of this ever-changing and growing maelstrom of human activity. It really is key to understanding, and seeking to come to terms with, the Anthropocene. Such stories, as she says, matter.

And if, all in all, among these stories, amid this interlacing of age-old and terribly new power struggles, the Earth is seen as a player and not simply a stage, then perhaps the Anthropocene can still remain Holocene-like enough to remain a mere epoch, rather than growing monstrously into a period, era, or eon. If it remains modest, it might perhaps remain, also, a friend to us.

FURTHER READING

Thomas, J. A., M. Williams, and J. Zalasiewicz. *The Anthropocene: A Multidisciplinary Approach.* Cambridge, UK: Polity Books, 2020.

Waters, C.N., J. A. Zalasiewicz, M. Williams, M. Ellis, and A. Snelling, eds. *A Stratigraphical Basis for the Anthropocene.* London, UK: Geological Society of London, Special Publication 395, 2014.

Williams, M., J. Zalasiewicz, A. Haywood, and M. Ellis, eds. "The Anthropocene: a new epoch of geological time?" *Philosophical Transactions of the Royal Society* 369A (2011): 833–1112.

Zalasiewicz, J. *The Earth After Us: The Legacy That Humans Will Leave In The Rocks.* Oxford, UK:Oxford University Press, 2008. 272 pp.

Zalasiewicz, J., C. N. Waters, M. Williams, and C. P. Summerhayes, eds. *The Anthropocene as a Geological Time Unit: A Guide to the Scientific Evidence and Current Debate.* Cambridge, UK: Cambridge University Press, 2019.

CHAPTER 2

Humanities and Social Sciences: Human Stories and the Anthropocene Earth System

Julia Adeney Thomas

People tell stories, and always have. Now that geologists are signaling a new chapter in Earth's story, humanists and social scientists are chiming in with their perspectives on the Anthropocene, and rightly so.[1] This extraordinary recalibration of the relationship between people and our only planet brings together the physical sciences and the human sciences in new ways, overcoming a century or more of discrete endeavors. Given the distinctive forms of knowledge, vocabulary, questions, and ways of speaking, dissonance among these approaches is hardly surprising. Different disciplines have been siloed from one another like vast towers above a harvested, mono-cropped plain. But now there's great eagerness on the part of non-scientists to engage the concept of the Anthropocene, and an eruption of different tales. To make sense of the cacophony in the humanities and social sciences, I suggest a loose typology of the narratives current among humanists and social scientists. What I ultimately emphasize is how important it is for us to find a common language based in the new reality revealed by Earth System

---

[1] Helmuth Trischler highlights the speed with which the concept of the Anthropocene entered non-scientific fields and the lively debates it has engendered. See Tricschler, "Introduction," in Helmuth Trischler, ed., *Anthropocene: Exploring the Future of the Age of Humans*, RCC Perspectives 2013, no 3. doi.org/10.5282/rcc/5603. For a full exploration of the term's use in many disciplines, see Jan Zalasiewicz, Colin N. Waters, Erle C. Ellis, et. al., "The Anthropocene: comparing its meaning in geology (chronostratigraphy) with conceptual approaches arising in other disciplines," *Earth's Future*, vol. 9 (2021). https://doi.org/10.1029/2020EF001896

scientists and geologists. As historian Libby Robin says, we need a common language for our debates.[2]

STORYTELLING

The point I want to make about the Anthropocene is, fundamentally, a humanist's point: reality does not dictate the stories we tell ourselves. Even the reality of the Anthropocene, all-encompassing though it is, gives rise to more than just one storyline. I'm not talking about fiction. With the true stories of history, anthropology, economics, and much else, reality has constrained narrative possibilities only loosely, if at all. For instance, it's a fact that we all die, but tales of transcending death and attaining immortality of one sort or another are everywhere. The discipline of history, philosopher Hannah Arendt argued, was founded by the ancient Greeks to ensure that some mere mortals – the heroes among us – might become as gods, living forever through verse.[3] It's also true that water flows downhill, but we dream up pulleys, pumps, and water wheels to move it in desired directions, telling ourselves tales about our conquest of nature.[4]

This talent for stories is both a boon and a danger, because stories aren't just glosses on reality: they also mold the real world. Undeniably, the story of modernity, with its narrative of individualism, infinite progress, and endless economic and technological growth, did much to create the Anthropocene, however unwittingly. For precisely this reason, as humanists and social scientists respond to the new Earth System story from Jan Zalasiewicz and his colleagues on the Anthropocene Working

---

[2] Libby Robin, "Histories for changing times: entering the Anthropocene?," *Australian Historical Studies*, vol. 44, no.3 (2013), 329–340, here 336. https://doi.org/10.1080/1031461X.2013.817455

[3] Hannah Arendt, "The concept of history," *Between Past and Present: Eight Exercises in Political Thought* (New York: Penguin Books, 2006).

[4] Historians evaluate this conquest differently. For instance, David Blackbourn, *The Conquest of Nature: Water, Landscape, and the Making of Modern Germany* (New York and London: W.W. Norton and Company, 2006) tells a fairly positive story of human interventions in Germany's riverways. Mark Cioc's history is rather darker. Mark Cioc, "The Rhine as world river," in Edmund Burke III and Kenneth Pomeranz, eds., *The Environment and World History* (Berkeley and Los Angeles: University of California Press, 2009).

Group (AWG), we need to reconsider our narratives. Better stories will not only help us understand how human activities came to wreak such havoc, but also how we might navigate the perilous conditions ahead. In this way, Anthropocene stories, like all stories, connect past, present, and future. But there's something fundamentally different about a good Anthropocene story as opposed to earlier stories in the humanities and social sciences. To be useful, they must contend with a much more restricted future. The dizzying range of stories once thought possible is narrowed by the Anthropocene. Indeed, our previous surfeit of true stories may well be an artifact of the Holocene itself, a form of "epistemological anarchy" only possible in the probabilistic universe of a relatively stable Earth System. Yet even so, even under the constraints of this fearsome new epoch, choices remain. The Anthropocene radically constricts potential plotlines, but does not dictate them, at least not yet.

For now, the humanist imperative to craft stories that open on future possibilities, however narrowed, still rules. At root, the commitment to narrative potential is a commitment to liberty. Stories are about choices. They describe a situation and show us how the protagonist responded to the genie's offer of three wishes or dealt with a threat to national security. Believing in the human capacity for decency and justice along with our talent for cruelty and destruction means believing in more than just one true story. The tradition of critical thought, as literary critic Ian Baucom rightly observes, "has long understood its vocation as simultaneously descriptive and transformative: a method oriented to mapping the situation in which we find ourselves and to making something emancipatory of that situation."[5] The truest stories of the Anthropocene will map our altered planetary system in accord with the science and, dire though the situation is, still try "to make something emancipatory" of it. These narratives can emerge from conversations across disciplines – geologists and Earth System scientists, on one hand, and humanists and social scientists on the other. Each side has to listen hard for the new rhythms of this dialogue.

[5] Ian Baucom, *History 4° Celsius: Search for a Method (Specters of the Atlantic: Volume Two)* (Durham, NC: Duke University Press, 2020), 8.

Three is an important number in stories: we tell tales of the three
sisters (weird and otherwise[6]), the three wishes, the three ages of man
(and woman) from infancy to old age, the three aspects of the Christian
god, the three vinegar tasters (the Buddha, Confucius, and Lao-tzu) and
on and on. Three seems particularly good for adventures and parables.
The Anthropocene, being both an epic adventure and a morality tale, has
also spawned triplicates. Three types of story can be discerned in the vast
literature inspired by this term. Each one brings Earth System science and
human history together to create a particular vision of where we've been
and where we're going. I have dubbed them "Anything Goes," "The
Singular Story," and "A Democracy of Voices." Naturally, this typology is
highly artificial (which typology is not?), but if stories are important both
for making sense of the world and for world-making, then analyzing the
types of stories available to us at this crucial moment is essential.

While all three types of narrative portray humanity in relation to
Earth in the Anthropocene, I call the first "Anything Goes" because it
makes little reference to the scientific literature. The result is an array of
imaginative terms and alternative planetary visions. But, because this way
of talking about the Anthropocene maintains the traditional separation
between Earth's story and modern human stories, it is deeply conserva-
tive. The Anthropocene changes little or nothing about the old ways of
plotting stories and judging protagonists.

The two other types of narrative take Earth System science and
geology seriously. Both recognize the new epoch's fundamental challenge to the ways we've thought about human values and destinies. They
also acknowledge the non-negotiable limits our altered planet puts on
our potential plotlines. What I call the "Singular Story" aims at interdisciplinary synthesis, making geology, poetry, politics, and everything else
speak the same language so that humanity can be included in large-scale
computational models of the Earth System. From this perspective, the
human story – the evolution of our species, animal domestication, the
efflorescence of agriculture, complex political societies, dreams, dance,

---

[6] The three weird sisters appear in Shakespeare's "Macbeth," and less weird sisters appear
in Giambattista Basile "The Three Sisters" (an Italian fairytale) in his 1634 work, *The
Pentamerone*.

economic forms, and values – evolved within the Earth System story until the mid-twentieth century when we – as a species – started overwhelming the great forces of nature. Now our collective activity is calculated along-side ocean dynamics, terrestrial ecosystems, tropospheric chemistry, and a host of other powerful forces. A new integrated story has begun.

The third group of stories promoting a "Democracy of Voices" also takes the science seriously, but argues that our best hope is not to insist on a single tale, but to play up the diversity of perspectives that has been the strong suit of our species, as well as the ace card of the humanities and social sciences. This multiplicity retains the resilience-building pluralism of diverse cultures and values, *but only to the extent warranted* by planetary boundaries. Both the Singular Story and the Democracy of Voices accept that humanity's Anthropocene narratives are restricted in ways they never were in the Holocene. Back then, the time and space for experimentation appeared limitless; now, our time is short, and our planet feels smaller. I argue here that as we struggle to bend the Earth System's trajectory toward a stabilized state, we will need both the singular global story and small-scale textured tales of Anthropocene experiences. We need the global narrative incorporating our species among the forces acting on the Earth System and also the many diverse, redundant experiments in resili-ence that might provide ballast as we lurch over thresholds and tipping points. Both these types of story are radical in their commitment to incorp-orating Earth System science into new human stories. They aim to be true both to our new reality and to our old powers of invention. Below I explore these three types, focusing especially on the second and third in relation to a particularly important recent paper on the Earth System's trajectory.[7]

STORY #1 ANYTHING GOES

The "Anything Goes" group, taking its cue from the eponymous musical, is the most fun.[8] With a pell-mell playfulness that often sets Earth System

---

[7] Will Steffen, Johan Rockström, Katherine Richardson, et al., "Trajectories of the Earth System in the Anthropocene," *PNAS*, vol. 115, no. 33 (August 14, 2018), 8252–8259.

[8] Zóltan Boldizsár Simon calls this phenomenon "runaway agonism" in *The Epochal Event: Transformations in the Entangled Human, Technological, and Natural Worlds* (London, UK: Palgrave Macmillan, 2020).

science and stratigraphy aside, writers respond inventively to the new word. Some adopt defensive postures, attacking the proposed geological epoch as a threat, even an existential threat, to their understanding of the world. Conversely, a few in this group take "Anthropocene" as inspiration for an Ecomodernist utopia where infinite growth and progress continues, uncoupled from the biogeophysical planet. Of this "Anything Goes" group, it may truly be said that "the Anthropocene is a concept that has as many definitions as the authors who write about it."[9] Essentially, the "Anything Goes" stories try to shoehorn our new Earth System reality into old Holocene categories.

The Anthropocene is hardly the first scientific recasting of human history to spark a hundred disparate tales and much dissent. A century and a half before Paul Crutzen proposed "Anthropocene," Darwin stirred up a hornet's nest with "evolution." Humanists and social scientists danced dizzy tangos with the idea that humans were descended from apes. Reformers Herbert Spencer and Beatrice Webb applied natural selection in the form of Social Darwinism to society. Anglo-American triumphalists applied the phrase "survival of the fittest" (one that Darwin had originally borrowed from Spencer) to justify empire and "their sort." Germans, with a keener grasp of Darwin's meaning, recognized that the form of "fitness" driving evolution had less to do with gunboats, finance, and colonies, and more to do with sex. Yet carnal love and the maximization of offspring were hardly suitable for state sponsorship, so German authorities also banned evolution from school books.[10] Japanese leaders redefined the term in yet another way, arguing that their up-and-coming nation could hop, skip, and jump over evolution's intermediary stages to join Western Imperial Powers.[11] Some of these Meiji oligarchs eagerly

---

[9] Robynne Mellor, "Review of *Economic Development and Environmental History in the Anthropocene: Perspectives on Asia and Africa* ed. by Gareth Austin; *The Birth of the Anthropocene* (Berkeley and Los Angeles: University of California Press, 2016) by Jeremy Davies; and "After nature: a politics for the Anthropocene by Jedediah Purdy," *Journal of World History*, vol. 30, no. 3 (September 2019), 441–448, here page 441.

[10] Alfred Kelly, *The Descent of Darwin: The Popularization of Darwinism in German, 1860–1914* (Chapel Hill, NC: The University of North Carolina Press, 1981).

[11] For Herbert Spencer's 1892 letter to cabinet minister Kaneko Kentarō (1853–1942), see Herbert Spencer, *On Social Evolution*, edited and with an introduction by J. D. Y. Peel (Chicago: University of Chicago Press, 1972), 253–257. See also, Julia Adeney Thomas,

presented their 1890 constitution, the first such instrument of government in modern Asia, to Spencer himself. The great Sage of the Tennis
Courts (said to dictate his sprawling books while knocking balls) immediately dismissed the Japanese effort as far too advanced for such a
backward people. The Japanese document had originally been penned
in German and was primarily modeled on the Prussian constitution.
The descent of social theory based on misconceptions of the "descent
of man" is too well known, and too grim, to bear repeating, as eugenics
exemplifies. Darwin's theory, or at least some its terms, were reima-
gined by social scientists as grounds for many things, including selfish
individualism, imperialism, racism, classism, utopianism, sexual pas-
sion, and social engineering. In response to evolutionary theory, anything went.

As with Darwinism, so too with the Anthropocene. It also threatens
long-held beliefs about the place of humanity in the world, the production of knowledge, and the possibilities for our future. One response is
to deflect attention from the evidence by focusing on the word. The
giddy multiplication of alternative terms for "Anthropocene" make
Humpty Dumpty look like an amateur in the world of wordplay.[12] In
2013 in French and then in English in 2016, the pioneering book *The*

Reconfiguring Modernity: Concepts of Nature in Japanese Political Ideology (Berkeley and Los
Angeles: University of California Press, 2001).

[12] Scientifically grounded precursors and additions include the following: In 1992, science
journalist Andrew Revkin used the term "Anthrocene" in a book on global warming.
(Andrew C. Revkin, *Global Warming: Understanding the Forecast* (New York: Abbeville Press,
1992.) In 1999, entomologist Michael Samways coined "Homogenocene" to highlight
the unprecedented scale and transglobal nature of species invasions. (Michael Samways,
"Translocating fauna to foreign lands: here comes the Homogenocene," *Journal of Insect
Conservation*, vol. 3 (1999), 65–66.) In 2000, Paul Crutzen's proposal of "Anthropocene"
at a conference was unpremeditated, although he subsequently learned that freshwater
ecologist Eugene Stoermer had been using the term informally since the 1980s, which
led to their joint publication. (See Will Steffen, Jacques Grinevald, Paul Crutzen, and
John McNeill, "The Anthropocene: conceptual and historical perspectives," *Philosophical
Transactions of the Royal Society*, vol. 369 (2011), 842–867. doi: 10.1098/rsta.2010.0327).
Fisheries biologists Dirk Zeller and Daniel Pauly suggested "Myxocene" in 2005, an age
of jellyfish and slime, to reflect human-driven changes to the oceans (Dirk Zeller and
Daniel Pauly, "Good news, bad news: global fisheries discards are declining, but so are
total catches," *Fish and Fisheries*, vol. 6 (2005), 156–159. doi:10.1111/j.1467-
2979.2005.00177.x).

Shock of the Anthropocene presented chapters on the Thermocene, Thantocene, Phagocene, Phronocene, Agnotocene, Capitalocene, and Polemocene.[13] But even so, this compendium looks scant compared with the more recent, encyclopedic list of a thousand alternative coinages gathered by Clémence Hallé and Anne-Sophie Milon.[14] These include Manthropocene, Chthulucene, Heterocene, and on and on. The reasons for trying to redefine the Anthropocene in ways at odds with the chronostratigraphic and ESS definition range from a desire to offer different models of explanation for the current ecological crisis to a distrust of science, partially manufactured by political and corporate interests. As literary scholar Elizabeth M. DeLoughrey notes, each word initiates a different storyline, featuring different protagonists, causes, and goals.[15]

Foreswearing wordplay, but still insisting that "Anything Goes," some social scientists have repurposed "Anthropocene" to accord with their own discipline's imperatives. For instance, anthropologist and political scientist James C. Scott refers to a "thin Anthropocene" that dates "from the use of fire by *Homo erectus* roughly half a million years ago and extends up through the clearances for agriculture and grazing and the resulting deforestation and siltation." However, as he admits, "there is no particular reason to insist on the label 'Anthropocene'." His point is "to insist on the global environmental impact of the domestication of fire, plants, and grazing animals," not to reorganize the Geological Time Scale.[16] As scientists have observed, having a global environmental impact is not the same as producing a new geological epoch or altering the Earth System. In a similar vein, global historian John McNeill

---

[13] Christophe Bonneuil and Jean-Baptiste Fressoz, *The Shock of the Anthropocene: The Earth, History and Us*, English translation by David Fernbach (Brooklyn, NY: Verso, 2016). The original French version (2013) did not include chapters on "Agnotocene" and "Capitalocene."

[14] Clémence Hallé and Anne-Sophie Milon, "The infinity of the Anthropocene: a (hi)story with a thousand names," in *The Science and Politics of Landing on Earth*, ed. Bruno Latour and Peter Weibei (Cambridge, MA: MIT Press, 2020), 42–43.

[15] Elizabeth M. DeLoughrey, *Allegories of the Anthropocene* (Durham, NC: Duke University Press, 2019).

[16] James C. Scott, *Against the Grain: A Deep History of the Earliest States* (New Haven, CT: Yale University Press, 2017), 19–20.

occasionally observes "the customs of historians" over those of geologists, in arguing that "the Anthropocene began at different times in different places. Some places, for example Venice or Mexico City, were well into their local Anthropocenes by 1750. People transformed swamps into cities in both places. Other places, such as the peaks of Patagonia or the depths of the Marianas Trench, which are (I imagine) very much as they were in recent centuries, may not have entered it yet." His use of the concept, as he rightly says, "would not suit geologists" whose standards require a near-synchronous global impact.[17] These appropriators of "the Anthropocene" part ways with Earth System scientists, happy to leave them to their own devices, while social science continues on its accustomed path.

Others in the "Anything Goes" camp are not so generous to geologists and Earth System scientists. For them, "the Anthropocene" is a provocative red cape waved by a devilish matador. The AWG and the discipline of geology are denounced as misguided, if not downright malicious, enterprises. Instead of ceding to stratigraphers their own conventions on planetary time and letting Earth System scientists have their say about the Earth System, this group presents them with a catalog of their errors. Among the misdeeds of the AWG is "defining the Anthropocene in order to meet stratigraphy's requirements."[18] Another is "the geologists' slow motion – dare one say glacial – assessment of the Anthropocene's claims," a pace said to have "eroded their authority over the outcome."[19] An environmental historian charges them with ignoring the biosphere:

---

[17] John R. McNeill, "Energy, population, and environmental change since 1750" in John R. McNeill and Kenneth Pomeranz, eds. *The Cambridge World History, Volume 7: Production, Destruction and Connection, 1750–Present, Part 1: Structures, Spaces, and Boundary Making* (Cambridge, UK: Cambridge University Press, 2017), 52. McNeill's approach in this essay diverges from his earlier work advocating a mid-twentieth century understanding of the Anthropocene which he has done both as a member of the AWG and in print. See for instance, the works cited above and John R. McNeill and Peter Engelke, *The Great Acceleration*, (Cambridge, MA: Harvard University Press, 2016).

[18] Jean-Baptiste Fressoz, "Does political ecology need the approval of geologists?" *IPPR Progressive Review*, vol. 24, no. 3 (2017), 172.

[19] Rob Nixon, "The Anthropocene: the promise and pitfalls of an epochal idea," in Gregg Mitman, Marco Armiero, and Robert S. Emmett, eds., *Future Remains: A Cabinet of Curiosities for the Anthropocene* (Chicago: University of Chicago Press, 2018), 15.

"in the rapid ascendency of planetary earth science, and the subsequent displacement of ecology as the sine qua non of environmental sciences, we risk losing sight of life, in all its diverse forms, human and nonhuman, that have shaped the planet."[20] But these supposed errors of geologists are nothing compared to their alleged ethical lapses. Anthropocene scientists stand accused of ascribing moral culpability to everyone equally, promoting a "human species-supremacist planetary politics," echoing "biblical dominion," and promulgating a "deeply problematic" and "ignorant" "philosophy of history."[21] Anthropologist Kathryn Yusoff believes that this science "is a praxis of exploitation, dispossession, subjection, and othering, closely tied to the slave mode of production."[22] "White Geology" seems a greater enemy than an altered planet.

Responding to these concerns on scientific grounds has availed little. Explanations of stratigraphy's standards and processes seem to fall on deaf ears. For instance, producing geology's foundational tool of global comparison – the Geological Time Scale – requires widespread agreement and precise forms of physical evidence, making stratigraphy the very heart of that enterprise. One might point out that the AWG's deliberations look almost swift if we remember that the Holocene was first proposed in 1867, formally submitted to the International Geological Congress in Bologna in 1885, and officially ratified by the

[20] Gregg Mitman, "Hubris or humility? Genealogies of the Anthropocene," in Gregg Mitman, Marco Armiero, and Robert S. Emmett, eds., *Future Remains: A Cabinet of Curiosities for the Anthropocene* (Chicago: University of Chicago Press, 2018), 61.

[21] Eileen Crist, "On the poverty of our nomenclature," *Environmental Humanities*, vol. 3 (2013), 129. See also Eileen Crist, *Abundant Earth: Toward an Ecological Civilization* (Chicago: University of Chicago Press, 2019); David Wallace-Wells, *The Uninhabitable Earth: Life After Global Warming* (New York: Tim Duggan Books, 2019), 20; Daniel Hartley, "Anthropocene, Capitalocene, and the problem of culture," in Jason W. Moore, ed., *Anthropocene or Capitalocene: Nature, History and the Crisis of Capitalism* (Oakland, CA: PM Press, 2016), 154–55.

[22] Kathryn Yusoff quoted on H-Environment, Call-for-Papers: Conference on "Inhuman Memory: Race and Ecology across Timescales," (26 October 2019) https://networks.h-net.org/node/19397/discussions/5170380/cfp-conference-inhuman-memory-race-and-ecology-across-timescales (accessed October 2021). See also Kathryn Yusoff, *A Billion Black Anthropocenes* (Minneapolis: University of Minnesota Press, 2019); Heather Davis and Zoe Todd, "On the importance of a date, or, decolonizing the Anthropocene," *ACME: An International Journal for Critical Geographies*, vol. 16 (December 2017), 761–80.

Committee of the International Union of Geological Sciences (IUGS) only in 2008. The idea that ESS ignores the biosphere has no basis. Most of what we know about Earth's life forms and their evolution is written in the rocks, so geologists rarely lose sight of life. The power of the biosphere to shape the planet's chemistry and geology is encapsulated in the very term "biogeophysical."[23] As the paleobiologist Jan Zalasiewicz and colleagues explained in 2014, five years after the AWG was established:

> "The significance of the Anthropocene lies not so much in seeing within it the 'first traces of our species,' but in the scale, significance, and longevity of change to the Earth System. Humans started to develop an increasing, but generally regional and highly diachronous, influence on the Earth System thousands of years ago. With the onset of the Industrial Revolution, humankind became a more pronounced geological factor, but in our present view it was from the mid-twentieth century that the worldwide impact of the accelerating Industrial Revolution became both global and near-synchronous."[24]

Often such explanations of scientific protocols and scientific definitions are brushed aside.

Ecosocialist Ian Angus has attempted to explain to detractors that "Anthropocene" refers not "to all humans, but to an epoch of global change that would not have occurred in the absence of human activity."[25] Scientists do not blame everyone (nor indeed anyone); they do not relish *Old Testament* dominion nor espouse a theory of human history; and nothing in the AWG's reports suggests that the proposed new epoch is cause for celebration or self-congratulation. The reason for calling it

---

[23] For ways in which ecology is key to the Anthropocene, see Sharon Kingsland, "The importance of history and historical records for understanding the Anthropocene," *The Bulletin of the Ecological Society of America*, vol. 98 (2017), 64–71. doi:10.1002/bes2.1296. See also the works of Stephen Jay Gould (1941–2002), professor of both biology and geology.

[24] Jan Zalasiewicz, Colin N. Waters, Mark Williams, et al., "When did the Anthropocene begin? A mid-twentieth century boundary level is stratigraphically optimal," *Quaternary International*, vol. 383 (2015), 201.

[25] Ian Angus, *Facing the Anthropocene: Fossil Capitalism and the Crisis of the Earth System* (New York: Monthly Review Press, 2016), 232.

"Anthropocene" is the accelerating dominance of human activities driving the Earth System.

The names geologists give to intervals of time in Earth's long history aren't meant as the be-all and end-all of their analysis, any more than referring to the "Age of Revolutions" in the late eighteenth and early nineteenth centuries suffices as historical analysis. In fact, these names are sometimes whimsical. For instance, the Silures, a fierce tribe who gave Roman invaders a hard time, are the namesakes of the Silurian Period (443 million to 416 million years ago) simply because the nineteenth-century Scottish fossil hunter Sir Roderick Murchison (1792–1871) remembered his Tacitus while digging in Wales. In no way was Murchison suggesting that he had discovered evidence of Welsh triumph in the layer of rock representing deep, trilobite-haunted seas. Naming the most recent strata formed on Earth's crust "Anthropocene" is certainly not a celebration of human supremacy. While a group called "Ecomodernists" proclaim a "Good Anthropocene" where "resource-efficient technologies" decouple humanity from reliance on planetary systems, the members of the AWG reject the idea that human beings can go our merry way without need for a rich biosphere, breathable air, and fresh water. They stress that we are irrevocably part of the Earth System, and few are sanguine about our future. In fact, some Earth System scientists are resorting to uncharacteristically emotive words like "emergency" and looking with dread to looming social, political, and economic dislocations.[26] There is nothing triumphalist about their bleak view.

Some writers get muddled about the science, perhaps because they rely for their information on popularizers. For example, one fanciful misconception is that "the signature characteristic of the Anthropocene ... is that it is declared from an imagined point in a future millions of years from now"[27] so that its "starting point [is] in a distant future in which all important events have already

---

[26] For example, the term "emergency" is used by Timothy Lenton et al., to describe our current situation. Timothy M. Lenton, Johan Rockström, Owen Gaffney, et al., "Climate tipping points: too risky to bet against," *Nature*, vol. 575 (2019), 596.

[27] Julia Nordblad, "On the difference between Anthropocene and climate change temporalities," *Critical Inquiry*, vol. 47 (Winter 2020), 336.

taken place."[28] While it's exciting to think of strata as future phantasms projected by feverishly imaginative geologists, strata – and geologists – are more grounded, quite literally. The durable, globally synchronous layers in the Earth's crust that mark the proposed start of the Anthropocene were laid down in the mid-twentieth century, where geologists dig them up, measuring the changes already evident. These geologists aren't wizards, living backwards like Merlin, treating the future as the past. Instead, like historians, they study what has already taken place, and when they think about the future, they do so as a matter of informed speculation because they cannot know whether people will decide to live within planetary limits in the next few decades or not.[29] No one knows. Most scientists are urgently concerned. Anthropocene science currently informs the work of the international bodies such as the IPCC and the United Nations Development Programme, trying to divert the worst outcomes. Understanding Anthropocene science is the bedrock of generative new political analyses.[30] It is therefore mystifying to read that the Anthropocene is "of little help for understanding what is at stake for politics in the current crisis. Treating the future as the past in effect means to end all openness of the future and thereby to stifle political thought and creativity."[31]

So what are we to make of the frivolity, distress, anger, and misconceptions of the "Anything Goes" stories? Perhaps there is an understandable reluctance to spend time digesting the complexities of the emerging science. It's

---

[28] Nordblad, 2020 (Footnote 27), 336.

[29] See, for instance, Jan Zalasiewicz, *The Earth After Us: What Legacy will Humans Leave in the Rocks* (Oxford: Oxford University Press, 2009) and Alan Weisman, *The World without Us* (New York: MacMillan/Thomas Dunne Books, 2007).

[30] Major contributions include Manuel Arias-Maldonado, *Environment and Society: Socionatural Relations in the Anthropocene* (New York: Springer, 2015); Manuel Arias-Maldonado and Zev Trachtenberg, *Rethinking the Environment for the Anthropocene: Political Theory and Socionatural Relations in the New Geological Epoch* (Abingdon-on-Thames, UK: Routledge, 2018); Mark Beeson, *Environmental Populism: The Politics of Survival in the Anthropocene* (London: Palgrave Macmillan, 2019); Frank Biermann and Eva Lövbrand, *Anthropocene Encounters: New Directions in Green Thinking* (Cambridge, UK: Cambridge University Press, 2019); Nigel Clark and Bronislaw Szerszynski, *Planetary Social Thought: The Anthropocene Challenge to the Social Sciences* (Cambridge, UK: Polity, 2021); John S. Dryzek and Jonathan Pickering, *The Politics of the Anthropocene* (Oxford, UK: Oxford University Press, 2019); Duncan Kelly, *Politics and the Anthropocene* (Cambridge, UK: Polity, 2019); and, Philipp Pattberg and Fariborz Zelli (ed.), *Environmental Politics and Governance in the Anthropocene: Institutions and Legitimacy in a Complex World* (Abingdon-on-Thames, UK: Routledge, 2017).

[31] Nordblad, 2020 (Footnote 27), 336.

easier to fall back on more familiar terms like "the environment" and "climate change" in the rushed atmosphere of publish-or-perish. It's also easy and more readily rewarded within the academic world to adhere closely to disciplinary protocols and ways of thinking. When humanists and social scientists stray into geology and ESS with their odd forms of citation, multiple-authored articles, and strange ways of telling stories, their colleagues are often bemused. The approach characterized here as "Anything Goes" may even reveal a sublimated fear of the situation illuminated by the AWG. Perhaps the *ad hominem* attacks on geologists confuse the messengers for the message. In any case, these "Anything Goes" narratives, at their heart, are not about the reality we face.

In fact, what is most striking about "Anything Goes" is its deep conservatism. These stories feature familiar villains and victims. Scientific hubris is once again denounced.[32] Disciplinary prerogatives are protected from the challenge posed by the Anthropocene which, like evolution, brings the study of humans and of the rest of nature together in deeply uncomfortable ways. "Anything Goes" relies on the disconnected forms of knowledge institutionalized in late nineteenth-century universities, and resists reimagining the relationship among them. Many adherents seem to hint that somewhere, somehow, there *must* be a way of retaining the old dream of ever-growing abundance for everyone. The Ecomodernists who denounce environmentalism for putting limits on human desires even insist that we can head toward greater opulence.[33] The old concepts of justice and liberty, the old economic forms, the old ways of thinking of our lives and what they mean must not be challenged, or so they imply. Don't listen to the scientists, don't take on this unprecedented vision of human impact on the planet, don't let the band stop playing.

---

[32] Historian of science, Naomi Oreskes, a member of the AWG, argues that this distrust of science is often politically generated. The trustworthiness of science arises from the social practices surrounding the vetting of its claims rather than abstract reliance on the "scientific method." The more inclusive these practices are in terms of types of evidence and social perspectives of the people involved, the better the science will be. See Naomi Oreskes, *Why Trust Science?* (Princeton, NJ: Princeton University Press, 2019).

[33] Ted Nordhaus and Michael Shellenberger, *Breakthrough: From the Death of Environmentalism to the Politics of Possibility* (New York: Houghton and Mifflin, 2007). For a critique of ecomodernism, see Clive Hamilton, "The theodicy of the 'Good Anthropocene'," *Environmental Humanities*, vol. 7, no. 1 (2016), 233-38. doi:10.1215/22011919-3616434.

As current AWG secretary Colin Waters notes (and the evidence of "Anything Goes" shows), "Anthropocene" has come to mean different things as it has spread to different groups, a situation that can only end in headaches: "We need a common understanding."[34] Without it, neither critique nor collaboration is meaningful; with it, there can be useful disagreements and concerted action. Naturally enough, with a scientific concept such as the Anthropocene, the fundamental definition comes from the science. In the preceding chapter, Jan Zalasiewicz presented the understanding that is now widely, though not universally, accepted within the geological community and increasingly outside it as well. As Zalasiewicz acknowledges, the proposed new epoch may never be formalized by the IUGS, but, even so, a clear definition will advance a multidisciplinary understanding. If the Anthropocene is truly as dangerous and unprecedented as it seems to be, taking guidance from the scientists on what it is and then forging a concerted way forward is surely the wisest route.[35] Thus armed, it is possible to speak truth to the powers that continue to force the Earth System's trajectory toward unpredictable tipping points.

NEW STORIES FOR A NEW REALITY

What would happen to our stories in the humanities and social sciences if we took Anthropocene science seriously? To explore this question, I'll focus on one paper, "Trajectories of the Earth System in the Anthropocene," which appeared in *PNAS* in 2018.[36] With this matter-of-fact title, Earth System scientist Will Steffen and his co-authors do not ring alarm bells, at least not initially. They begin by laying out the

---

[34] Quoted in Ian Sample, "Anthropocene: is this the new epoch of humans?" *The Guardian* (16 October 2014) www.theguardian.com/science/2014/oct/16/-sp-scientists-gather-talks-rename-human-age-anthropocene-holocene (accessed October 2021).

[35] For an insightful analysis of why political science should take Anthropocene science seriously, see Manuel Arias-Maldonado, "Bedrock or social construction? What Anthropocene science means for political theory," *The Anthropocene Review*, vol. 7, no. 2 (August 2020), 97–112, doi:10.1177/2053019619899536.

[36] Steffen, et al., 2018 (Footnote 7), 8256.

evidence that the planet has left not only the relative warmth of the Holocene's interglacial interlude, but perhaps even the glacial–interglacial cycles of the Quaternary Period beginning 2,588,000 years ago. Our planet, they say, is on a new trajectory toward "Hothouse Earth."[37] If the planet continues along the current business-as-usual pathway, feedbacks, tipping points, and non-linear dynamics may plunge the Earth System across a dangerous threshold. Crossing this threshold, possibly reached when the globally averaged temperature rises of 2 degrees Celsius (3.6 degrees Fahrenheit) above pre-industrial levels (as is expected to occur before the end of the century), is "likely to produce uncontrollable and dangerous conditions."[38] To cross it "poses severe risks for health, economics, political stability (especially for the most climate vulnerable) and, ultimately, the habitability of the planet for humans."[39] At that point, all bets are off (Figure 2.1).

The better hope is to stabilize the Earth System before that threshold is reached. Success wouldn't return us to the pleasant conditions of the Holocene. This *PNAS* paper is not modeled on the trope of the Prodigal Son where all is forgiven. Alas, there can be no "repeal the Anthropocene."[40] Instead, "stabilized Earth will likely be warmer than any other time over the last 800,000 years at least" and probably won't avoid the activation of some triggers that would lead to "abrupt shifts at the level of critical biomes that support humanity."[41] What this means is that in the best case scenario we should expect green and pleasant lands to become deluged scenes of death and places that once were merely lethargically hot to be scorching and unlivable for ourselves and many other species. Perhaps most frightening of all is that the Earth System does not tend to be stable at approximately 2 degrees Celsius above pre-industrial levels. A stabilized planet at that temperature would be highly artificial. Constructing and maintaining it would require orchestrating our social systems to manipulate

---

[37] These cycles have waxed and waned throughout the past 2.6 million years known as the Quaternary Period. www.ncdc.noaa.gov/abrupt-climate-change/Glacial-Interglacial%20Cycles (accessed October 2021).

[38] Steffen et al. 2018 (Footnote 7), 8256.   [39] Steffen et al. 2018 (Footnote 7), 8256.

[40] Marcia Bjornerud, *Timefulness: How Thinking like a Geologist Can Help Save the World* (Princeton, NJ: Princeton University Press, 2018), 177.

[41] Steffen et al. 2018 (Footnote 7), 8257.

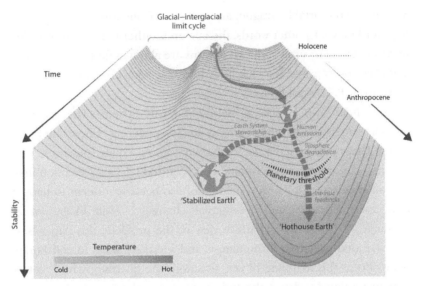

2.1. Earth System pathways. Stability landscape showing the pathway of the Earth System out of the Holocene to its present position in the hotter Anthropocene. The "fork in the road" represents two divergent pathways of the Earth System in the future (broken arrows). Currently the Earth System is on a "Hothouse Earth" pathway beyond which the system follows an essentially irreversible pathway driven by intrinsic biogeophysical feedbacks. The other pathway leads to "Stabilized Earth," a pathway of Earth System stewardship guided by human-created feedbacks to a quasi-stable, human-maintained basin of attraction (Steffen et al. 2018).

the Earth System and deflect it from the business-as-usual trajectory. That said, it would be better than the Hothouse alternative.

In story-telling terms, what's interesting about this study is that it provides only two plotlines. Unlike research based on climate models that project a range of intermediate scenarios, the authors of "Trajectories of the Earth System" argue that non-linearities in feedback processes reduce potential pathways – or plotlines – to two. Tipping points either occur and change the whole system, or they don't. Our choice is thus between a bucking Hothouse Earth marked by abrupt state shifts leading to "a much higher global average temperature than any interglacial in the past 1.2 million years and to sea levels significantly higher than at any time in the Holocene,"[42] with a markedly diminished biosphere, or, on the other hand, a carefully managed Stabilized Earth

---

[42] Steffen et al., 2018 (Footnote 7), 8252.

System, uncomfortable, fragile, and different from anything our species has ever known. In other words, the tale ends either horrendously or less horribly. These severely reduced options are about as far from "Anything Goes" as you can get. No kick lines here. No songs by Cole Porter. No input from P.G. Wodehouse.[43]

How might we achieve a stabilized Earth System? The scientists' answer entails more than science-and-engineering since, they say, "a fundamental reorientation of human values, equity, behavior, institutions, economies, and technologies is required."[44] This revolution in all human systems is a tall order, made more so because it needs to happen right away: "gradual or incremental change ... will likely not be adequate."[45] Given this expansive view of the problem, this paper is an open-handed invitation to humanists and social scientists to collaborate. If we accept this mapping of our situation, the question is how to twist human plotlines to bend the trajectory of the planetary system toward the limited freedom of a harsh but habitable planet. The so-called *positive* feedback loops pushing the Earth System along its dangerous business-as-usual trajectory must be turned, somehow, into *negative* feedback loops producing a stabilized state. (To be clear, "stabilized" in this sense means being relatively constant within certain variables. In no way does it imply stasis or lack of circulation.) The story we need to figure out how to tell will not be a comedy, but it could avoid tragedy. The quest, in other words, is to avoid the tyranny of "Hothouse Earth" and create something emancipatory, even of this terrible exigency.

So how do we choose the less bad option? "Trajectories of the Earth System" suggests two ways. Primarily, Will Steffen and his co-authors call for the Singular Story: a "deep integration of knowledge from biogeophysical Earth System science with that from social sciences and the humanities."[46] Although they foresee that unifying diverse fields will be

---

[43] The musical "Anything Goes" had input from both Porter and Wodehouse and featured a love affair between a wall street broker and a girl named Hope.

[44] Steffen et al. 2018 (Footnote 7), 8258.   [45] Steffen et al. 2018 (Footnote 7), 8257.

[46] Steffen et al. 2018 (Footnote 7), 8253.

difficult, they hope it will produce "more effective governance at the Earth System level."[47] To many, advocating top-down global governance sounds alarmingly totalitarian or simply naive, a misunderstanding of politics as the practice of negotiation. (This is a problem to which I'll return.) But, on close reading, the essay also calls, more quietly, for a second type of story, one that encourages diverse, local efforts directed toward the same shared end, the very reverse of top-down governance.[48] The reasoning here is that because the tipping points caused by non-linear dynamics cannot be forecast with any degree of certainty, no global dictate can ensure survival. More flexible, community-controlled measures with lower built-in costs could also help build resilience. These "resilience-building strategies," the authors say, "include developing insurance, buffers, redundancy, diversity, and other features"; a multiplicity of efforts more nimble in the face of the unforeseeable surprises inherent in a destabilized system.

In other words, alongside the recommendation that we commit to the "Singular Story," this paper also recognizes the value of a "Democracy of Voices." Both are true to the science, but they suggest very different political and social narratives, the first founded on the logic that equates the single stabilized Earth System with a single humanity and even a single governing authority; the second encouraging a range of human systems, all resonating with the Anthropocene imperative of redirecting Earth's trajectory but in different ways. In political terms, we might call the first "benevolent totalitarianism" and the second a "multicultural empire" where pluralism *up to a point* is permitted. Neither are ideal political forms in terms of most late Holocene logics, but then no society in the Anthropocene enjoys the latitude of Holocene conditions.

---

[47] Steffen et al. 2018 (Footnote 7), 8257.

[48] Critiques of top-down governance include Giovanna Di Chiro, "Environmental justice and the Anthropocene meme," in Teena Gabrielson, Cheryl Hall, John Meyer, and David Schlossberg, eds. *The Oxford Handbook of Environmental Political Theory*, (Oxford, UK: Oxford University Press, 2016); John S. Dryzak and Jonathan Pickering, *The Politics of the Anthropocene* (Oxford, UK: Oxford University Press, 2019); and, Mark Beeson, *Environmental Populism: The Politics of Survival in the Anthropocene* (Singapore: Palgrave MacMillan, 2019).

STORY #2 THE SINGULAR STORY

Particularly on large scales, the human story is easily integrated into the biogeophysical one. The evidence is everywhere. From this perspective, we are fundamentally beings of rock, water, and air. Like all our fellow creatures, we arise from the Earth System. Our species' story of perhaps 300,000 years can be fitted snugly within the Earth's 4.5 billion year history.[49] In the very *longue durée*, the mastery of fire in Africa by our ancestral species *Homo erectus*, the domestication of the dog, our hand-prints on cave walls from Borneo to Spain, the traps dug to capture and kill mammoths in Mexico some 15,000 years ago, and the invention of pottery and agriculture in many different places, all attest to creativity. Our ability to bend our environments to meet our desires has conquered oceans, leveled mountains, and rearranged the living world from fungi and microbes to flora and fauna. We have invaded every continent with our companion species, some purposely brought along, some hitch-hikers with their own destinies. As historian Kyle Harper shows in Chapter 4, we've both accumulated disease-causing viruses and bacteria in extraordinary numbers compared with our chimpanzee cousins (who have only about two dozen), and also worked, both consciously and unconsciously, to disinfect the planet, suppressing many terrible diseases and building up immunities, to allow our population to soar beyond 8 billion.[50]

---

[49] David Christian has led the way in developing "Big History" which puts the human story within the larger story of Earth and even the universe. See David Christian (with William McNeill), *Maps of Time: An Introduction to Big History* (Berkeley and Los Angeles: University of California Press, 2005); David Christian, Cynthia Stokes Brown, and Craig Benjamin, *Big History: Between Nothing and Everything* (New York: McGraw-Hill Education, 2014); and David Christian, *Origin Story: A Big History of Everything* (New York: Little, Brown Spark, 2018). For an incisive critique of this form of history, see Ian Hesketh, "The Story of Big History," *History of the Present*, vol. 4, no.2 (Fall 2014), 171–202.

[50] Kyle Harper, "What makes viruses like COVID-19 such a risk for human beings? The answer goes back thousands of years," *Time* (March 11, 2020) https://time.com/5800558/coronavirus-human-civilization/ (accessed October 2021); and Ariane Düx, Sebastian Lequime, Livia Victoria Patrono, et al., "The history of measles: from a 1912 genome to an antique origin," (preprint, March 2020) *bioRxiv* 2019.12.29.889667; https://doi.org/10.1101/2019.12.29.889667 (accessed October 2021).

We struggle. We create. We colonize. We dominate, like all species, to the extent that we can until the environment can no longer support our activities. Our foods taste of the soils in which they are grown, from the *terroir* of French wines to the volcanic sting of true wasabi; our bodies, in the words of the English burial service (and a David Bowie song) go "from ashes to ashes." Few humans eat rocks *per se*, but we are not all that far removed from the newly discovered type of shipworm that munches stone.[51] When we integrate the human story and the Earth System story, we orchestrate vast scales of time and space along with intimate biogeophysical interactions. I don't doubt that the story can be told this way.

This story's giant protagonist is the combination of humanity-and-Earth-System that has been lumbering for millennia toward the Anthropocene, "the sum total of human impacts on the system," which needs "to be taken into account for analysing future trajectories."[52] To study this Leviathan, proponents of the "Singular Story" argue for the merger of disciplinary perspectives and a unity of knowledge. Sometimes this integration takes the form of calls for collaboration among human and natural scientists with new institutions to support their joint work.[53] Sometimes an even more intense synthesis is promoted, one that "fully integrates different approaches and different types of scholarly experience."[54] This unity of knowledge has been long heralded. In *Economic and Philosophic Manuscripts of 1844*, Karl Marx prophesied, "Natural science will in time incorporate into itself the science of man, just as the

[51] Bob Yirka, "Shipworm that eats rock instead of wood found in river in the Philippines," *Phys.Org* (19 June 2019) https://phys.org/news/2019-06-shipworm-wood-river-philippines.html (accessed October 2021). For more information, see J. Reuben Shipway, Marvin A. Altamia, Gary Rosenberg, et al. "A rock-boring and rock-ingesting freshwater bivalve (shipworm) from the Philippines," *Proceedings of the Royal Society B: Biological Sciences*, vol. 286, no. 1905 (2019): 20190434. doi: 10.1098/rspb.2019.0434.

[52] Steffen et al. 2018 (Footnote 7), 8252.

[53] E.S. Brondizio, Karen O'Brien, Xuemei Bai, et al., "Re-conceptualizing the Anthropocene: a call for collaboration," *Global Environmental Change*, vol. 39 (2016), 318–327.

[54] Michael A. Ellis and Zev Trachtenberg, "Which Anthropocene is it to be? Beyond geology to a moral and public discourse," *Earth's Future*, vol. 2 (2013), 124.

science of man will incorporate into itself the natural science: there will be one science."[55]

Recent conferences and policy forums also emphasize "the need for radical interdisciplinary collaboration between the nature and the human sciences."[56] Along these lines, but from a slightly different perspective, geoscientist Peter Haff adds up all human–Earth interactions, describing the aggregate as the "technosphere." Borrowing an approach from the physical sciences called "coarse graining," Haff adopts a level of resolution in his analysis that captures the overall system's behavior, beyond the operations of its individual components. This technosphere, he claims, has now become autonomous, appropriating mass, energy, and information on its own.[57] We must either serve the technosphere or suffer the consequences. The aim of unifying knowledge is to master the planet more thoroughly – or in Haff's terms, cope with the technosphere more skilfully – so as to avoid the current Hothouse trajectory. This unified story both *maps* our situation and *makes something emancipatory* of it. The Singular Story and "governance at the Earth System level" offer an escape route away from the deterministic business-as-usual road leading us to ruin.

But there are cautions too, from many sides. One warning points to the wondrous complexity of ourselves and our planet, and asks how we can know enough to govern from above. Such coarse-grained analysis of the total Earth System discounts the contingencies of myriad small-scale entanglements, yet it is doubtful that the Earth System functions independently of them. Certainly human existence cannot be understood only in global aggregate. The world, to borrow poet Louis MacNeice's phrase, is "incorrigibly plural," socially, but also physically and

[55] Quoted in Jürgen Renn, *The Evolution of Knowledge: Rethinking Science for the Anthropocene.* (Princeton: Princeton University Press, 2019), 408.

[56] Poul Holm and Verena Winiwarter, "Climate change studies and the human sciences," *Global and Planetary Change*, vol. 156 (2017), 115.

[57] Peter Haff, "Technology as a geological phenomenon: implications for human well-being," in Colin Waters, Jan Zalasiewicz, Mark Williams, Mike Willis, and A.N. Snelling, eds., *A Stratigraphical Basis for the Anthropocene*, Special Publications 395 (London: Geological Society, 2014), 301; Peter Haff, "Humans and technology in the Anthropocene: six rules," *The Anthropocene Review*, vol. 1, no. 2 (2014), 126–136.

biologically. E.O. Wilson argues that mathematical models in ecology, as in economics, are of limited use given the "ubiquitous nonlinearities that twist and turn like escaping eels when you put together the actions of real players." "Overall," he says, "theorists have not been able to grasp the near-bottomless complexity of the real world."[58] These intricate dynamics will not easily submit to a single master narrative, and even if they might, the costs of a mistake would be high. Committing to the wrong global governance regime or megascale project could very well lead to higher costs and horrific suffering, as Clive Hamilton warns when he critiques geoengineering for "Promethean recklessness."[59] Naturally, megascale projects gone wrong are much harder to correct than smaller-scale, more locally controlled schemes.

Another related caution is the untranslatability of one form of knowledge to another. If translating among human languages poses irresolvable difficulties (just compare English-language versions of the *Tao Te Ching!*), then translating, for instance, the language of rocks into the language of social justice is bound to throw up obstacles. What language, what mode of representation is appropriate for a single narrative combining histories of human endeavors with changes in the Earth System? Policy attempts to combine knowledge from the natural and human sciences have produced mixed results. For instance, the languages of the humanities and the metrics of climate models rarely mesh. The official remit of the United Nations International Panel on Climate Change (IPCC) includes considering "socio-economic" factors, but in practice, as historians Poul Holm and Verena Winiwarter have shown, the IPCC resists "major insights from cultural theory and historical analysis."[60] Holm and Winiwarter quote a particularly revealing passage from the 2014 IPCC report complaining that research on social change can't be used because of "the difficulty in representing these processes in

---

[58] Edward O. Wilson, *Half-Earth: Our Planet's Fight for Life* (New York and London: Norton, 2016), 102. Wilson, interestingly, confuses the Ecomodernist view of the Anthropocene for that of the AWG and therefore argues against the concept of the Anthropocene.

[59] Clive Hamilton, *Earthmasters: The Dawn of the Age of Climate Engineering* (New Haven: Yale University Press, 2013).

[60] Holm and Winiwarter, 2017 (Footnote 56), 115.

models."[61] This dismissal appears to have deeper roots than the difficulty posed by modeling social change. Some in the IPCC community are ideologically wedded to a narrow range of technical solutions. One editor, responding to an external reviewer's comment on the need for more social science to understand people's conduct, declared, "Changes in behavior may play a role; maybe not ... it is really tech change that matters."[62] In short, calls for collaboration, if not outright disingenuous, frequently insist that the humanities and social sciences conform to scientific modes of research and representation.

To the extent that humanistic knowledge can be made to conform to scientific protocols, the melding of knowledge seems to work best on discrete problems such as eliminating ozone-depleting fluorocarbons. Al Gore's 2006 film, *An Inconvenient Truth*, created just such a story. Top-down solutions such as governmental restrictions on fluorocarbons or over-fishing have their uses in limited arenas, but for the more complex challenges of the Anthropocene, a "Democracy of Voices" offers a better way forward than benevolent totalitarianism. The fact that the Anthropocene is global, systemic, and near-synchronous is not – and should not be taken as – a prescription for a single global, systemic, and near-synchronous solution. Reality, even the singular reality of the Anthropocene, does not dictate only one human story.[63] The aim of Anthropocene story-telling is to bend Earth's trajectory away from the worst of all possible worlds, but we hamper ourselves if we insist only on unified knowledge, a single protagonist, and an integrated narrative synthesizing all disciplinary perspectives.

STORY #3 A DEMOCRACY OF VOICES

There is only one Earth System, but there are many textured, contingent, and small-scale stories within it, human and otherwise. Some of these stories are congruent with the global story, others are not; some are both

---

[61] Holm and Winiwater 2017 (Footnote 56), 121.

[62] Quoted in Holm and Winiwater 2017 (Footnote 56), 121.

[63] Lisa Sideris, "Anthropocene convergences: a report from the field," *RCC Perspectives*, vol. 2016, no. 2 (2016), doi: doi.org/10.5282/rcc/7450.

depending on the timescale and the magnitude involved. The problem begins, I think, with defining the Anthropocene as "the cumulative history of local and regional social change operating in various and evolving forms of connections to global processes."[64] While partly right, this cumulative history necessarily ignores all the things that people did that never contributed to the forcings on the Earth System. Many still do these things: a fallen branch becomes a flute played at dawn, a community gathers to deliberate shared water rights, milkweed is planted to nourish monarch butterflies, communities organize ways to share clothes, school supplies, tools, seeds, and transportation. These activities point to virtuous cycles of reuse, repair, and regeneration. Although these actions are now overwhelmed by the dread emergence of the Anthropocene, which cannot be reversed, recuperating and strengthening them may help stabilize the Earth System. Another point in their favor is political. A cumulative politics to contend with history's cumulative outcome pulls power out of local hands and centralizes it, but thinking in terms of local cycles helps make space for a "Democracy of Voices" and a wider range of inventive possibilities. In the end, it will be necessary to keep both levels in view, and do the political work to negotiate the tension between them. Chapters 5 (Howe and Boyer), 7 (Arias-Maldonado), and 8 (Brown) speak to this problem of connecting local experiences and politics with the overarching planetary goal.

Above, I showed how a single human story can be integrated into the Earth System narrative at the macro level by highlighting our species' restless, avaricious, inventive actions. During the Pleistocene, the activities that laid the foundation for the twentieth-century Anthropocene include moving out of Africa and spreading across the continents. Whether or not this was accompanied by extinctions, perhaps even including that of our near hominin relatives, is hotly debated.[65] In the

---

[64] Eduardo S. Brondizio, Karen O'Brien, Xuemei Bai, et al, "Re-conceptualizing the Anthropocene: a call for collaboration," *Global Environmental Change*, vol. 39 (2016), 323.

[65] Julien Louys, Todd J. Braje, Chun-Hsiang Chang, et al., "No evidence for widespread island extinctions after Pleistocene Hominin arrival," *PNAS*, vol. 118, no. 20 (2021), e2023005118.

Holocene, domesticating animals, plants, and microbes, salinizing and eroding soil, and burning jungles and forests set the stage for the Great Acceleration, even before the very-late-Holocene rise of imperialism, fossil fuels, industrialization, fertilizers, antibiotics, and extreme global inequality. This cumulative history brought us to the Anthropocene, but, crucially, not everything done by everyone everywhere worked against the feedback loops that kept our planet within Holocene boundaries.

Take ideas. Not all people want to accumulate ever-greater wealth at the cost of social cohesion and their environment. The Bushman of the Kalahari guarded against community-destroying jealousy by customs for the distribution of food, especially meat, throughout the group and with neighbors.[66] Some say that the First Nations of the Canadian and American Pacific Coast strengthened coastal management regimes and much else by great feasts called potlatches where the powerful gave away or destroyed valuables. The original people of Australia went further, not just creating sustainable communities, but actively managing the whole continent to produce a bounteous, variegated landscape through the skillful deployment of fire. According to historian Bill Gammage, strategic burning allowed them to encourage desirable plants and preferred animal habitats so that people "travelled to known resources and made them not merely sustainable, but abundant, convenient, and predictable."[67] This coordinated management of an entire continent to foster enhanced biodiversity, moisture-retaining soils, cleaner water, and a range of habitats is an example of what paleogeologist and AWG member Mark Williams terms "mutualism" in Chapter 12. Going beyond sustainability, mutualism is the active enrichment of the environment.

More recent examples of the human potential for enforcing negative feedback loops include the systemic use of night soil as fertilizer in early modern Japan which resulted in cleaner, healthier cities, more fertile soil, and more nutritious produce.[68] Early modern Japanese also appear

---

[66] Elizabeth Marshall Thomas, *The Old Way: A Story of the First People* (New York: Picador, 2006), 101–103.

[67] Bill Gammage, *The Biggest Estate on Earth: How Aborigines Made Australia* (Crows Nest, NSW, Australia: Allen and Unwin, 2012), 3.

[68] See, for instance, Susan Hanley, *Everyday Things in Premodern Japan* (Berkeley and Los Angeles: University of California Press, 1997); Kayo Tajima, *The Marketing of Urban*

to have taken active measures to ensure population stability in the eighteenth century. Family size was calibrated to the goal of providing for the next generation by limiting births through a range of methods, including late marriages, compulsory non-marriage for the heir's siblings, young people working away from home, abstinence, and infanticide. The result was a steady population slightly below 30 million for a century.[69] Frugality, even though not always practiced, was preached as a samurai virtue by Neo-Confucian scholar Kumazawa Banzen (1619–1691).[70] Cultures around the early modern world felt the appeal of simplicity, even where people could have chosen greater opulence and ease as Puritan, Amish, and Mennonite tenets reveal. The admonition "waste not, want not" has roots going back to at least the sixteenth century, and practices such as quilting, based on reusing materials and incorporating scraps have a central place in English and American folkways. Not so very long ago, having a vegetable garden was a normal part of life, even in towns.

But we need not look back to pre-modern periods for alternatives to today's business-as-usual production and consumption. Even today, there are examples of alternative storylines discordant with the overall trajectory. While industrial agriculture diminishes soil quality and biodiversity, and creates ocean and river dead zones due to chemical fertilizer runoff, an estimated 50 percent of the world's population still depends on small-holder farms, some of which are now being managed to produce better soils, more nutritious crops, and stronger local

Human Waste in the Edo/Tokyo Metropolitan Area: 1600–1935 (Medford, MA: Tufts University, 2005); and David Howell, "Fecal matters: prolegomenon to a history of shit in Japan," in Ian J. Miller, Julia Adeney Thomas, and Brett L. Walker, eds. *Japan at Nature's Edge* (Honolulu: University of Hawai'i Press, 2017, pp. 137–151). See also Donald Worster, "The good muck: toward an excremental history of China," *RCC Perspectives*, vol. 2017, no. 5 (2017) www.environmentandsociety.org/perspectives/2017/5/good-muck-toward-excremental-history-china (accessed October 2021).

[69] See Fabian Drixler, *Infanticide and Fertility in Eastern Japan: Discourse and Demography, 1660–1880* (Cambridge, MA: Harvard University Press, 2008).

[70] James McMullen, "Twenty-first-century ecology lessons from seventeenth-century Japan: climate change, deforestation, and moral regeneration," *Japan Forum*, (2020). doi: 10.1080/09555803.2020.1806902

communities.[71] This movement has sprung up in developed countries such as Japan, Germany, and the United States, as well as less developed countries.[72] Some cities are beginning to deliberately foster wildlife by new building techniques and setting aside land, as in Chicago's wildlife corridor. Even universities can become green oases, as the 40-year long effort of Tsai Jen-Hui, architect at National Taipei University of Technology, has shown. These projects exemplify the "slow hope" that historian Christof Mauch recommends as our best way of putting the skids on business-as-usual.[73]

As we look to the future, harnessing local ingenuity to build multiple, redundant systems of different sorts in different environments at different levels may help us cope better with tipping points and unexpected events on our destabilized planet. Most especially, if we are to galvanize communities to work toward ecological reflexivity, drawing on useful patterns in their pasts that accord with their particular traditions and remaining ecosystems can help meet the global goal. In this way, bringing together the singular new reality of our planetary situation with diverse local initiatives gives us more than just one social Anthropocene story. More voices, more stories, more options.

Going local is not just a matter of place-bound cultural knowledge. It's also about resilient scientific practices. Take, for instance, something as superficially uncontroversial as tree-planting on a global scale to reduce carbon dioxide in the atmosphere. The headline-grabbing research of

---

[71] Sarah K. Lowder, Jakob Skoet, and Terri Raney, "The number, size, and distribution of farms, smallholder farms, and family farms worldwide," *World Development*, vol. 87 (November 2016), 16–29.

[72] Examples of these experiments include Fukuoka Masanobu, *The One-Straw Revolution: An Introduction to Natural Farming* (Emmaus, PA: Rodale Press, 1978); Barbara Kingsolver, *Animal, Vegetable, Miracle: A Year of Food Life* (New York: Harper Perennial, 2007); Liz Carlisle, *Lentil Underground: Renegade Farmers and the Future of Food in America* (New York: Penguin Random House, 2015); Vandana Shiva, *Soil Not Oil: Environmental Justice in an Age of Climate Crisis* (Brooklyn: South End Press, 2008); and Ramachandra Guha *The Unquiet Woods: Ecological Change and Peasant Resistance in the Himalaya* (Berkeley: University of California Press, 2000).

[73] Christof Mauch, "Slow hope: rethinking ecologies of crisis and fear," *RCC Perspectives: Transformations in Environment and Society*, vol. 2019, no. 1 (2019), 21–23. www .environmentandsociety.org/perspectives/2019/1/slow-hope-rethinking-ecologies-crisis-and-fear (accessed October 2021).

Thomas Crowther's lab promoted an "additional 0.9 billion hectares of canopy cover ... as one of the most effective solutions at our disposal to mitigate climate change," yet this work sparked dissension due to its global level of analysis.[74] *Science* published six critiques, many pointing to regional and local "environmental or socioeconomic constraints," including different soils and small farms.[75] The Olympian perspective of a global computer model of forests may help, but it is limited, perhaps severely, by the incorrigible pluralism of interactions between life forms and inorganic cycles at non-global levels. When we move away from the narrowness of a climate change analysis to the more complex, systemic problem of the Anthropocene, there's an even stronger imperative to tell stories with many protagonists, each with different impulses and aims.[76] What works at one level in some places may not work at all universally.

Anthropocene science tells us that we have a single Earth System and that stabilizing it is our best hope, but it also helps us see that we still need many voices and many disciplinary tools to tackle this enormous challenge. In short, we need both the "Singular Story" and a "Democracy of Voices" – and the means to negotiate between them.

CONCLUSION

My chapter puts a brave face on things. I have tried to convince you – and myself – that there are stories that do not end in Hothouse Earth. I have tried to make the case that our first step – everyone's first step – is to

---

[74] Jean-Francois Bastin, Yelena Finegold, Claude Garcia, et al., "The global tree restoration potential," *Science*, vol. 365 (2019), 78.

[75] Eike Luedeling, Jan Börner, Wulf Amelung, et al, "Forest restoration: overlooked constraints," *Science*, vol. 366 (18 October 2019), 315. For a general overview, of this controversy, see Gabriel Popkin, "Growing pains: ecologist Thomas Crowther is having a bumpy rise to prominence," *Science*, vol. 366 (25 October 2019), 412–415.

[76] For the importance of the difference between climate change and the Anthropocene, see Julia Adeney Thomas, "Why the 'Anthropocene' is not 'climate change' and why it matters." *AsiaGlobal Online*, (10 January 2019) www.asiaglobalonline.hku.hk/anthropocene-climate-change/ (accessed September 2021)and Michael Ellis, "Climate-change and the Anthropocene," *Inhabiting the Anthropocene*, (January 23, 2019) https://inhabitingtheanthropocene.com/2019/01/23/climate-change-and-the-anthropocene/ (accessed October 2021).

grasp the nature of our challenge as described by the AWG and Earth System scientists. Then, and only then, can we begin to craft useful human stories of how to navigate the reality of the Anthropocene. That reality, limiting though it is in comparison with the Holocene, is not yet deterministic. There is still more than one possible true story, and even more than one possible *emancipatory* story. Collectively, we can – and indeed must – attempt to steer the Earth System by mirroring its totality with forms of global cooperation and with acceptance of our strange new political agency as a species. This story is an epic on the largest scale, unifying all forms of knowledge, peoples, and planet. But, alongside this epic tale, we can – and indeed must – attempt to foster a thousand experimental parables. Each could make changes to local ecosystems, values, and institutions so that they don't push us ever more rapidly into dangerous territory. These allegories of local goodness would need to be orchestrated toward the same end of stabilizing the Earth System. Despite their contrasting protagonists, both the "Singular Story" and "Democracy of Voices" begin and end with a common understanding of our daunting new challenge.

All the while, as we ponder our way forward, the business-as-usual storyline swiftly propels us on a trajectory headed toward the Niagara Falls of a planetary threshold. If the *PNAS* article by Will Steffen and his co-authors is correct, we have little time and much to do. Once the Earth System cascades over the precipice, there's no crawling back. Our collective story at that point, on an uninhabitable planet, can offer no emancipatory narrative for human societies. Responding to the Anthropocene with an "Anything Goes" attitude that refuses to take the science seriously is complicit in business-as-usual. If this approach, the "normal one" we're used to, prevails, tragedy looms. For individuals amid the tumult of Hothouse Earth, I can imagine stories of both courage and failure. A few will face death with the clarity of a Stoic or a Buddhist, many will be kind to fellow sufferers, but most, in the words of W.H. Auden, will "die as men before their bodies die."[77] After that, all our stories will be over.

---

[77] The phrase is from "The Shield of Achilles" but the past tense of the poem is, here, made future.

PART TWO

ONE ANTHROPOCENE; MANY STORIES

CHAPTER 3

Earth System Science: Gravity, the Earth System, and the Anthropocene

Will Steffen

There are many things about the Earth that we used to take for granted – clean air, water without microplastic particles, ungenetically modified food, and gathering comfortably with friends and strangers. Air and water pollution, large-scale changes to food production, and COVID-19 have all forced us to rethink these features and many more of life on Earth. We now see how we had once taken them for granted – always there at our disposal.

Gravity, however, is not one of these features that we have had to rethink. It is indeed 'always there', it hasn't been affected by recent changes, and, if you're like most of us, you wouldn't give it a second thought. Gravity is a property of the geosphere, the non-living part of the Earth. Even if Earth was a lifeless planet, it would still have gravity.

This is an essay about what we have learned about our home planet – its fundamental characteristics, how it has changed and continues to change, and how it operates as one big system. In the natural sciences, we have recently come to call our home the 'Earth System', with system in the singular. It is arguably the most complex entity scientists have ever attempted to understand. We have made some progress but the 'science of the Earth' still has a long way to go. Although natural scientists often describe our work in terms of somewhat abstract phenomena (like gravity), mathematical equations, and complicated computer models, visual representations of the Earth System play an important role and are a good platform on which to explore our home planet, both inside and outside of the natural sciences. This essay focuses on the very wide variety of visual approaches that are used to describe our home planet and how it operates, but perhaps more challenging, to describe the invisible, intangible forces and processes that are central to the functioning of the Earth System.

The 2013 movie *Gravity* is a good place to start. Although the film is replete with death-defying jaunts in outer space that only Hollywood can conjure up, it is a gripping visual account of a human leaving the Earth System and then returning to it again. Rookie astronaut Sandra Bullock is on a routine space mission when a rogue asteroid destroys the vehicle, leaving her hanging onto a piece of space debris while fellow astronaut George Clooney flies off into the dark void never to be seen again. Bullock then miraculously debris-hops from one piece of space junk to another before finally returning safely back to Earth, landing in a lush green patch of pristine nature complete with fresh air, liquid water, and croaking frogs. She is overwhelmed just to be able to breathe naturally again, to be alive, and to be immersed in life. In fact, she has just experienced the three great 'spheres' that comprise the current Earth System – gravity, one of the most powerful forces of the geosphere; the beauty of the biosphere, the living part of the Earth; and the technology of the anthroposphere that propelled her out of the Earth System and then delivered her back into it, albeit on a rather treacherous and frightening pathway.

Terms and concepts like the *Earth System,* the *geosphere,* the *biosphere,* and the *anthroposphere* would be unfamiliar even to NASA astronauts. They would never have gone through Sandra Bullock's character's mind as she breathed in an atmosphere rich in oxygen when she arrived back at the Earth's surface. They arise from a natural scientist's view of our home planet. The term geosphere coincides with the origins of the planet itself about 4.5 billion years ago. It shares its first syllable with geology, the field of natural science that studies planetary history and the forces that have shaped the physical Earth from its formation. Solar radiation, volcanoes, drifting continents, great polar ice sheets (which are very recent in Earth history) and other 'great forces of nature (e.g., the biosphere)' have moulded Earth, leaving their traces in sediments and rocks, allowing stratigraphers to piece together a continuous history of Earth in the Geologic Time Scale (GTS).

Even before humans were trying to piece together the long history of the physical Earth, they were puzzling about the bigger picture – where did Earth fit in the vastness of space and the infinity of time? Tackling such questions – the so-called Copernican Revolution of the 1500s – was a critical step in the evolution of the natural sciences as we know them today. Visualization played a key role in that scientific revolution. The invention of the telescope was the technological breakthrough that allowed scientists like Nicolaus Copernicus to peer into the heavens in great detail, following the rotations of stars and planets, ultimately leading Copernicus and his contemporaries to discern the correct positioning of the Earth in the cosmos. Explaining this breakthrough involved further visualizations – for instance, new maps of the heavens and the three-dimensional models of the heliocentric solar system called orrery.

But something was missing. Science was building the capability to understand how the physical Earth had evolved and had discerned that the Earth revolved around the Sun, not the other way around, but it hadn't yet developed an equivalent understanding of the thin, complex, living skin on the surface of the planet, the home for humanity and the rest of life on this unique planet. Earth System scientist H.J. [Hans Joachim (John)] Schellnhuber, in his influential essay 'Earth system analysis and the second Copernican revolution', published in 1999, tackled this lacuna head-on in a striking visual way. Figure 3.1 shows what he calls the second Copernican revolution. In the first Copernican revolution, shown in part a of the figure – from a fifteenth-century woodcut – the invention of the telescope allowed humans to break through the veil surrounding the planet and peer out into the great universe.

In part b of the figure, an Earth System scientist of the twenty-first century is depicted as a planetary physician. She is peering into the machinery of Earth's surface in an attempt to understand how our own life support system works. The visual analogy is striking. Using a vast array of modern instrumentation, a physician can peer in great detail into the organs and circulation systems of the human body, itself an amazingly complex system, and diagnose the health of the system. But note that our planetary physician in Figure 3.1b is outside of the Earth System, attempting to unveil the secrets of our planetary home.

Just as the scientists in the time of Copernicus used a new instrument, the telescope, to unlock secrets of the universe, in the past few decades a

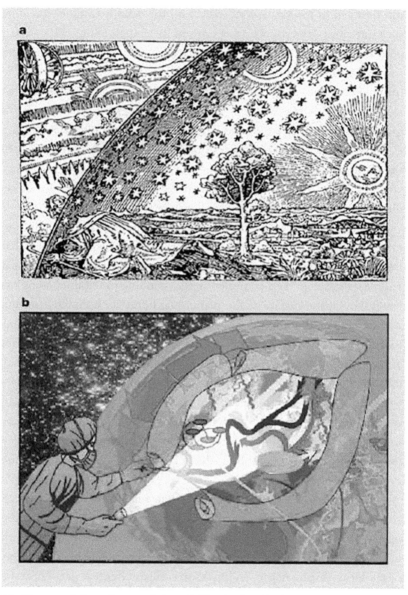

3.1. The second Copernican revolution: (a) The shock of the Enlightenment as expressed in a fifteenth-century woodcut. (b) Earth System diagnostics in the twenty-first century (Schellnhuber 1999).

vast array of new scientific instruments and approaches – particularly space-based observation – is allowing scientists to exit the planet in a virtual sense and peer down through the atmosphere, just as the planetary physician in Figure 3.1b. From a position outside of the Earth System, they can now routinely observe many features of the Earth – large weather features such as tropical cyclones, the intricate patterns of human agricultural systems, the waxing and waning of the Arctic sea ice with the seasons, and much more. It is not quite correct, however, to attribute the beginnings of contemporary Earth System science to our ability to exit the system and look down on it from above.

Many accounts of the evolution of Earth System science (e.g., Steffen et al. 2020, and references therein) put its beginnings in the 1920s, with the pioneering work of Vladimir Vernadsky, a Russian geochemist who focused on the importance of the biosphere – life – as a fully interactive component of the Earth System, not simply a passenger going along for the ride with the physics and chemistry of the geosphere doing all the hard work in the engine room that kept Earth evolving (Vernadsky 1998). Fast forward to the 1970s. James Lovelock introduced Gaia, a highly controversial concept that argued for the central role of life in the functioning of the Earth System (Lovelock 1979). Lovelock directly challenged the dominant paradigm of that time by proposing that the Earth was not a 'Goldilocks planet' that just happened to have the right conditions for life to prosper, but rather that life got a tenuous toehold on the planet and then shaped Earth for its own purposes. This caused an uproar in the geophysical research community, many of whom had little understanding of biosphere dynamics or complex system theory. Even more controversially, Lovelock suggested that life had jumped into the driver's seat, and was now steering the Earth via a complex set of feedbacks that guaranteed that the planet would remain in a stable, habitable condition. Gaia – the Earth – was a living entity.

Again, the brewing scientific controversy over the role of life in the functioning of the planet was shaken by a visual image. In 1972, in fact on 7 December 1972, the American spacecraft Apollo 17 sent back to Earth an image of the whole planet from space. The image, quickly dubbed the 'Blue Marble', was an instant hit, not just in the scientific community but with humanity in general. It was an emotional intervention in our lives – a psychological jolt. For the first time, we could now view the Earth System from outside the system! Several features of the Blue Marble changed our view of the Earth forever:

- The Earth appeared small and isolated, floating in the infinite blackness of space. Many interpreted the image as showing the Earth as somewhat fragile or vulnerable, with no exit strategy should the planet become less hospitable for humans.
- The Blue Marble showed the Earth in its entirety as a single entity. The swirling white clouds, deep blue oceans, white ice, and brown lands all fit together as one whole. There were no artificial lines and colours that demarcated nation-states, or any visible evidence of human activity.
- In contrast to the vast amount of space-based data that began to pour in as research satellites increasingly probed parts of the planet, this one striking image intuitively showed our home planet as a single integrated system – a unified whole – and fundamentally challenged the reductionist approach that dominated the natural sciences.
- But more than anything else, the Blue Marble was a highly emotional image, changing our view of our place in the cosmos. As Earth System scientist Johan Rockström says, 'We are no longer a small world on a big planet. We are a big world on a small planet.' (Rockström and Klum 2015).

However, perhaps the most striking prose triggered by the view of Earth from space was that of Carl Sagan, describing 'Pale Blue Dot', an image taken of Earth by the Voyager 1 space probe from a distance of 6,000,000,000 kilometers (Sagan and Druyan 1994):

> 'The aggregate of all our joys and sufferings, thousands of confident religions, ideologies and economic doctrines, every hunter and forager, every hero and coward, every creator and destroyer of civilizations, every king and peasant, every young couple in love, every hopeful child, every mother and father, every inventor and explorer, every teacher of morals, every corrupt politician, every superstar, every supreme leader, every saint and sinner in the history of our species, lived there – on a mote of dust, suspended in a sunbeam.'

The Blue Marble image, and many more space-based observations, were a core driving force for the blossoming of Earth System science

(ESS) in the 1980s. Thus, it was no surprise that the American space agency NASA played a central role in the rapid development of ESS at that time (NASA 1986). But the NASA role was far more than sending up a plethora of satellites to monitor the Earth from space. It also established a broad spectrum of research on the ground – or rather, the surface of the Earth – which, together with space-based measurements, began to piece together how the planetary machinery actually operates. ESS quickly became international, driven first by the formation of the World Climate Research Programme (WCRP) and then by the International Geosphere-Biosphere Programme (IGBP) along with companion programmes on the human dimensions of global change and on biodiversity (Steffen et al. 2020). Although these research efforts made significant progress in understanding the Earth System, they were still largely grounded in the siloed approach to research that had reigned supreme for the last several centuries. This siloed approach examines particular aspects of our world, on their own, in ever greater detail, without placing them within the Earth System as a whole. It has provided an in-depth understanding of individualized phenomena through the development of disciplinary tools. For instance, an ichthyologist may study lampreys, a vulcanist investigate Hawaiian eruptions, a paleoanthropologist look at the hominid mastery of fire, an art historian examine the Japanese ink and wash paintings of Sesshū Tōyō, a political philosopher the thinking of John Locke, an economist the views of Adam Smith, and an engineer the differences among types of load-bearing walls, all without considering how they might ultimately be interlinked into one system. Negotiating these distinctive ways of knowing raises philosophical – and narrative – challenges of the first order (as discussed in Chapter 2 and see Thomas, 2014; Renn, 2019; Thomas et al., 2020). The Blue Marble, though, remained as a strong visual image of our planet as a single, integrated system, challenging the research community to rise above the dominant fragmented approaches to understanding our home planet.

The next great shock to our perception of the Earth came in 2000 when atmospheric chemist Paul Crutzen proposed that the Earth had left the 11,700-year-long geological epoch of the Holocene and entered a proposed new epoch that he called, in a spur-of-the-moment outburst, the 'Anthropocene' (Crutzen 2002). At the time, only geologists and some Earth System scientists thought much about the geological time interval that the Earth occupied. Most people simply assumed that the Earth would continue to provide the stable, accommodating conditions that have allowed humanity to develop agriculture, villages, cities, and great civilizations across the planet – the Ethiopian kingdoms, the Incas in South America, the great Chinese and Indian civilizations of Asia, the Egyptian, Greek, and Roman empires of the Mediterranean region, and so on. The fundamental planetary life support system that had allowed human societies to develop, thrive, and prosper was out of sight, out of mind, and people carried on as though it would always be there – like gravity.

Crutzen's outburst shook that fundamental assumption to its core. He argued that humans had now become so numerous – and, in aggregate, so economically and technologically powerful – that we were overwhelming the great forces of nature. Without even recognizing it, we were changing our own planetary life support system at a rate of change that had rarely been seen before in Earth's 4.5-billion-year history. The proposal of the Anthropocene quickly generated a mass of discussion, debate, confusion, and controversy in the broad research community. Underlying much of the debate was the confusion between the human imprint on the face of the planet, which could be clearly seen for centuries and millennia deep into the past, and the human-driven trajectory of the Earth System outside of the relatively stable conditions of the Holocene. The latter was not only of significance for the young ESS research community, but it also challenged the venerable geological research community, and more specifically the stratigraphers – the time-keepers of planet Earth, as embodied in the GTS.

This was not the first time that the notion that humans were changing the geology of the planet caught the attention of the geological community. Back in the 1920s, Vernadsky argued for the importance of the biosphere in steering the trajectory of the Earth System and, even earlier, scholars like George Perkins Marsh, who in his 1864 book *Man and Nature* had documented the irreversible impacts of human activity on the Earth (Marsh 1864). The work of Marsh, Vernadsky, and others triggered a response from the American palaeontologist and botanist Edward Wilber Berry in 1926:

'No one would gainsay the magnitude and multifarious effects of human activity, but these are scarcely of geological magnitude. (Significant human impacts are)... not only a false assumption, but altogether wrong in principle, and ... really nurtured as a surviving or atavistic principle from the holocentric philosophy of the Middle Ages ...'

Compared to the early arguments that Berry railed against, the Anthropocene put forward a far more formidable case for a human-driven alteration to the path of Earth history and hence for inclusion in the GTS. The key was a set of graphs, produced as part of IGBP's synthesis project in the early 2000s and first published in 2004, that came to be known as the Great Acceleration graphs[1] based on Hibbard et al. (2007) and Steffen et al. (2004) (Figure 3.2). They were intended to show the evolution of what was called 'the human enterprise' and, on the same time scale, the changes in the Earth System, both the geosphere and the biosphere.

The first version of the graphs spanned the 1900–2000 period, because the term 'global change', as defined in IGBP research, was strongly focused on the twentieth century. However, Crutzen's proposal for the Anthropocene in February 2000 and its initial publication in May 2000 (Crutzen and Stoermer 2000) challenged that assumption. When he first suggested the concept, Crutzen proposed that the Anthropocene began with the advent of the Industrial Revolution in England in the late 1700s. This demanded a change in the time scale of the Great Acceleration graphs, with the start of the graphs pushed back to 1750 to capture the beginning of the Industrial Revolution and its evolution up until the present.

When the graphs were extended back to 1750, we expected to see the curves sweeping smoothly upwards from the late 1700s to 2000. We were in for a surprise. What we actually found, as shown in Figure 3.2a, were only very modest rates of change from 1750 to about 1950, after which there was a sharp increase in the rate of change in nearly every individual graph of socio-economic change. In general, the same patterns emerged from the 12 companion graphs showing changes in the Earth System

---

[1] The term 'Great Acceleration' was coined in 2005 by twentieth-century historian John McNeill at the Dahlem Conference 'Sustainability or Collapse: An Integrated History and Future of People on Earth'.

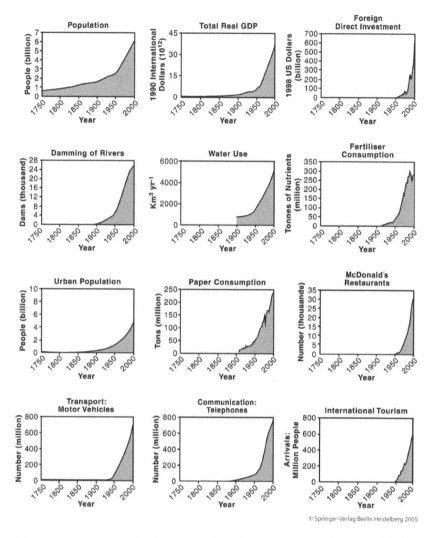

3.2. (a) The original Great Acceleration graphs: socio-economic trends (Steffen et al. 2004).

itself (Figure 3.2b), the top six individual graphs showing indicators for the geosphere and the bottom six showing indicators for the biosphere. A mass of evidence points to two fundamental conclusions that arise visually from the Great Acceleration graphs (Steffen et al. 2004):

- The Earth System is no longer within the Holocene envelope of variability. Starting from the mid-twentieth century, we are now

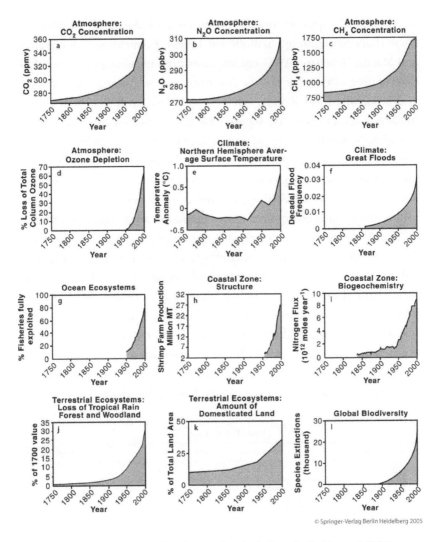

3.2. (b) The original Great Acceleration graphs: physical trends (Steffen et al. 2004).

accelerating into planetary *terra incognita*. No longer did the evidence point to a late 1700s starting point for the Anthropocene.

- Human activities, not natural variability or other non-human forces within the Earth System, are the dominant drivers propelling the Earth System away from the Holocene.

The challenge that Crutzen had laid out to the geological community was answered in 2009 with the formation of the Anthropocene Working Group

(AWG), which operates under the auspices of the Subcommittee for Quaternary Stratigraphy. Skilfully led by Jan Zalasiewicz, Colin Waters, and Martin Head, the AWG encompasses not only geologists focused on determining whether or not the Anthropocene was stratigraphically real, and if so, when did it start, but also included Earth System scientists, historians, legal experts, ecologists, biologists, archaeologists, and anthropologists. In addition to its primary task of meeting the traditional standards for establishing a new time interval, the group has taken a broad, inclusive approach to exploring the reality of the Anthropocene, including a range of fascinating visual approaches from museum exhibits to AWG t-shirts and an impressive visual array of potential stratigraphic markers.

The Anthropocene poses equally significant challenges to the Earth System science community, demanding a change in how we fundamentally conceived of the Earth System itself. Figure 3.3a is the now-iconic 'Bretherton diagram', named after Francis Bretherton, a NASA scientist who was one of the leading figures in NASA's pioneering Earth System science programme of the 1980s (NASA 1986). This is a classic box-and-arrow 'wiring diagram' for which natural scientists are notorious. It aims to show how a system – in this case, the Earth System – works by dissecting it into its component parts and then linking them with arrows to show

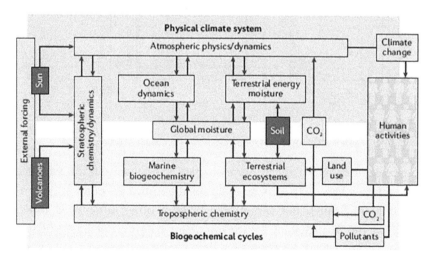

3.3. (a) The NASA Bretherton diagram of the Earth System. The focus is on the interactions between the geosphere and the biosphere, with human forcings represented as an outside force affecting the geosphere-biosphere system. (NASA 1986).

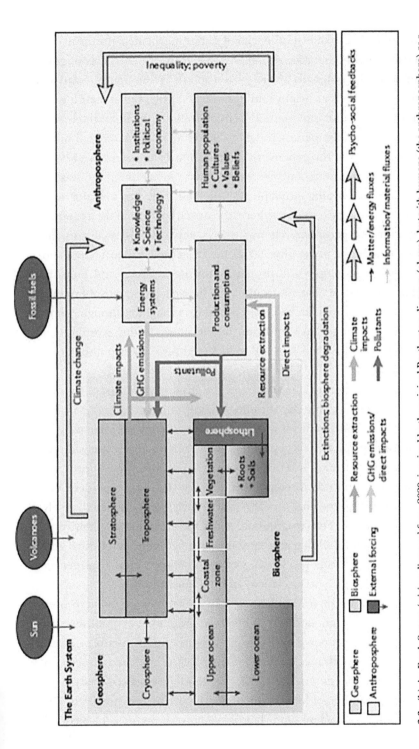

3.3. (b) An Earth System 'wiring diagram' from 2020, inspired by the original Bretherton diagram (above), but with humans (the anthroposphere) as a fully integrative, interacting sphere. Interactions between the Anthropocene and the rest of the Earth System are two-way, with human greenhouse gas emissions, resource extraction and pollutants driving impacts that reverberate through the geosphere-biosphere system. Feedbacks to the anthroposphere are also important, including direct impacts of climate change and biosphere degradation but also psycho-social feedbacks from the rest of the Earth System and within the anthroposphere. (Steffen et al. 2020).

how they connect to one another. It is a rather mechanical portrayal of a multi-scale, multi-dimensional complex system in which the emergent properties of the system as a whole – not shown by the figure – actually give the system both its beauty and its functional role. But at least it is an attempt to go beyond the twentieth century trend in the natural sciences to focus on one's discipline – roughly aligned to a part of a much more complex system – at the expense of understanding the system as a whole.

The Bretherton diagram was revolutionary for its time, and was an inspirational organizing principle for the IGBP. It was a major step forward in that it gave the biosphere, the lower half of the figure, equal billing with the geosphere. It was a first step towards rectifying the dominant paradigm in the physical sciences that the Earth just happened to have the right geophysical properties for life to evolve and flourish, and that geophysical changes would drive impacts in the biosphere in a unidirectional manner. In the 1986 Bretherton diagram, though, there were arrows pointing back up from the biosphere to the geosphere, a sort of 'tip of the hat' to James Lovelock and his Gaia hypothesis of a decade earlier.

Perhaps the most striking feature of the Bretherton diagram was the position of humans and our societies, rapidly being recognized in the 1980s as the dominant driver of the climatic and land use changes that were becoming apparent around the world. Humans appear only in one box – 'Human activities' – at the side of the figure, giving the impression that they are an outside forcing factor, like the sun and volcanoes (and curiously 'soil'), perturbing an otherwise orderly, well-connected, nicely functioning system. Perhaps, though, at the time this was probably revolutionary enough. Building at least some links between the physical and biological sciences was challenging enough without even considering how to deal with the social sciences and the humanities.

Building on the rapid developments in global change research over the past 30 years, an updated Bretherton diagram was published in 2020 as part of a paper describing the origins and evolution of Earth System science (Steffen et al. 2020) (Figure 3.3b). Modelled directly on the Bretherton diagram of the 1980s, this new figure reflected advances in our understanding of how the biophysical Earth System functions. For example, the geosphere and biosphere now have a soft, blended boundary rather than being separated into sharply distinct boxes. The coastal zone, linking land and ocean, now appears explicitly in the 2020 figure. Most surprisingly, the large polar ice sheets, which are crucial for the functioning of the Earth System, do not appear at all in the original Bretherton diagram. In the updated version, they are prominent in a box of their own (the cryosphere) as a major part of the geosphere along with the atmosphere. Finally, climate change appears in the original Bretherton diagram as a small box in the upper right corner, not central to the figure, whereas in the 2020 update climate change is depicted as a large arrow representing a major process influencing the functioning of the Earth System as a whole. Likewise, at the bottom on the diagram, a large arrow indicates that biosphere degradation is also a major global phenomenon.

Although these features represent important developments in our understanding of the Earth System, the most dramatic and important advance in the 2020 diagram is the inclusion of humans and our activities as an entire sphere, called the anthroposphere, within the Earth System, on the same level as the geosphere and the biosphere. Together, these three spheres – and the myriad ways in which they interact – describe how our planetary home functions as a single complex system with emergent properties characteristic of the system as a whole. As shown in the 2020 Earth System diagram, we humans are no longer embedded in the biosphere as part of a stable and very accommodating planet, but have recently emerged from being only part of the biosphere to now becoming the dominant driving force of the Earth System trajectory over the next decades, centuries and, indeed, for many millennia into the future. We have clearly created the Anthropocene.

Three other major differences stand out visually in a comparison of the 1986 Bretherton diagram and the 2020 updated version:

- There are more arrows of varying strengths that connect the Anthroposphere with the rest of the Earth System in both directions. One of the most important is the arrow from fossil fuels into the energy systems of the Anthroposphere. Importantly, fossil fuels are not part of the Earth System; like the sun and volcanoes, they are external entities that influence the functioning of the system.

They are external to the system because they are locked away, inert, from the active carbon cycle and would remain that way if humans did not mine and burn them, sending the gases from combustion – mainly carbon dioxide – into the atmosphere and thus into the dynamics of the Earth System. Thus, unlike the sun and volcanoes, fossil fuels affect the functioning of the Earth System only through their activation by humans.

- Three large, heavier arrows – climate change, biosphere degradation (extinctions) and inequality/poverty – represent high-level, emergent phenomena of the Anthropocene. These are all planetary-scale trajectories, arguably the most significant changes now occurring in each of the three major spheres of the Earth System and each, without a doubt, driven by human activity. Together, they have pushed the system out of the Holocene and onto a trajectory towards an unknown future state of the Earth System.

- The anthroposphere contains important detail in the form of three boxes: (i) knowledge, science, technology, (ii) institutions, political economy, (iii) cultures, values, beliefs. These boxes are an attempt to represent the ultimate driving forces of the Anthropocene – the human desires, ingenuity, and historical contingencies that have given rise to ever more elaborate energy systems, transport, built infrastructure, agriculture and so on. These human factors are the software that drives the hardware of the anthroposphere, and ultimately drives the trajectory of the Anthropocene.

The 2020 Earth System diagram, however, has a serious flaw, obvious from its visual representation. It is made up of individual boxes and arrows that connect them, and, as noted earlier, it is a rather reductionist, mechanical view of a single, complex system. Perhaps this is to be expected, given that contemporary ESS is still a small, nascent field of enquiry embedded in a large ocean of disciplinary sciences, as shown by the individual boxes. While disciplinary research is still very important and contributes much useful understanding to how various aspects, human and otherwise, of the Earth System functions, the challenge now is to bring these distinct ways of knowing into conversation with one another, a difficult task due to problems of scale and value. As this

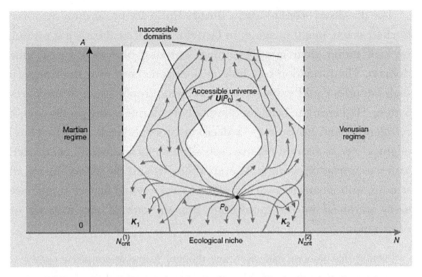

3.4. A 'Theatre world' representing pathways of sustainable development (arrows). Catastrophe domains, such as the 'Hothouse Earth' state are represented here as the spaces labelled K_1 and K_2 (Schellnhuber 1999).

book shows, one approach is to highlight the narrative form – the stories – used by almost all disciplines to convey their understanding and analysis. Another approach is through visual representations that aim to integrate insights into an emerging understanding of the Earth System as a whole.

A striking example of such a visualization is that of 'catastrophe domains', introduced by John Schellnhuber in his 1998 book *Earth System Analysis* (Figure 3.4). Creating a 'theatre world' for the future of humanity, Schellnhuber depicts the Earth System as a comfortable eco-logical niche nestled between an ultra-cold, dry 'Martian regime' and an ultra-hot, gaseous 'Venusian regime'. There are many possible pathways that humanity could take into the future within our accessible universe, as depicted by the multitude of arrows in the space labelled 'Accessible universe'. However, a few of them wander into areas that he calls 'catas-trophe domains', regions in which the Earth System does not flip into ultra-hot ('runaway greenhouse') or ultra-cold states, but nevertheless are regions so different from the Holocene that the human population would crash to much lower levels than today, with the survivors eking out a miserable existence on a hostile planet.

The threats of Schellnhuber's theatre world are not as esoteric or far-fetched as one might imagine. In fact, humanity has already just missed, by luck rather than good planning, entering one such catastrophe domain. The formation of a hole in the ozone layer over the southern high latitudes could easily have led to a catastrophic state of the Earth System. Had bromine been used instead of chlorine in the production of refrigerants and insulation – a decision probably made by a mid-level engineer on the basis of relative costs – humanity would have been faced with a catastrophic ozone hole everywhere around the planet during all seasons, without any forewarning. Paul Crutzen noted that we could have easily stumbled into a catastrophe domain without any warning or preparation:

> 'Noting that nobody had given any thought to the atmospheric consequences of the release of chlorine or bromine before 1974, I can only conclude that mankind has been extremely lucky.' Crutzen (1995)

Crutzen wasn't so lucky when he attended a scientific meeting in Punta Arenas, Chile, in January 2003. Punta Arenas is one of the very few human settlements that are far enough south that their residents could be affected by the ozone hole. The residents were well aware of the health risks of the ozone hole and, under the mistaken belief that Crutzen had *caused* the ozone hole instead of unravelling the atmospheric chemistry that caused it, took to the streets in anger when they heard he was in town. A hastily called press conference and some behind-the-scenes negotiation by Chilean government officials averted a show-down that could have led to a personal catastrophe domain for Crutzen.

A more complex catastrophe domain looms on the horizon for humanity as a whole. A group of Earth System scientists, employing a complex systems framework, carried out an assessment of the future pathways that the Earth System could take. The research was illustrated in a 'stability landscape' (see Figure 2.1), in which the system's recent past and possible futures are laid out as a sphere – the Earth System – rolling across an undulating landscape of hills, valleys, large plains, and a potentially catastrophic cliff or waterfall beyond which lies a deep, hot pit from which escape would be very difficult (Steffen et al. 2018).

The comfortable warmth and stability of the Holocene appears as a small valley at the far end of the figure, sitting above the larger, deeper valley of the ice ages. But the Earth System has already been pushed out of this comfortable home, and is now rolling away from it into a rather broad, shallow valley of increasing heat. This shallow valley is already a region of instability, but the Earth System is rolling onwards towards a deepening, more well-defined valley of stable but very much hotter conditions. In fact, it is likely poised very close to a 'bifurcation point' – a fork in the road.

Beyond the fork, one pathway – the one that the Earth System is currently tracking – takes the system on an accelerating trajectory down a steepening valley towards a critical point beyond which plunging over the planetary threshold becomes inevitable. This point-of-no-return occurs upstream from the planetary threshold itself. Beyond the point-of-no-return, intrinsic feedback processes in the Earth System become the dominant drivers of the system trajectory. Once irreversibly committed to going over the cliff, a 'Hothouse Earth' future awaits us:

> 'Hothouse Earth is likely to be uncontrollable and dangerous to many, particularly if we transition into it in only a century or two, and it poses severe risks for health, economies, political stability (especially for the most climate vulnerable), and ultimately, the habitability of the planet for humans.' Steffen et al. (2018).

Although the fork in the road may be looming in our immediate future, it is unlikely that we've already crossed it. But time is rapidly running out to move the Earth System onto the 'Stabilized Earth' pathway. How can we get there? It won't be easy, and will likely require what could be called a *global social tipping point*. Creating this beneficial tipping point would require redirecting a host of human activities toward the goal of stabilizing the planetary system. These new practices would include institutional and social innovation from the global governance level all the way down to decisions made by local communities and individuals, along with changes in demographic patterns to lower the human population, the end of an economic system based on continuously expanding production and consumption, greater philosophical dedication to collective wellbeing, educational and civic institutions supporting regenerative activities, and technologies attuned to stabilizing the planetary system as a whole rather than fixing discrete problems (Steffen et al. 2018; Thomas et al. 2020).

To conclude, we leave the complex, unsettling world of stability landscapes and catastrophe domains and come back 'down to Earth' to the more immediate, tangible world of 2021 and beyond. To do this, we turn to our old friend, gravity, and its critical role in returning Sandra Bullock back into the Earth System in the Hollywood portrayal of a catastrophic space accident. Space travel has now become somewhat routine, but no less insightful in experiencing the Earth System from outside – its intrinsic beauty, the increasing human imprint on the system, and the dangers that still threaten the space traveller when gravity inevitably pulls her back down into the Earth System.

By chance, at a scientific meeting in San Francisco in 2015, I met a real-life space traveller, a NASA astronaut who had made several trips to the International Space Station and then back to Earth. I asked him what struck him about seeing the Earth from above and, in particular, what struck him about the continent of Australia, where I live. One of his answers was expected, but the other was totally unexpected.

It came as no surprise to hear that the Great Barrier Reef, stretching for 2,300 kilometres along Australia's east coast, appeared as a dazzling, multi-coloured jewel from out in space. That was in 2015, and, unfortunately, mass coral bleaching events in 2016, 2017, and again in 2020 have now killed about 50% of the hard corals, leaving large swathes of ghostly white coral skeletons along the reef. The view from space would likely be quite different now – a scar from the Anthropocene.

The other answer was actually a question. Each time he passed over Australia from west to east, he noted an absolutely straight north-south line, stretching all the way from Australia's north coast down to the Southern Ocean. The line lay about a third of the way across the continent from the west. He knew that it was not a highway or a railway line, as no such human-made features existed. He also knew that it could not be natural, as nature does make such absolutely straight features for thousands of kilometres. He had been unable to obtain an explanation from anyone for this weird feature, always present when he crossed over Australia.

It had me puzzled too, until I recalled some early ecological studies that I had done. The answer then became immediately obvious – it was the rabbit-proof fence. The settlement of Australia by Europeans could be interpreted, perhaps a little too harshly, as one ecological disaster after another. One of them was the introduction of rabbits. With no natural enemies, their numbers exploded and they quickly ate their way westward across the continent. Not even the central arid zones could stop them. To prevent the western territories from suffering the ecological disaster that the rabbits had wrought in the east, it was decided to build a north–south wire mesh fence across the entire continent, with the fence also buried into the ground to prevent the rabbits from digging their way underneath it.

The fence was a success, stopping the rabbits in their tracks. To the east, the vegetation had been largely removed by the voracious rabbits, leaving vast sand dunes. To the west, however, the vegetation survived and a semi-arid open savanna stretched towards the Indian Ocean. From space, the demarcation was clearly visible as more light was absorbed on the more vegetated western side. Here was yet another striking marker of the Anthropocene, this time in one of the most remote areas of the planet.

Before we parted ways, the astronaut made one last comment, this time about the dangers of gravity, albeit rather indirectly. On one mission, he was launched into space with Russian cosmonauts from the Russian space centre in southern Siberia. Just before entering the launch vehicle, he and the cosmonauts were issued with rifles. His colleagues noted his puzzled look and explained that the rifles were for the wolves. If the launch had to be aborted soon after lift-off, the cosmonauts would be ejected and would land somewhere to the east, deeper in Siberia. Unlike the beautiful forests, ponds, and chirping frogs that welcomed Sandra Bullock back to Earth, the cosmonauts would face packs of hungry wolves and would need to defend themselves.

Despite its dangers, be they manufactured by Hollywood or experienced in reality, space travel has given an increasing number of humans the experience of leaving the Earth System and then returning to it. A common experience is awe, the deep emotional feeling of soaring silently above the globe, with its swirling white clouds, deep blue oceans and brown/green land masses – all connected in intricate ways to form one vibrant whole. The Earth – the tangible sphere that we inhabit – may be our planetary house, but the intangible, complex, living, evolving system that natural scientists call the Earth System is our planetary home.

REFERENCES

Berry, E.W. (1926), quote provided by Professor Jan Zalasiewicz, Chair of the Anthropocene Working Group.

Crutzen, P.J. (2002) Geology of mankind: the anthropocene. *Nature* **415**: 23.

Crutzen, P. (1995) *My Life with O_3, NO_x and other YZO_xs. Le Prix Nobel (The Nobel Prizes) 1995*. Stockholm: Almqvist & Wiksell International, pp 123–157.

Crutzen, P.J. and E.F. Stoermer (2000) The Anthropocene. *Global Change Newsletter*, **41**, 17–18.

Hibbard, K.A., Crutzen, P.J., Lambin, E.F., et al. (2007) Decadal interactions of humans and the environment. In: Costanza, R., Graumlich, L. and Steffen, W. (eds) *Integrated History and Future of People on Earth*, Dahlem Workshop Report 96. Cambridge, MA: MIT Press, pp 341–375.

Lovelock, J. (1979) *Gaia: A New Look at Life on Earth*. Oxford: Oxford University Press, 176pp.

Marsh, G.P. (1864) *Man and Nature: Physical Geography as Modified by Human Action*. London: S. Low, Son and Marston.

NASA (National Aeronautics and Space Administration) (1986) *Earth System Science Overview: A Program for Global Change*. Prepared by the Earth System Sciences Committee, NASA Advisory Council. Washington, DC: The National Academies Press, 48pp.

Renn J. (2019) *The Evolution of Knowledge: Rethinking Science for the Anthropocene*. Princeton, NJ: Princeton University Press, 561pp.

Rockström, J. and Klum, M. (2015) *Big World, Small Planet: Abundance within Planetary Boundaries*. Newhaven, CT: Yale University Press, 208pp.

Sagan, C. and Druyan, A. (1994) *Pale Blue Dot: A Vision of the Human Future in Space*. New York: Random House, 429pp.

Schellnhuber, H.J. (1998) Earth System analysis: the scope of the challenge. In: Schellnhuber, H.J. & Wentzel, V. (eds) *Earth System Analysis. Integrating Science for Sustainability*. Berlin, Heidelberg, New York: Springer-Verlag, pp. 3–195.

(1999) 'Earth system' analysis and the second Copernican revolution. *Nature* **402**, C19–C23.

Steffen, W. Sanderson, R.A., Tyson, P.D., et al. (2004) *Global Change and the Earth System: A Planet Under Pressure.* The IGBP Book Series. Berlin, Heidelberg, New York: Springer-Verlag, 336 pp.

Steffen, W., Leinfelder, R., Zalasiewicz, J., et al. (2016) Stratigraphic and Earth System approaches to defining the Anthropocene. *Earth's Future* **4**, 324–345.

Steffen, W., Rockström, J., Richardson, K., et al. (2018) Trajectories of the Earth System in the Anthropocene. *Proceedings of the National Academy of Sciences (USA)*, **115**(33), 8252–8259.

Steffen, W., Richardson, K., Rockström, J., et al. (2020) The emergence and evolution of Earth System Science. *Nature Reviews: Earth and Environment* 1:54–63.

Thomas, J. A. (2014) History and biology in the Anthropocene: problems of scale, problems of value. *American Historical Review* 119(5), 1587–1607.

Thomas, J.A., Williams, M., and Zalasiewicz, J. (2020) *The Anthropocene: A Multidisciplinary Approach.* Cambridge, UK: Polity Press, 233 pp.

Vernadsky, V.I. (1998) *The Biosphere [1926]* (complete annotated edition: Foreword by Lynn Margulis and colleagues, introduction by Jacques Grinevald, translated by David B. Langmuir, revised and annotated by Mark A.S. McMenamin). New York: Copernicus (Springer-Verlag), 192 pp.

CHAPTER 4

Deep History and Disease: Germs and Humanity's Rise to Planetary Dominance

Kyle Harper

THE ABUNDANT APE

The story of the Anthropocene is inseparable from the rise in human population.[1] There are, at time of writing, roughly 7.8 billion humans on Earth. By contrast, our nearest surviving relative, the chimpanzee, numbers only a few hundred thousand. Habitat loss over the last century has reduced chimp numbers, but even at the best of chimp times, there were probably never more than a million or two of our ape cousins. Why such disparity? Why is it not a planet of some *other* ape? For that matter, why are there not billions of gibbons, or geese, or geckos?[2]

The basic answer, from the perspective of a population ecologist, is that in nature all populations of animals are regulated. The flow of energy through ecosystems ensures that rates of population change are controlled by density-dependent mechanisms. As a population grows, energy availability (i.e. food) declines. Or other organisms, namely predators and parasites, are more able to take energy from successful species. Chimpanzees, for instance, are well adapted to win food from their forest environment, eating insects, fruits, and occasionally the small monkey. If they multiply too rapidly, food is harder to find, and mortality increases or fertility decreases. Chimps are also eaten by the big cats that prowl the forest, and they are killed or weakened by the microbes they

---

[1] AWG Press release, "Results of Binding Vote by AWG" (May 21, 2019) http://quaternary .stratigraphy.org/working-groups/anthropocene/ (accessed October 2021).

[2] On ape numbers, Strindberg, S., Maisels, F., Williamson, E., et al. 2018. "Guns, germs, and trees determine density and distribution of gorillas and chimpanzees in Western Equatorial Africa." *Science Advances* 4: 2964.

swap with each other and other forest fauna. (A parasite, in the memorable phrase of E.O. Wilson, is a predator that eats its prey in units of less than one). So chimp populations are constrained, and they cannot experience runaway increase.[3]

The human population has effectively escaped these ecological constraints, and we must look to ecology to understand why. We would never consider any other organism – its evolutionary history, its distribution, abundance, and ecosystem impacts – without attending to the fundamental questions of what it eats and what eats it. It is self-flattery if we imagine that we are really so different. It is true that already in the deep past, more than a million years ago, the mastery of fire gave our hominin ancestors a tool for ecological manipulation that makes us distinctive. Fire – a "species monopoly" of humans – means that *Homo sapiens* alone consumes energy through metabolism and combustion, using fire to do work like cooking, clearing forests, powering machines, fueling vehicles, and so on. Fire also gave us the upper hand over predators, which, despite the occasional mishap, have never played a major role in regulating human numbers.[4]

Fire may also have facilitated the evolution of humanity's big brains through the many advantages and downstream effects of cooking.[5] Even so, the mastery of fire – along with humanity's promethean intelligence – did not let our ancestors burn through all ecological limits. Food availability and parasites remained, for most of the human past, strong regulating factors on human populations. The importance of food availability in regulating human demography was theorized by Thomas Robert Malthus, whose famous theory of human population (first

---

[3] For the concept in general, see Turchin, P. 2003. *Complex Population Dynamics: A Theoretical/Empirical Synthesis*. Princeton, NJ: Princeton University Press. Parasites are predators: Wilson, E. O. 2014. *The Meaning of Human Existence*. New York: Liveright, at 180.

[4] Species monopoly: Goudsblom, J. 2015. "Fire and fuel in human history," in D. Christian, ed., *The Cambridge World History*, vol. 1. Cambridge, UK: Cambridge University Press, 185–207, at 185.

[5] Wrangham, R W. 2009. *Catching Fire: How Cooking Made Us Human*. London, UK: Profile Books.

published in 1798) is an essentially ecological theory.[6] He argued that when populations outstripped their food supply, death's scythe would cut their numbers through starvation (or its sequelae, like pestilence and war). However, the importance of parasites in controlling human numbers has not always been equally recognized, even though, into the twentieth century, infectious diseases were the primary cause of death, and waves of epidemic mortality repeatedly reduced human populations. Only recently have increased food production and control of infectious disease allowed human numbers to escalate to their current, potentially unsustainable, level.

This essay focuses on infectious disease as integral to understanding the Anthropocene. Even though this topic takes us away from the stratigraphic questions rightly at the heart of defining the Anthropocene as a geological epoch, it is an essential part of the story. It helps to explain the rise to planetary dominance of a single, particularly voracious species of primate: ourselves. Human population dynamics are a major driver of the forces that have precipitated the Anthropocene (see, for instance, the place of human population in Will Steffen's refined Bretherton diagram, Chapter 3, Figure 3.3b), and in turn infectious diseases have been a primary factor in human demographic history. In essence, infectious disease was an imperfect but non-trivial ecological buffer limiting human population growth for the vast majority of our history; humanity's sudden attainment of control over infectious disease (registered in the decline of infectious diseases as the leading causes of death) is part and parcel of our species' dominance of the planet. This is a part of the Anthropocene story that is often missing, perhaps because of the dissonance between the plot-lines of liberating humanity from much suffering and early death (a good thing) and environmental degradation and loss of biodiversity (a bad thing). The two are, however, uncomfortably inseparable, and an honest narrative requires us to confront directly the connections between human preeminence over microbes and its planetary consequences.

---

[6] On the intellectual context of Malthus, see Bashford, A. and J. Chaplin. 2016. *The New Worlds of Thomas Robert Malthus : Rereading the Principle of Population.* Princeton, NJ: Princeton University Press.

We cannot fathom how our species became an agent impacting the Earth System without giving our microbial companions and adversaries their due. This ecological history extends deep into the past. Even in the Pleistocene, our ancestors started to accumulate an unusually wide array of microbial enemies. However, with Holocene conditions and the invention of settled agriculture and cities, we created the ecology for a truly "unnatural," so to speak, portfolio of infectious diseases. Nevertheless, by the eighteenth century, humans started to gain the upper hand. In 1800, the global human population stood at roughly one billion, an astounding number in comparison with chimps and most large mammals. And since then, there's been little stopping us. Human population growth, along with the resource usage that it entails, is the proximate cause of the Anthropocene, and the control of infectious disease is the proximate cause of the modern population explosion. The Great Acceleration was enabled by a massive project of bioengineering aimed at preferentially eliminating the microorganisms that cause us suffering and death.

The control of infectious disease also highlights the precarity of human planetary supremacy. We now live in the shadow of global pandemics. Even if we cannot anticipate exactly when, where, and how new biological disruptions will emerge, these events in some form are now inevitable because human expansion has, paradoxically, accelerated the emergence of novel threats to human health. Like so many dimensions of the Anthropocene predicament, this feature of the complex Earth System's response to delirious human expansion reminds us of our ecological embeddedness – and the unintended and often undesirable consequences of human dominance.

HUMAN DISEASE FROM AN ECOLOGICAL PERSPECTIVE

Infectious disease is a state of impaired health caused by an invasive agent. Agents that cause disease are *pathogens* (from Greek roots meaning "disease" and "to cause to be"). *Germ* is a good colloquial word for a pathogen, usually implying a microbial one. *Parasite* (also from a Greek root, meaning someone who eats at the expense of another) is an ecological term, meaning any organism that takes energy from another species (the host) while causing it harm. In English, parasite sometimes connotes *macroparasites*, like worms, to the exclusion of microparasites, like bacteria, but it can also carry a broader meaning that encompasses *microparasites*. We should recognize that all of these terms are handy rather than precise. For instance, something so basic as whether an organism is a pathogen can depend on context.[7]

Pathogen, parasite, and germ are not taxonomical terms, and precisely because parasitism is a strategy that has evolved countless times, the organisms that exploit humans are taxonomically diverse. For convenience, we can categorize them into five groups. Some *fungi* cause disease in humans, although most cause severe disease only in immunocompromised individuals. *Helminth* is a catch-all category for various worms, several of which, like hookworm, are a major burden on human health. *Protozoa* are single-celled organisms (with an organized nucleus) that cause important diseases like malaria. *Bacteria* are single-celled organisms (without an organized nucleus) that cause major diseases like tuberculosis, plague, typhus, typhoid, etc. *Viruses* are nucleic acids protected by protein; they do not perform metabolism but invade the host's cell and insert themselves into the host's replication machinery. Although they are subject to Darwinian selection, it is debatable whether viruses are "alive." They indisputably cause some of our worst diseases, like smallpox, measles, yellow fever, polio, AIDS, COVID-19, and so on.[8]

These organisms exist because of evolution – because their ancestors were successful in transmitting their genes. Like any organism, they are under constant evolutionary pressure and will go extinct if they cannot pass their genes on to future generations. Because they have short generation times – especially viruses and bacteria – they acquire genetic mutations rapidly. A single host cell infected with poliovirus, for example, can produce 10,000 new virus particles in the space of 8 hours. The error rates vary from virus to virus, but in some small viruses they are as high as one mistake in every 1,000 base pairs (the "letters" that make up the genetic code). Some viruses mutate even faster, so nature is

---

[7] Thomas, J. A. 2014. "History and biology in the Anthropocene: problems of scale, problems of value." *American Historical Review* 119(5), 1587–1607.

[8] Schmid-Hempel, P. 2013. *Evolutionary Parasitology: The Integrated Study of Infections, Immunology, Ecology, and Genetics.* Oxford, UK: Oxford University Press.

constantly trying new genetic arrangements. All pathogens face strong evolutionary pressures, not least from the host's immune system, so pathogen evolution is fast and unforgiving, Darwinism in hyperdrive.[9]

Every organism has pathogens and parasites. Even bacteria are exploited by viruses, "bacteriophages," which are probably the most abundant entity in the biosphere. All mammals suffer from pathogens falling across the same taxa that cause disease in humans. Yet we should not underestimate how strange the human disease pool really is. Controlled comparison is impossible, since humans have an inordinate proclivity, and medical interest, in studying ourselves. But chimpanzees have been intensely observed by scientists for decades, and primatologists have called attention to the striking if impressionistic differences. Humans have vastly more parasites than our primate relatives – even relatively old (in evolutionary terms) parasites like worms. Even more striking is the number of bacteria and viruses that cause disease in humans, especially the number of directly transmissible pathogens, the number of pathogens that cause acute disease, and the number of pathogens that have a narrow host range – in other words, that specialize in infecting us. Our germs are unusual in their number, their nastiness, and their narrowness.[10]

Humans and chimpanzees shared a common ancestor six to nine million years ago. This common ancestor was ape-like, adapted to life in the forest environment. We can safely infer, on ecological grounds, that it would have suffered a humdrum primate disease pool. The distinctive human disease pool is a product of our distinctive ecological history. And increasingly, we have the tools to probe that history and understand humanity's unusual relationship with the microbes that have parasitized our success.

[9] Sanjuan, R., M. R. Nebot, N. Chirico, L. M. Mansky, and R. Belshaw. 2010. "Viral mutation rates." *Journal of Virology* 84: 9733–9748.

[10] e.g. Nunn, C. and S. Altizer. 2006. *Infectious Diseases in Primates: Behavior, Ecology and Evolution.* Oxford, UK: Oxford University Press. See also S. Calvignac-Spencer, S. A. J. Leendertz, T. R. Gillespie, and F. H. Leendertz 2012. "Wild great apes as sentinels and sources of infectious disease." *Clinical Microbiology and Infection* 18: 521–527. On the formation of the human disease pool, Harper, K. 2021. *Plagues upon the Earth: Disease and the Course of Human History.* Princeton, NJ: Princeton University Press.

ARCHIVES OF EVOLUTIONARY HISTORY

For the vast majority of the human past, infectious diseases (both in "normal" times and during epidemic crises) accounted for most human deaths. But as the COVID-19 pandemic has shown, it is not simple to know, measure, and report death, even in countries with advanced health bureaucracies. Efforts to measure worldwide causes of death (known as by-cause mortality) only go back to the 1990s. In most countries, national mortality statistics do not go earlier than the twentieth century. For the United States, national by-cause mortality data only go back to around 1900. In a few countries like Britain the data go earlier, and for a few cities, there are "Bills of Mortality" that can take us back a little further still. But with both public records as well as medical and other historical texts, the challenge of "retrospective diagnosis" – of understanding the biological cause of diseases perceived in very different cultural categories and terms – is a daunting challenge. In short, it is hard to know how people in the past died.[11]

We live at a time when a new kind of archive is rapidly helping to cast light on questions of evolutionary history: genomes. Genomes are the instructions of life encoded in nucleic acid inside every living cell. They are passed from generation to generation, with slight variation. These patterns of variation are a way to trace evolutionary relationships. Your genome is a record of your ancestry, a fact that commercial ancestry companies have cashed in on. The same is true of microbial pathogens. The COVID-19 pandemic, for instance, is being tracked in real time through an unprecedented amount of genome sequencing and global data sharing.[12]

In 1976 the first complete genome of a virus was sequenced. Not until 1995 was a complete bacterial genome published. But over the last ten years, advances in genome sequencing technology have changed the

---

[11] Alter, G. C. and A. G. Carmichael. 1999. "Classifying the dead: toward a history of the registration of causes of death." *Journal of the History of Medicine and Allied Sciences* 54: 114–132.

[12] For a rich overview focused on human population history from genomics, see Reich, D. 2018. *Who We Are and How We Got Here: Ancient DNA and the New Science of the Human Past.* Oxford, UK: Oxford University Press. For SARS-CoV-2, see nextstrain.org.

game by increasing the speed and decreasing the cost of sequencing genomes. The result is a staggering amount of data, which represents a vast new archive of evolutionary history. One unintended spinoff of high-throughput sequencing has been the rise of *paleogenomics* – the study of ancient fragments of DNA recovered from archaeological samples. Paleogenomics makes it possible, sometimes, to identify the specific pathogens responsible for death in the past. High-throughput sequencing has also dramatically improved the study of *phylogenomics*, that is the creation of evolutionary "family trees" (phylogenies) based on patterns of genetic relatedness discerned from enormous datasets.[13]

The sequencing revolution is starting to tell us bits and pieces of the story of how humans have shaped the evolution of pathogens. Evolutionary trees can give us a sense of *when* pathogens emerged. Sometimes we can infer *where* evolutionary events occurred, and often we can glean clues about *what ancestral hosts* the forebears of our germs infected. When archaeological DNA can be sequenced, it obviates many of the challenges of retrospective diagnosis to tell us what pathogens were present at specific points of the human past. Notably, for instance, the bacterial agent of bubonic plague (*Yersinia pestis*) has been definitively confirmed as the cause of historic pandemics like the Plague of Justinian and Black Death, resolving intense scholarly debates.[14]

The genomic evidence does not replace the conventional kinds of evidence, both documentary and archaeological. Rather it complements and enriches what can be done with the more familiar sources for studying the human past. And it should be underscored that we are still in the early days of the genomics revolution. Over the coming years the methods will develop and some of the giant gaps in our knowledge will be filled in.

---

[13] For a recent effort to assess what these methods mean for historians, K. Harper. 2020. "Germs, genes, and global history in the age of COVID-19." *Journal of Global History* 15: 350–362.

[14] For the importance of *Y. pestis* paleogenomics and phylogenetics, M. Green. 2020. "The four Black Deaths." *American Historical Review* 125: 1601–1631, also making the case that the Second Pandemic started earlier than the traditional narrative, based on written sources from the Near East and Europe, proposes. The impact (and chronology) of the Black Death in Africa and China are lively open questions at the moment, as the literature cited by Green shows.

HUMAN EXPANSION DRIVES PATHOGEN EVOLUTION

For better and for worse, humans are uniquely powerful ecosystem engineers, and consequently our species has outsized and complex effects on biodiversity at every scale. Humanity's role in shaping the ecology and evolution of our parasites is a special case, due to the fact that our own bodies *are* the primary environment for our parasites. Thus, human population growth throughout our history has been the most basic ecological change driving the evolution of parasites. But almost everything about the way we live and use nature – sedentary lifestyles, the domestication of plants and animals, the adaptation of commensal species to human habitation and food production, the development of transportation networks – shapes the ecological context for our pathogens.[15]

When our ancestors still had chimp-like lifestyles, they would have had chimp-like germs. Several of our helminth parasites, like whipworm and hookworm, have evolved with us on the deepest timescales. Similarly, a number of relatively avirulent, chronic infections like those caused by herpes viruses seem to be millions of years old. Humans, for instance, serve as host to two herpes simplex viruses. One of them (HSV-1) is as old as the split between our ancestors and chimps; it primarily causes lesions in the mouth. All primates seem to have one herpes simplex virus, while humans alone are cursed to carry two. The second, bonus species (HSV-2, the cause of genital herpes) was acquired around 1.6 million years ago by a now extinct *Homo* ancestor, ultimately contracted from chimpanzees, subsequently handed down to us.[16]

Humans spent 95% of our history as hunter-gatherers during the Pleistocene epoch. This long period of the human past is often glossed over in histories of disease, which rush to emphasize the Neolithic Revolution as a turning point. It is right to emphasize that the ecological dynamics of hunter-gatherer societies limited the kinds of pathogens that

[15] This narrative summarizes the arguments presented more fully in a monograph, *Plagues upon the Earth*, forthcoming by the author from Princeton University Press.

[16] Wertheim, J., M. D. Smith, D. M. Smith, K. Scheffler, S. L. K. Pond. 2014. "Evolutionary origins of human herpes simplex viruses 1 and 2." *Molecular Biology and Evolution* 31: 2356–2364. Underdown, S. J., K. Kumar, and C. Houldcroft. 2017. "Network analysis of the hominin origins of herpes simplex virus 2 from fossil data." *Virus Evolution* 3: vex026.

could establish in human populations, relative to what came later. Technological innovation was limited and slow for most of our history, and humans depended on wild food sources, a stark constraint on our numbers and density. When population densities are low, and societies are mobile, then acute, virulent, directly transmissible pathogens will go extinct. Nevertheless, infectious diseases were already important in the Pleistocene past. It is notable, for instance, that infectious diseases are the leading cause of death in virtually every observed hunter-gatherer society, and account for a greater proportion of deaths than in studied chimpanzee populations. Germs were a powerful factor in regulating human numbers, already in the Pleistocene.[17]

The most important class of parasites to adapt to humans in the Pleistocene were vector-borne diseases. Using a blood-eating insect as an intermediary transport vehicle is a bold evolutionary gambit, but it has paid off handsomely for parasites like the single-celled parasite that causes vivax malaria (*Plasmodium vivax*). Transmitted by the bite of certain mosquitos in the genus *Anopheles*, malaria is one of the great human diseases, and the vivax form is an evolutionary product of the Pleistocene. The phylogenetic evidence of the parasite itself suggests that it emerged from a chimpanzee parasite during the Pleistocene. The human genome bears witness to this history; many African populations carry a genetic variant in the red blood cell (known as Duffy negativity) that is highly advantageous because it confers resistance to vivax malaria. This variant rose to high frequency in the late Pleistocene, unfortunately for much of humanity only *after* the out-of-Africa migrations were well underway. The humans who first migrated to Asia and Europe lacked this protective variant.[18]

---

[17] Gurven, M. D and C. M. Gomes. 2017. "Mortality, senescence, and life span." In M. N. Muller, R. W. Wrangham, and D. R. Pilbeam, eds. *Chimpanzees and Human Evolution.* Cambridge, MA: Harvard University Press, 181–216.

[18] See most recently on the evolution of vivax, Arisue, N., T. Hashimoto, S. Kawai, et al. 2019. "Apicoplast phylogeny reveals the position of *Plasmodium vivax* basal to the Asian primate malaria parasite clade." *Scientific Reports* 9(1): 7274. On human adaptation, McManus, K.F., A. M. Taravella, B. M. Henn, et al. 2017. "Population genetic analysis of the DARC locus (Duffy) reveals adaptation from standing variation associated with malaria resistance in humans." *PLoS Genetics* 13: 1006560.

Vector-borne pathogens were able to transmit successfully even in low-density, mobile populations. One of the really distinctive dynamics of human population history is that vector-borne diseases are geographically discriminatory, and have been since the Pleistocene. We use the language of "tropical diseases" to express the reality that many major infectious diseases are limited to the lower latitudes, where, for instance, vector species exist in greater abundance. Other primates are not cosmopolitan, and in consequence do not have radically dissimilar disease environments between populations. Health inequality is one of the primordial sources of difference between human societies, and throughout our past has often played into other configurations of power and exploitation.

While the Pleistocene disease package was more dangerous than once believed, the transition to sedentary lifestyles and the domestication of plants and animals were transformational. It turns out that what V. Gordon Childe famously called the Neolithic Revolution was in reality more of an evolutionary process. Moreover, because domestication arose independently in around a dozen places, it would be even more accurate to speak of revolutions (or evolutions). Nevertheless, domestication was an energy breakthrough. Human societies learned to turn over landscapes to the capture of solar energy by a few preferred species, most importantly grasses with big, edible seeds (e.g. wheat, rice, maize). Sunlight was converted into more human bodies. At the start of the Holocene, there were maybe 10 million humans on Earth – awfully successful for a primate, but hardly a premonition of what lay ahead. Farming created an ongoing population boom.[19]

Farming caused greater population densities, reduction of biodiversity, and closer proximity to domesticated animals, but maybe its most immediate ecological consequence for infectious disease was sedentism. Among other things, life in a permanent settlement meant that humans were now surrounded by their own waste, as well as the

---

[19] Barker, G. 2006. *The Agricultural Revolution in Prehistory: Why Did Foragers Become Farmers?* Oxford, UK: Oxford University Press. Because they are based on so little actual evidence, estimates of human population at the beginning of the Holocene have varied widely, from as low as 1 million to as high as 20 million (see HYDE 3.1, favoring an estimate of 2 million, which is probably too low).

waste of large numbers of domesticated mammals and birds. A human settlement is a unique waste environment, probably the greatest aggregation of inter-species scat in all of nature. Pathogens that rely on transmission via the fecal–oral route came to thrive in such environments. Diarrheal disease has been and remains one of the great burdens on human health, and it is a bit of an oddity that the respiratory diseases have famous and memorable names (tuberculosis, measles, smallpox, whooping cough, diphtheria, scarlet fever), while diarrheal diseases are lumped together and their biological agents languish in obscurity (rotavirus, Shigella, paratyphoid fever, and so on, hardly being household names).[20]

As populations continued to grow, and technologies like metallurgy, writing, and the domesticated horse were developed, it allowed cities, states, and eventually empires to form. The result was the evolution of the so-called "crowd diseases," directly transmissible pathogens that require large populations of humans to sustain transmission. Probably, such pathogens had emerged continuously throughout our past, but just as quickly gone extinct. What changed was that big, dense populations now provided a network where aggressive pathogens could emerge *and* establish permanently in an endless sequence of human hosts, thereby avoiding extinction.

For earlier generations of medical historians, the Neolithic Revolution was a transformational moment in the history of disease because it brought us into close contact with domesticated animals, thought to be the source of new diseases. For example, human and bovine tuberculosis are caused by closely related bacteria, so it was inferred that cows were the source of this human disease. Genome-based phylogenies have flipped this story on its head, for it turns out that human TB is ancestral to bovine TB. But the point is more general, that the simplistic story of the derivation of human diseases from domesticated animals needs to be rewritten. We now have a better understanding of how constant and pervasive host-switching and cross-species

---

[20] Webb, J. L. A. 2020. *The Guts of the Matter: A Global History of Human Waste and Infectious Intestinal Disease.* Cambridge, UK: Cambridge University Press, finally gives these germs their due.

transmission are in nature, and we can see that wild animals have been the major source of new infectious diseases. Our domesticates were more often a bridge for new diseases – a proximate rather than ultimate origin. What changed with domestication, then, was the place of humans in the broader web of animal life – and animal disease.[21]

These patterns have become beautifully clear in the case of measles, the ultimate crowd disease. Caused by a small RNA virus, measles is one of the most contagious diseases known. It has a critical population threshold of around 250,000, so in populations below this size it will run out of susceptible hosts and go extinct. Measles emerged around 2500 years ago when it diverged from a common ancestor shared with the Rinderpest virus, a pathogen that causes a devastating disease in cattle. Remarkably, the timing aligns with the moment in human history – the early Iron Age – when human settlements first passed ca. 250,000. Measles and Rinderpest are closely related to the virus that causes *peste des petits ruminants*, a disease of sheep and goats. This might seem like a classic story of Neolithic domestication and disease transmission to humans. But broader surveillance of wild animals has shown that all of these viruses are related to a family that is widely spread among bats and rodents. The deeper story, then, is that the aggregation of sheep, goats, and cattle formed the ecological context for the adaptation of this virus of wild animals to our domesticates, and then to our city-building ancestors.[22]

In general, the genomic evidence is starting to reveal that many of the major infectious diseases are young. The evolution of plague, tuberculosis, leprosy, falciparum malaria (the even more evil cousin of vivax malaria), measles, smallpox, whooping cough, and so on, all belong to the last several thousand years. Moreover, the advance of transportation technologies, from the horse to transoceanic shipping, has facilitated the global dispersal of pathogens. The most explosive example is the microbial dimension of the Columbian Exchange, the human-mediated

[21] Harper, K. [Kristin – not the present author], and G. J. Armelagos. 2013. "Genomics, the origins of agriculture, and our changing microbe-scape: time to revisit some old tales and tell some new ones." *American Journal of Physical Anthropology* 57: 135–152.

[22] Düx, A., S. Lequime, L. V. Patrono, et al. 2020. "Measles virus and Rinderpest virus divergence dated to the sixth century BCE." *Science* 368: 1367–1370.

biological transfer of flora and fauna allowed by trans-Atlantic shipping. Old World pathogens like smallpox, measles, and (probably) typhus were imported to the Americas. Moreover, most of the tropical diseases of the Old World, such as falciparum malaria and yellow fever, were transplanted to the neotropics, creating a powerful geographical gradient of infectious disease with far-reaching consequences.[23]

Although this is not yet rigorously demonstrable, it seems likely that the last several centuries have witnessed the acceleration of disease emergence and dispersal. A much more virulent strain of smallpox emerged in the sixteenth century and disseminated globally. Typhus is suddenly visible and devastating from the late fifteenth century onward. Cholera emerged in these centuries and went global in the age of steamship. Polio and AIDS were also new in the nineteenth and early twentieth centuries. In short, the control that humans have achieved over infectious disease in modern times should be seen as an accomplishment that occurred against the backdrop of a steadily *more*, not less, challenging environment.[24]

DISINFECTING THE PLANET

In the twentieth century, the average human lifespan more than doubled, thanks largely to the control of infectious disease. Life not only became longer, but also more predictable. The control of infectious disease is such an integral and intimate part of modernity that it is hard to imagine a counterfactual world where the other signature transformations of modernity – modern economic growth, mass education, the fertility decline, and empowerment of women – progress without concomitant control over infectious disease. Even though its mortality toll pales in comparison to historic plagues, the COVID-19 pandemic is disruptive and traumatic precisely because so many of our social systems (especially in developed economies) are predicated on the control of infectious disease.

---

[23] See McNeill, J. "Disease Environments of the Caribbean to 1850: A Tale of Two Syndemics," forthcoming, for an up-to-date synthesis focused only on the Caribbean.

[24] Gillings, M. R., and I. T. Paulsen. 2014. "Microbiology of the Anthropocene." *Anthropocene* 5: 1–8.

How did humans gain the upper hand? The short answer is twofold: science and state power. There is a longstanding temptation to locate the key moment in the control of infectious disease in the later nineteenth century, with the rise of "germ theory" and the implementation of public health policies by modern states. That temptation is understandable, since permanent increases in human longevity begin around the 1860s in western Europe. This narrative is buttressed by the arrival, for the first time, of decent national statistics – gathered by the same increasingly powerful states – that allow important quantitative insights. But such a shallow perspective on the modern health transition is distorting in important ways.[25]

Public health efforts *avant la lettre* go back at least to the later middle ages in some parts of Europe and Asia, and the efforts to improve population health via environmental control went hand-in-hand with the empowerment of states. Urban sanitary policies were particularly important, and in places like Italy rudimentary health bureaucracies emerged along with population-level surveillance practices, such as mortality registration. In early modern Japan, the immense city of Edo, now Tokyo, commercialized the removal of human waste to make green fertilizer; the result was a virtuous cycle of cleaner streets, cleaner water, better food, and healthier people.[26] Moreover, quarantine and forcible isolation (or "lockdown") developed through experience with bubonic plague and helped in the elimination of plague from western Europe in the later seventeenth and early eighteenth centuries.[27]

The eighteenth century was a turning point, at least in western Europe and its colonial offshoots. Epidemic mortality was brought under control. (The last really severe mortality crisis in England, for example,

[25] Deaton, A. 2013. *The Great Escape: Health, Wealth, and the Origins of Inequality.* Princeton, NJ: Princeton Unversity Press; Weil, G. 2015. "A review of Angus Deaton's *The Great Escape: Health, Wealth, and the Origins of Inequality.*" *Journal of Economic Literature* 53: 102–114.

[26] Hanley, S. 1997. *Everyday Things in Premodern Japan.* Berkeley: University of California Press; Howell, D. 2013. "Fecal matters: a prolegomenon to a history of shit in Japan," in I. J. Miller, J. A. Thomas, and B. L. Walker, eds., *Japan at Nature's Edge: The Environmental Context of a Global Power,* Honolulu: University of Hawaii Press. 137–152.

[27] Geltner, G. 2019. *Roads to Health: Infrastructure and Urban Wellbeing in Later Medieval Italy.* Philadelphia: University of Pennsylvania Press.

were the epidemics of the 1740s, probably caused by typhus). Life expectancies increased modestly. For the first time, persistent class inequities in health emerged, as social advantage was translated into longer life. Enlightenment medicine was empiricist in approach, and it promoted preventative methods to thwart disease. Medical scientists preached sanitation, ventilation, water filtration, hygiene, and so on, in the name of health. At century's end, Edward Jenner demonstrated the possibilities of vaccination against smallpox, a dramatic improvement over the already important technique of inoculation that had spread globally, probably from China.[28]

Rapid urbanization and industrialization overwhelmed these efforts in the early nineteenth century, however. Increases in life expectancy stalled or even reversed, as old enemies like tuberculosis and new ones like cholera took advantage of the ecology of an urbanizing and inter-connected world. These challenges helped to galvanize the public health movement and inspired the scientific advances that unraveled with dizzy-ing speed in the later nineteenth century. Louis Pasteur and Robert Koch are the avatars of "germ theory," which was a loosely connected series of discoveries that progressively illuminated the microbiological dimensions of human disease. In 1850, the idea that disease was caused by invisible living agents was marginal. By 1900 or so, it was a dominant consensus.[29]

Some of the interventions allowing human control of infectious dis-ease preceded germ theory and did not intellectually depend on it, while

---

[28] In a classic treatment, Omran, A. 1971. "The epidemiologic transition: a theory of the epidemiology of population change." *Milbank Memorial Fund Quarterly* 49: 509–538, described the "age of receding pandemics." For an enlargement of this idea, as presented here, see Harper, K. 2021. *Plagues upon the Earth: Disease and the Course of Human History.* Princeton, NJ: Princeton University Press, Chapter 10. The mortality crisis of the 1740s was triggered by a series of anomalously cold years and ensuing harvest failures: Post, J. D. 1984. "Climatic variability and the European mortality wave of the early 1740s." *Journal of Interdisciplinary History* 15: 1–30. The precise origins of inoculation are not entirely clear, and it is possible that it was discovered independently in different regions. See Harper, K. 2021. *Plagues upon the Earth: Disease and the Course of Human History.* Princeton, NJ: Princeton University Press. 363, for discussion and further literature.

[29] Walker, J. 2003. *Discovery of the Germ (Twenty Years That Transformed the Way we Think about Disease).* New York: Colombia University Press.

others – like vaccinations and antibiotics – were decisively advanced by microbiology. The control of infectious disease is a massive bioengineering project to eliminate the subset of microbes that cause us harm, as well as the insects that serve as vectors of important diseases. We manipulate environments at various scales, from the proteins and cells of our own immune system (via vaccination) to entire landscapes (think of DDT sprayed over millions of square miles).[30]

Consider one everyday example of a chemical intervention that preserves human health: the treatment of drinking water. Drinking water contaminated with feces was one of the biggest threats to human health. Industrialization had only made a bad problem worse. Above all, typhoid fever stood as one of the leading causes of death. Its causes were gradually deciphered, and the need for water treatment was made evident. Sewer systems and water filtration helped, but the real breakthrough was chlorination. The most important reason many of us can drink a glass of water today and not feel even a hint of dread that it carries deadly typhoid bacteria is because it has been treated with chlorine. With almost unbelievable speed, this scourge was brought under control in the developed world (Figure 4.1).[31]

The effort to disinfect the planet for our benefit is multifaceted. The hygiene revolution of the late nineteenth century required a quasi-religious campaign. The "gospel of germs" was preached to create a cultural awareness of disease-causing microbes. Many of our personal routines and private spaces – kitchen and bathroom tile floors, hand-washing, the use of household chemical disinfectants, screen doors and windows, fly-swatting, and so on – have been shaped by the imperatives of engineering domestic environments that are unwelcoming to disease-causing microbes.[32]

---

[30] For the deployment of insecticides and "war" on insects, see Russell, E. 2001. *War and Nature: Fighting Humans and Insects with Chemicals from World War I to Silent Spring.* Cambridge, UK: Cambridge University Press.

[31] Melosi, M. 2008. *The Sanitary City: Urban Infrastructure in America from Colonial Times to the Present.* Baltimore: John Hopkins University Press; McGuire, M. 2013. *The Chlorine Revolution: Water Disinfection and the Fight to Save Lives.* Denver: American Water Works Association.

[32] Tomes, N. 1998. *The Gospel of Germs: Men, Women, and the Microbe in American Life.* Cambridge, MA: Harvard University Press.

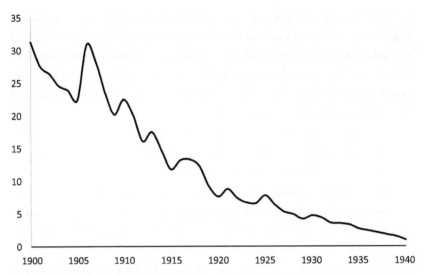

4.1. Typhoid deaths per 100,000, United States. (Data: United States Public Health Service, National Office of Vital Statistics.)

It has sometimes been emphasized that biomedical interventions like pharmaceuticals and vaccinations arrived too late to account for the mortality decline. But it is important to underscore the role of pharmaceuticals and vaccines in holding humanity's dominance in place against microbial threats. (Think of the polio virus, which spread terrifyingly, even in the antiseptic societies that had started to control infectious threats, until it was stopped in its track by two effective vaccines.) Even more importantly, biomedical interventions, along with insecticides, were critical to the globalization of good health in the twentieth century.[33]

As the demographer Samuel Preston demonstrated, over the course of the twentieth century, the structural relationship between per capita income and life expectancy shifted, as it became possible to achieve longer life at lower levels of economic income. The reason why is that scientific understanding of infectious disease increased, and the technologies to prolong life – "magic bullets" like insecticides, vaccines, and

---

[33] Biomedicine was famously downplayed by McKeown, T. 1976. *The Modern Rise of Population.* New York: Arnold. See Davis, K. 1956. "The amazing decline of mortality in underdeveloped areas." *American Economic Review* 46: 305–318.

oral rehydration therapy – spread globally. The sudden increases in life expectancy in the mid-twentieth century are astonishing. Processes that had taken decades if not centuries in societies pioneering the control of infectious disease were accomplished in the space of years in most of the world. The globalization of good health was the domino that tipped humanity into the Great Acceleration.[34]

The increase in human numbers in the course of the twentieth century has depended on expanded global food production. Global population in 1900 was 1.6 billion; in 2020, humans numbered 7.8 billion. But the mortality decline, driven by the control of infectious disease, was the primary and proximate cause of global population growth. After all, the mortality decline eventually triggered the fertility decline (always in that order, with some lag, during which populations grew explosively). In short, human beings multiplied deliriously not because they "suddenly started breeding like rabbits: it is just that they stopped dying like flies."[35]

The escapes from poverty and premature death, as globally uneven as they still are, represent twin accomplishments of modernity, and they have the same ultimate source – humanity's knowledge of nature and ability to manipulate it for the narrow and short-term benefit of our species. In the words of the economist David Weil, "The contemporaneous advance of income and health in the leading countries over the last several centuries (after millennia of stagnation) is explained largely by changes in know-ledge. More specifically, productive knowledge and health knowledge advanced together, driven by the underlying advance of science and the spirit of experimentation born of the Enlightenment."[36] Sadly, the unin-tended consequence of our liberation from the constraints that hold other

[34] Preston, S. H. 1980. "Causes and consequences of mortality declines in less developed countries during the twentieth century," In R. Easterlin, ed., *Population and Economic Change in Developing Countries.* 289–360. Chicago: University of Chicago Press. See generally Riley, J. C. 2001. *Rising Life Expectancy: A Global History.* Cambridge, UK: Cambridge University Press.

[35] Lean, G., D. Hinrichsen, A. Markham. 1990. *Atlas of the Environment.* London: Hutchinson Reference. Generally, Dyson, T. 2010. *Population and Development.* London: Zed Books Ltd.

[36] Weil, D. N. 2015. "A review of Angus Deaton's *The Great Escape: Health, Wealth, and the Origins of Inequality.*" *Journal of Economic Literature* 53: 113.

species in check has been the degradation of the environment and loss of biodiversity, possibly beyond the limits that made the old Earth System so conducive to human civilization.

EMERGING DISEASES NOW

In 1991, the Institute of Medicine (now the National Academy of Medicine) commissioned a panel to study microbial threats. The panel's report, published as *Emerging Infections: Microbial Threats to Health in the United States*, was a broadside against "complacency." One of its co-chairs, the Nobel-prize winning microbiologist Joshua Lederberg, was a pioneering expert in microbial evolution. He knew better than anyone that nature does not stand still. "In the context of infectious diseases, there is nowhere in the world from which we are remote and no one from whom we are disconnected." The arsenal of magic bullets had given humans the upper hand, but this advantage was unstable. "Because of the evolutionary potential of many microbes, however, the use of these weapons may inadvertently contribute to the selection of certain mutations, adaptations, and migrations that enable pathogens to proliferate or nonpathogens to acquire virulence."[37]

The report gave "emerging infectious diseases" a place in both scientific and public consciousness. Complacency and alarm have co-existed in an uneasy mix for the last generation. Sometimes, our anxiety has been rational, leading to smarter investments in disease surveillance, global public health, international development, and basic science. Anxiety also manifests itself in collective fascination with new diseases, in sensationalist journalism, in lurid fiction and films, even zombie apocalypses. Prophets in the line of Lederberg have continuously forewarned us that new diseases were one of the most fundamental risks we face as a species. And the COVID-19 pandemic made it all too evident that their alarms were both prescient and unheeded.

The pandemic was, in some sense, inevitable. The evolution of pathogens is the great threat and the basic reason why we can never entirely escape the risk of global pandemics. Evolution is the source of new

---

[37] Lederberg, J., R.E. Shope, and S.C. Oaks (eds.) 1992. *Emerging Infections: Microbial Threats to Health in the United States.* Washington, D.C.: National Academies Press.

diseases and new strains of old diseases. New diseases emerge when microorganisms that infect animals cross the species barrier and adapt the ability to transmit between humans. New strains of old diseases evolve in response to selective pressures that we place upon them. In some instances, new strains emerge as human populations develop immunity to old strains, as is constantly happening with the influenza virus. In other instances, evolution picks new strains because they have mechanisms that allow them to evade or subvert our extended immune system. Antibiotic resistance, for instance, is a form of evolutionary response to our ample use of chemical weapons against bacteria. Those strains that adapt the ability to survive and reproduce in such an environment will pass on their genes to future generations.

In the Anthropocene, humans have become "the dominant animal." Organisms adapt to the human-dominated planet, or they go extinct. *Homo sapiens* now drives patterns of evolution across the biosphere, directly and indirectly. We favor some species intentionally (cows, chickens, pigs), others unintentionally (squirrels, pigeons). We harm some species deliberately (cockroaches, bedbugs), others inadvertently (polar bears, black rhinos, and the thousands of other animals going extinct). Pathogens are a special case, because we harm them intentionally, but benefit them inadvertently, since our own biological success is an opportunity for organisms that can exploit us.[38] We can identify five major risk factors that loom over our struggle to control the threat of infectious disease. The first is population growth itself. From a parasite's perspective, we are simply hosts, bundles of energy and nutrients there for the taking. The global human population today is a feast laid out on a banquet table. There are now nearly eight billion of us, and by mid-century there will be over ten billion of us. We also live more densely than at any time in the past. As discussed in Chapter 12, a number of cities have populations above twenty million. The population of Tokyo alone is more than double the number of humans that existed on the planet at the beginning of the Holocene.[39]

---

[38] "Dominant animal": Ehrlich, P. R. and A. H. Ehrlich. 2009. *The Dominant Animal: Human Evolution and the Environment*. Washington D.C.: Island Press.

[39] Population projections: Lutz, W. and K. C. Samir. 2010. "Dimensions of global population projections: what do we know about future population trends and structures?" *Philosophical Transactions of the Royal Society B: Biological Sciences* 365: 2779–2791.

Our voracious consumption habits are a second risk factor. The great enrichment of humanity rests on the usage of exhaustible resources. The most obvious correlate of human consumption is land-use. Not only does land-use for human purposes reduce biodiversity but it brings us into direct contact with virtually every ecosystem on the planet. Moreover, industrial agriculture is itself a source of grave risk. The hundreds of millions of cows, pigs, and chickens brought together in unnatural aggregations are a stewpot of new germs. The overuse of antibiotics in farm animals, largely to promote weight gain, promotes the spread of genes conferring antibiotic resistance.[40]

Jet travel is a third risk factor. The jet airplane is a transportation technology of fundamental epidemiological significance, on par with the horse, the steamship, and the railroad. Civil aviation has made long-distance travel ordinary. Consequently, human populations around the globe are more thoroughly inter-mixed than at any time in our past. Jet travel means that distance is now biologically negligible, in that it has become possible to travel between any two points on the planet during the incubation phase of any infection. For directly transmitted diseases – especially acute respiratory infections – distance has disappeared.

There are two final risk factors that bear mentioning, even though both are true wild cards. The first is climate change. Climate change could influence the disease environment in various ways, but maybe the most palpable is by expanding the territorial range of vector species. Mosquitos that transmit malaria, dengue fever, chikungunya fever, yellow fever, Zika fever, and so on may find that they can thrive at higher latitudes for more of the year. Similarly, regional changes in patterns of precipitation are likely to alter the breeding habitats of mosquitos and thus affect the geography of infectious disease. The links between eco-logical change and infectious disease are astonishingly complex and often incompletely understood: it has been hypothesized, for instance, that the increasing prevalence of the tick-borne infection Lyme disease is due to expanding numbers of the white-footed mouse, which is in turn

---

[40] For an evocative case study, McKenna, M. 2017. *Big Chicken: The Incredible Story of How Antibiotics Created Modern Agriculture and Changed the Way the World Eats.* Washington, D.C.: National Geographic.

explained by declining numbers of red foxes in the northeastern United States.[41]

The last wild card is biological warfare. The intentional weaponization of biological agents is within our species' technical capacity. In principle, existing or potential pathogens could be genetically manipulated in the laboratory to be made more deadly or more contagious. While the deployment of biological weapons violates international law and moral norms, the ability of global institutions to enforce these legal and ethical standards is limited. The democratization of knowledge means that a growing number of states have or will become players in biological research relevant to the weaponization of disease. Moreover, the potential for non-state actors to develop or deploy biological weapons will continue to increase.[42]

COVID-19 stands in an unbroken line of new diseases. Before COVID-19, the impact of most new pathogens (like Ebola and the first SARS) was kept in check, due to a combination of good policy and good luck. The virus responsible for the COVID-19 pandemic has a set of insidious biological features that make it hard to control and moderately virulent. The response of global health institutions was bumbling and incompetent. Countries with weak public health infrastructures have struggled to contain the virus, while countries with low social capital, poor leadership, or both, have struggled to slow transmission. The virus has already shown us how entangled are the fundamentals of biology and the politics of health. As with the climate crisis, solutions will require both technical ingenuity *and* political wherewithal and creativity.[43]

Finally, the Anthropocene has been marked by the rise of novel non-infectious threats to human health that follow from our manipulation of the environment. Although aging and death are natural for all organisms, we should resist seeing the way we die now as normal. The receding

---

[41] McMichael, A. J. 2017. *Climate Change and the Health of Nations: Famines, Fevers, and the Fate of Populations.* New York: Oxford University Press. On Lyme disease, Levi, T., A. M. Kilpatrick, M. Mangel, and C. C. Wilmers. 2012. "Deer, predators, and the emergence of Lyme disease." *Proceedings of the National Academy of Sciences* 109: 10942–10947.

[42] Casadevall, A. 2012. "The future of biological warfare." *Microbial Biotechnology* 5: 584–587.

[43] Jones, K. E., N. G. Patel, M. A. Levy et al. 2008. "Global trends in emerging infectious diseases." *Nature* 451: 990–993.

tide of infectious disease did not just leave behind good, natural deaths. Our diets, and consequent cardiovascular and metabolic diseases, are highly unnatural. Toxins, plastics, radiation, and atmospheric pollution are pervasive. Cancer has become a preeminent threat to human health; the regulatory processes of our cells are disturbed by the artificial environments we inhabit. Moreover, our sterile habitats, our pervasive use of antimicrobials and artificial preservatives, and our heavy dependence on antibiotics, have done extensive damage to our symbiotic microbes; the human microbiome in the Anthropocene is radically different from the microbiomes of our forebears. One upshot of the collateral damage done to our "good bacteria" is a sharp increase in autoimmune disorders. And, finally, ever more powerful synthetic compounds – like pharmaceutical-grade opioids – are unprecedentedly addictive psychotropic chemicals that have frayed the social fabric and even reversed gains in life expectancy in the United States.[44]

Perhaps most threatening of all, it would be foolish to assume that COVID-19 is the last painful pandemic we will face. The unsettling truth is that it could have been much worse. Our freedom from infectious disease is less secure now than it was half a century ago. Thankfully, more virulent diseases, like Ebola or the first SARS, have so far proven less effective at transmitting, or more susceptible to our interventions. So far. The "big one" is still out there. The Anthropocene undoubtedly has new ways of dying, both natural and unnatural, in store for its dominant species.

---

[44] Langston, N. 2011. *Toxic Bodies: Hormone Disruptors and the Legacy of DES.* New Haven: Yale University Press; Walker, B. 2010. *Toxic Archipelago: A History of Industrial Disease in Japan.* Seattle: University of Washington Press.; Freinkel, S. 2011. *Plastic: A Toxic Love Story.* New York: Mariner Books; Obregon-Tito, A., R. Y. Tito, J. Metcalf, et al., 2015. "Subsistence strategies in traditional societies distinguish gut microbiomes." *Nature Communications* 6: 6505. Case, A. and A. Deaton. 2020. *Deaths of Despair and the Future of Capitalism.* Princeton: Princeton University Press.

CHAPTER 5

Anthropology: Colonialism, Indigeneity, and Wind Power in the Anthropocene

Cymene Howe and Dominic Boyer

In the physical and natural sciences, the Anthropocene has become the accepted designation for the mid-twentieth century transformation of the Earth System; the role of the social sciences is to look at the human antecedents of this recent event, some of them very distant in time and some more recent. One of the most important questions for social scientists concerns when and how "anthropos" began transforming the planet, and who that "anthropos" was. The reason for assigning responsibility for Earth System impacts is in part to figure out how to ameliorate the dangers in the fairest possible way without causing further harm to communities already damaged by the processes leading to the Anthropocene and, further, to ensure that the views of these dispossessed communities are central to mitigation efforts. Climate change, a centrally important facet of the Anthropocene, is a case in point. For many scholars, European colonial expansion beginning in the fifteenth century was crucial to the human trajectories leading to the Anthropocene because it tied together the Old World and the New, leading to a globalized economy and ultimately to the development of industrialization, starting in the late eighteenth century, and the rising use of fossil fuels. Framed in this way, European imperialism, settler colonialism, and carbon-reliant, mechanized economies are culpable for speeding planetary transformation beginning in the early modern period. Indigenous peoples who suffered from territorial displacement, resource extraction, genocide, and disease were victims of these processes. Today, intensive energy production continues primarily to harm the poor, but many proposals for "solving" climate change through "green energy," instead of overturning economic and political inequality, replicate old patterns. For Indigenous communities, both the causes of climate change and the so-called solutions are all of a piece. As Potawatomi philosopher and activist Kyle Powys Whyte puts it, "the hardships many non-Indigenous people dread most of the climate crisis are ones that Indigenous peoples have endured already due to different forms of colonialism," including, "ecosystem collapse, species loss, economic crash, drastic relocation, and cultural disintegration" (Whyte 2018: 226). These multiple sites of ongoing suffering and survival are immense in their scope (Callison 2014).

There are of course other ways of describing how human forces became an overwhelming planetary force creating the Anthropocene. In Chapter 4, Kyle Harper describes the epic struggle between human beings and our microbial enemies since the dawn of our species. Our astonishing victory over many diseases allowed the human population to reach unprecedented heights and commandeer vast resources, though this victory, like any other in the long evolution of life, is precarious. In Chapter 8, looking at very recent events, Kate Brown focuses on the nuclear weapons and nuclear power plants that have irradiated the planet, creating a new background "normal" that damages human health and gives us *inter alia* geostratigraphic evidence for the new epoch. Following the lead of Indigenous scholars, the Anthropocene story in our chapter starts about 500 years ago with the rise of Western imperialism. Half a millennia ago, a sliver of the anthropos, western Europeans, began to colonize the rest of the world, often using violence to take Indigenous land, extract resources, and force mobilization of labor to supply the European homelands with precious products like timber, gold, silver, spices, sugar, tea, and coffee. Imperialism set in motion European industrialization and modernization, and ultimately the globalization we know today.

Our framework highlights the enduring power of colonialism and the expansionary, indeed predatory, tendencies of the capitalist relations that followed in its wake. Industrial capitalism – fueled first by coal and later by oil, gas, nuclear energy, and more – naturalized the luxuries of modern life, making them appear to be necessities. It also produced, and now helps maintain, the striking global inequities driving the Anthropocene trajectory. It did so primarily by obscuring the negative environmental and social externalities of biodiversity loss, intensive agriculture, land-use change, and high carbon energy use because of its blind obsession with two things: economic growth and technological advancement. In the past 50 years the world has slowly awakened to see that these "externalities" are in fact intimate disasters ranging from new diseases to extinctions and climate-fueled disruptions, all increasing in frequency and intensity. Across the world, anthropologists and activists have watched as the communities they work with are threatened, and even displaced or destroyed by these disasters – and also, as we will show, by some of the misplaced efforts to mitigate them. As Julia Thomas and Will Steffen discuss in Chapters 2 and 3, addressing the dangerous shift in the Earth System's trajectory and stabilizing our planet are increasingly urgent. It is equally certain that this shift has to be about more than just limiting greenhouse gas emissions; a holistic reckoning with the legacies of European colonialism, and the indulgences afforded to some among anthropos, is finally upon us.

The reason for framing the story in this way is not only to understand how we got to the Anthropocene but also to show how recent efforts to create a "green capitalist revolution" in renewable energy can fall back into the habits and patterns of colonial dispossession and fail to address the systemic danger posed by the commitment to infinite growth and consumption (Howe and Boyer 2020). Just as lands were commandeered and ways of life destroyed in the earlier imperialist search for unending wealth, so too does the new imperialism of green tech and green entrepreneurs raze the remaining vestiges of ecosystems and social systems resistant to global demands for ever more energy. Mexico's Isthmus of Tehuantepec is a highly Indigenous region which has found itself at the leading edge of these renewable energy efforts. It is a microcosm of these global developments in terms of both its productive potential and its political challenges and possibilities. Our fieldwork there allows us to tell this tale from the bottom up, adding to the "democracy of voices" (Chapter 2) that need to be heeded in the Anthropocene.

WHERE THE WIND BLOWS

Mexico's Isthmus of Tehuantepec has become home to the densest concentration of wind turbines anywhere on Earth. As cultural anthropologists, we want to understand how local Indigenous and mestizo communities are contending with a massive transformation of their lands and livelihoods. Our research on the rise of wind power addresses a central question for Anthropocenic times: what are the political forces that shape the possibilities for low carbon futures? Who sets the agenda for transitions and who – human and otherwise – is affected by massive infrastructural shifts to energy systems? In this chapter, we show how various forces – political, economic, and cultural – operate along with the wind itself to shape local futures in both positive and negative ways. Throughout, we pay special attention to Indigenous philosophies and experiences because they help us see better possibilities at the nexus of energy, environment, and human thriving.

Between roughly 2009 and 2016 there was a wind boom in the Isthmus. Its tumultuous rollout has offered new opportunities and instigated new conflicts at local, national, and international levels. Harnessing the wind's potential has shifted alliances between political parties and within local communities depending on their support for, or rejection of, wind development. Those opposed to wind development have made accusations of economic imperialism against foreign capitalists who have come, once again, to colonize the region with their extractive methods. Local landowners who receive usufruct rents, *caciques* (local bosses), and politicians are also accused of taking bribes or embezzling funds and are viewed with suspicion. Questions about Indigenous peoples' sovereignty and *campesinos'* (farmers') rights loom large in claims against the wind parks, especially given that the decades-long usufruct contracts appear to be just the sort of contractual tool that will forever displace poor and Indigenous peoples from the bits of land that they have preserved, often in communally managed forms. On this isthmus, older, frugal, more communitarian ways of life confront the hierarchical array of powers that seek, from one perspective, to do good: to create "green" energy. There are (at least) two different versions of "good" at play.

The story we tell is based on the stories of hundreds of residents, officials, and business people. Our research took place over 16 months of collaborative ethnographic fieldwork as we spoke with Indigenous and *mestizo* landowners, farmers, fisherfolk, and activists in the Isthmus of Tehuantepec. Over the course of about 200 interviews, we also talked with municipal, state, and federal government officials, representatives of renewable energy corporations, development bankers, and financiers in the state capital (Oaxaca City) and the nation's capital (Mexico City). In our study, we draw upon local knowledge and local concerns to call attention to the dangers of allowing – whether in the name of urgency, expediency, or inevitability – renewable energy development to repeat the inequalities seen in fossil extractivism. In this chapter, we show not only that there is "more to be done" in the reduction of carbon emissions but also that *how* that "more" is undertaken is of critical importance. As Earth System scientists are also saying, to mitigate the worst outcomes of the Anthropocene, "a deep transformation based on a fundamental reorientation of human values, equity, behavior, institutions, economies, and technologies is required" (Steffen et al., 2018: 8258). Our central argument is that it is essential to use energy transitions as opportunities to rethink dominant political, economic, and social institutions. Energy is not just about energy; it concerns values and relations of power. To ignore these dimensions is to imperil our ability to dislodge fossil fuels's dominion and the many inequalities that high carbon modernity helped to cement between the global North and South and between metropoles and resource-rich hinterlands.

Across the Isthmus of Tehuantepec we followed the wind through its many energetic and ethical possibilities exploring two aspects in particular. The first concerns the cosmological value of wind in the Isthmus of Tehuantepec among *Binnizá* (Zapotec) residents of the region. Here, the wind has shaped lives through its formidable, physical force, and it has been recognized for particular powers that oscillate between destruction and respite. The second aspect is how energy transitions rest on assumptions about how sustainable forms of energy ought to evolve and whose moral barometer ought to be used to measure the outcomes (Gardiner 2006; High and Smith 2019). As global carbon reduction mandates are instituted through protocols devised in United Nations' meetings and state policies, they raise not only political considerations but philosophical questions about collective ethics. Do our moral principles float above us in a collective atmosphere of climatological harm or are they grounded in the soils and livelihoods of the people and non-human others who live in the places bearing the brunt of energy transitions? Or is it both at once and if so, how do we establish and balance our priorities? In lieu of an easy response or moral certitude about these questions, here we explore how wind – as an elemental force – becomes part of an ethical negotiation: how and for whom is the wind to be used as a resource to dislodge the current trajectory of the Anthropocene?

IN THE CULTURE OF WIND

Victor Terán is a poet and a teacher. He is also a man wholly opposed to the spread of wind power projects across the Isthmus of Tehuantepec, his native land. Victor's renown as a literary figure and proponent of *Binnizá* (Zapotec) cultural and linguistic preservation preceded his fame as an outspoken critic of the parks. When we meet with him on a hot and blustery day in the Isthmus town of Juchitán de Zaragoza, Victor is contemplative, choosing his words carefully and thoughtfully, as a poet would. "The wind has many meanings," he begins. In Zapotec the word is *bi*. And *bi* is what designates the air and the breath. "It is the soul of a person," he says staring intently as he does so, "and it animates everything." Linguistically, Victor explains, the concept of *bi* is used to describe and name all animate beings. It is for this reason that nearly all of Binnizá words used to designate an animal or a plant begin with the prefix *bi*, including *Binnizá* (the "people") itself. *Bi* is etymologically inherent to expression in the same way that it is fundamental to life. "Without air there is no life and for this reason we use this prefix, *bi*, for everything," he explains. "It is very important because *bi* is the soul, the air, the breath, and the wind as well; it is a bundle of meanings." *Bi* is much more than a prefix and Victor depicts it with plain elegance. "Without the air we would not exist. Without the wind we would not exist."

In *Binnizá* cosmology, a trinity of winds are present across different seasons in the Isthmus: two from the north and the other from the south. *El viento viejo* (the old north wind) or *biyooxho*, should not be mistaken for a feeble wind. It is in fact the opposite: the wind that made the world through its astounding force and its primal intensity. *Biyooxho* is the northern wind of ancient genealogy that, at the very beginning of time, "pushed the world into existence." A less storied wind, but one that all Istmeños know equally well is *biguiaa*, the wind from the north that is less powerful than *biyooxho* but still insistent when it blows. And finally, there is the southern wind, *binisá*. This is the wind of the sea and the water, a revitalizing breeze that soothes the skin in the formidable heat of the day. It gathers across the *Laguna del Mar Muerto* just to the southeast of the *Laguna Inferior* on the edge of the Pacific in the Gulf of Tehuantepec. Here, *bi*, the air/life, is married to *niza* (breeze/breath) and in this union becomes cool, wet and full of abundance. *Binisá* is often described as a feminine wind, as a tender sensation, especially when compared to each of the northerly winds, which are inversely described as *masculino*.

In more than a few instances we have heard the gusting northern wind, *el viento viejo, biyooxho*, described as "the devil's wind." Its heat and intensity make it seem as though it has come directly from Lucifer's lips. When asked about this Devil's wind, Victor rejects that interpretation. It is no devil for him. He describes how the arrival of Christianity in the Isthmus changed many things, including the deities. For him it is only a Christianized mentality that can conceive of the wind as belonging to the devil. As we finish speaking with Victor about the wind he knows so well, he ends with the recognition that although the isthmus wind is invested with all sorts of cosmological meanings, it is also simply, sold. The wind has become a marketable commodity. Victor knows that as it moves rapidly across land and sky, the isthmus wind now promises economic and developmental salvation in the region. The turbines and the wind that drives them are regularly heralded as a boon for the climate and for the community. Victor is not convinced. As he stares off toward an unmarked horizon, Victor assures us that indeed, "there are many kinds of wind."

THE GHOSTS OF EXTRACTION IN LATIN AMERICA

The transition from fossil fuels to cleaner energy forms is widely regarded as one of the most pressing environmental and social challenges facing humanity and other planetary life in the twenty-first century. Certainly this is true, but it is only part of the truth of the

Anthropocene conundrum. As the chapters of this book argue in many ways, we need to do vastly more than alter the means of production in one sector of our economy; we must, as Mark Williams describes in Chapter 12, learn to live "mutualistically," in communities that enhance their environments, melding with the biota and landscape – and even the winds – around them. Yet even accomplishing greener energy is a challenge. It remains unclear how this goal can be achieved, especially given the proliferation of neoliberal economic and social policies across the world in the past three decades. These policies in Mexico, and elsewhere, often openly question the legitimacy and effectiveness of state-led programs of development, let alone the value of local customs and values, and instead turn to the private sector as the only possible means to prosperity. They are also dedicated to the ideology of perpetual economic growth, albeit "green growth." In this sense, Mexico is a critical, even paradigmatic case. Especially during the presidency of Felipe Calderón (2006–2012), the Mexican government has produced unusually ambitious legislation to address climate change and support energy transition. However, these projects remain vulnerable to internal and external forces beyond the government's control, ranging from transnational investors' desire for profit to local landowners' concerns about contracts with transnational renewable energy corporations that they fear will ultimately deprive them of their land and livelihood. We want to underscore that the commitment Mexico has made to climate remediation is laudable, especially given that the country was never compelled to do so by any international protocol such as the Kyoto Agreement. In their commendable efforts to address climate harm, however, Mexican officials and industry leaders have largely failed to link sustainable energy projects to more robust benefits for local populations, many of whom live on the margins of the state and in places where the wind blows the fiercest.

Latin America has a long and complicated history with energy resources and environmental management. Much of that history has been defined by colonial and corporate interests that have resulted in both human and environmental degradation (Galeano 1997). "Traditional" extractivism – the securing of hydrocarbon and mineral resources, since colonial times (Bebbington 2009) – has been the norm in the region, although whether extractivism has contributed to national development overall remains contested (Gudynas 2009). Amid calls to reduce carbon incineration practices that have spurred the Anthropocene, the "resources" of Latin America and the Caribbean have figured heavily. The South American continent is the most biodiverse in the world and the region has been at the forefront of renewable energy production, particularly hydroelectricity. Brazil and Colombia are generally accepted as the most biodiverse countries on the planet (assuming one includes plants in one's calculation), and while China boasts that 18% of its hydroelectricity comes from dams, 65% of Brazil's electricity comes from hydroelectric dams. Much more renewable potential remains on the horizon – in the form of solar and wind – and on the ground in the form of geothermal and biomass. Although many renewable energy projects aim to generate benefits and increase access to electricity in the area immediately around them, that doesn't always happen. Especially when the power being generated is being channeled to national elites in the metropole or toward the bottom line of transnational corporations' profits, suspicion is quick to set in among local populations in places with cruel histories of extractivism. The laudable intention to prevent further climatological harm and produce cleaner energy can look very different when viewed from the bottom-up. It can easily slip into the familiar maneuvers of hydrocarbon exploitation, including projects of massive scale and inadequate community consultation or consent (McNeish and Logan 2012). It can also devastate local ecosystems and denude the landscape of arable soil.

The effects of climate change are being acutely felt in Mexico, often in locations where economic and labor prospects are already sparse, leaving rural and agrarian populations doubly vulnerable (Eakin 2006). Mexico's climate legislation and the growth of renewable energy infrastructures are initiatives aimed at both mitigation and adaptation: securing an *adaptive* energy future through the forces of wind, solar, and hydroelectric power and *mitigating* the contaminative, warming effects of adding more greenhouse gasses to the atmosphere. The acceleration of renewable energy development in Mexico is also an indicator that among the country's leaders that adaptation to changing weather and water conditions is crucial and that renewable energy resources, if usefully tapped, will not only result in less carbon contamination and more green power, but will further enhance Mexico's reputation as a leader in climate adaptation and mitigation in the developing world (Boyer 2019).

MAKING POLICY FRAMEWORK FOR THE ANTHROPOCENE

The inauguration of the Piedra Larga wind park was the last of President Felipe Calderón's many ribbon-cutting ceremonies for wind parks across the Isthmus. When he served as the Secretary of Energy, Calderón was an important supporter of renewable energy in Mexico. As his presidential term neared its end, wind power counted as a key pillar of Mexico's clean development mechanisms. Calderón's speech was not triumphant, nor was it a swan song. Instead it pivoted between hope and precarity. He began with droughts, the most severe ever seen in Mexico and to the north in Texas. "This is climate change" he said to an audience of several hundred seated in front of him. "Carbon dioxide is like a sweater surrounding the earth, heating the ocean's waters and making for both more and less rain that is, overall, differently distributed." "However," he went on, "we cannot stop using electricity or building factories. Instead we need to make electricity with less smoke. We need to reduce emissions." And here, in the heart of the Isthmus is where much of this task was already occurring. The president called attention to the engineering careers that wind power had brought to the state of Oaxaca, and to the jobs in the supermarkets, now more plentiful because of the "economic spillover" of wind power. But Calderón's climatological intervention and wind power's role in it represent more than local jobs in Isthmus towns. "Mexico," he says, "is an important part of all humanity, the twelfth most populous country in the world." Although the country continues to extract, use and sell oil through the state-owned oil company, PEMEX (*Petróleos Mexicanos*), Calderón was right to note Mexico's important role in the world of renewable energy production.[1] Mexico's federal policies

---

[1] Petróleos Mexicanos (or Pemex) is Mexico's state-owned oil petroleum company, created in 1938 under President Cárdenas (1934–1940) through the nationalization of all private, foreign, and domestic oil companies. Pemex is the second largest enterprise in Latin

to reduce emissions from electricity production are, especially for a nation with an emergent economy, particularly impressive, including a federal mandate to have 35% of the country's electricity production come from renewable sources by 2024.

The Mexican Ministry of Energy (SENER, the *Secretaria de Energía*) is also a major proponent of renewable energy projects. From the perspective of SENER, wind power specifically offers extraordinary potential locally, nationally, and globally. The powerful winds of Oaxaca are, according to the official position of SENER:

- an opportunity to reduce emissions without compromising national economic development
- an opportunity to contribute to climate change mitigation
- an opportunity to attract investment to Mexico
- an opportunity to develop local capabilities
- an opportunity for technological development
- an opportunity to increase the nation's global competitiveness (SENER 2007: 32–33).

One of the reasons that "opportunity" moves so fluidly through state discourses is that in addition to being home to some of the best wind in the world, Oaxaca is also one of the poorest states in the country. For many local, state, and national officials, their mission to promote economic development through sustainable means – such as wind power – is, in part, an ethical calling to bring greater prosperity to the region. The future of the Isthmus is, in this way, married with the development plans of private capital in a tidy moral tale since wind power is developed and sold by private corporations with government

America (after Petrobras, the Brazilian national oil company) and it supplies a high percentage of revenue to the Mexican federal government. It is also considered to be among the top ten most polluting companies in the world. Renewable energy projects and policies in Mexico have operated under public/private partnership agreements wherein national and transnational companies build and run renewable energy plants with electricity sold through contracts with large companies (e.g. Coca Cola, Walmart) and for public consumption through the Comisión Federal de Electricidad (CFE), which operates the Mexican electric grid. Electricity generation and oil extraction in Mexico are generally separate enterprises.

institutions and infrastructures serving only a mediating function as in Public-Private Partnership (PPP) models elsewhere in the world.[2] By this calculus, the Indigenous people of Oaxaca will be embraced by global green capital, and benefit from this new wind power sweeping the Isthmus, one at odds with the three older winds of Victor Terán's cosmology.

In this context wind power is positioned as curative, even salvational, a method of ecological care and a generator of economic value. It is also the material manifestation of an ethical exercise intended, at least nominally, to benefit the "greater good" of local populations, the Mexican nation and, ultimately, all human inhabitants of Earth now imperiled by Anthropocenic conditions. The narratives of state offices and government representatives illustrate how the economic development aspirations of state agencies cannot be disentangled from a larger moral mission that Mexico created with its climate legislation, namely, to be a leader in renewable energy in the developing world.

QUESTIONING TRANSITION AND PREFIGURATIVE POLITICS

Opposition to wind park development, or as it is known in the Isthmus, the *anti-eólico* resistance, began in the mid 2000s. Bettina Cruz Velázquez, one of the key figures in the resistance has long roots in the Isthmus, in both her kinship and her activism. As a 14-year-old she famously marched through the streets of Juchitán as a *militante* for the COCEI (*La Coalición Obrera, Campesino y Estudiantil del Istmo*, The Coalition of Workers, Peasants and Students of the Isthmus [of Tehuantepec]). A Binnizá woman, it is she who is credited with making many of the initial pronouncements against green capitalism and the neoliberal

---

[2] In contrast to developments in the Global North that reflect NIMBY (Not in My Backyard) positions, the debates around wind power in the Isthmus of Tehuantepec do not center on the aesthetic "look" of wind turbines on the landscape, although Isthmus residents are also concerned about potential health impacts for those living in close proximity to wind parks. More significantly, Isthmus residents often do not have the financial resources to litigate against infrastructural developments in the region and many felt that the benefits of wind power, while positive for the global climate overall, did not translate into much-needed local benefits in the form of profit-sharing, community development, and infrastructural improvements.

qualities of the wind parks that have appeared across the lands where she was born and raised.

Opposition to wind parks transformed local politics. For many years, national parties and their operatives had fomented conflict in Oaxaca. But, in 2013, there was a return to an older political form known as *asambleas comunales* (communal assemblies) based on Indigenous customary law and collective land management (Howe, Boyer and Barrera 2015). The return to these institutions created the opportunity to build coalitions across long-held divides. Binnizá people and Ikojts (or Huave) populations in the Isthmus have sometimes been at odds with one another over the centuries, but opposition to wind power united them in a battle to save land and livelihoods from encroachments by the wind parks. Many local mestizo and Indigenous landowners decry the proliferation of turbines as an injurious, industrial occupation of their land. They worry about the effect on local plants and animal populations, about the water tables that nourish their crops and their families, and about the long-term impact of many megatons of steel and concrete. In short, the wind has operated in these environments to move politics in a particular direction: away from formal political parties and toward lateralist modes of collective action under the rubric of *asambleas*. It has renewed Indigenous political institutions.

While the growth of wind power has raised ecological and human rights concerns across the Isthmus, it has also revealed other political and philosophical questions. As we speak with Bettina in the shade of the little concrete patio outside her home, she wonders out loud about the idea of energy transition in principle. In fact, she asks us, "Can you even call this 'transition' at all?"

> "Maybe we are seeing a transition in the forms of energy... but there is a clear continuity in the form of resource exploitation. These huge companies we have here, sure, they are investing [in the region] but they are taking our raw materials without paying for them. Resources that should be going toward social benefits for people in the region, all of these benefits are going to the multinational corporations.
>
> The financial means that these companies have is being used to extract resources and to exploit people. And it is not just here. It is around

everything that they call 'energy.' Energy can be petroleum, but now it is the wind. One of the things we question is the fact that it is all the same companies that have plundered the world for millennia and which have now contaminated it. The fact that there is a phenomenon called 'global climate change' is because of [their] externalization of costs. These same companies have now gotten hold of renewable energy. And so, I have to ask what 'transition' is there? I don't feel that there is a transition. What change is there? There is no change here. Only talk."

Histories of colonial extraction and exploitation inform Bettina's position. But her attention to the ways that wind energy companies may be capitalizing on climatological crisis raises more pointed ethical critiques for the future of renewable energy and for responses to the Anthropocene. She explicitly questions whether the mechanisms and logics that have fueled the extractive fossil economy over the last three centuries are, in fact, being replicated here despite the putatively noble objectives of sustainable development and cleaner forms of energy.

Wind in the Isthmus can be the cosmological "breath of life"; wind, like other natural resources elsewhere, can be the basis for a development boon for an impoverished population; it can be used to enrich renewable energy corporations and their investors; it can sweep away old political tensions and revive communitarian politics. Wind embodies a multiplicity of ethical "goods" and at the same time it reveals deep sociopolitical challenges, making it a paradoxical force. In the wind we see more than a struggle between older forms of electricity generation (based on oil and coal) and newly developed ones (such as utility-scale wind power). Instead, we see the rifts between two ecological rationales: one insisting on the need for reducing greenhouse gasses in our shared skies and the other promoting the preservation of local ecoystems and social systems in the face of these megaprojects (Howe 2019). On this Mexican isthmus, we see small-scale versions of the political and economic green alternatives explored in Manuel Arias-Maldonado's essay in Chapter 7.

In these changing energetic times, the political and philosophical negotiations are just as important, if not more so, than the economic and engineering challenges so routinely highlighted in renewable energy debates. Any approach to reducing carbon pyrotechnics will have local impacts, and local acceptance or resistance will determine the possibility of global success. All life is local, even while the Anthropocene is global. We cannot lower CO_2 emissions on the planetary and regional level while ignoring or sacrificing the diversity of cultures and biomes, landscapes and stories that are the foundation of natural and social resilience. To look solely at any mitigation effort from the top-down – the Singular Story described by Thomas in Chapter 2 – will undermine the hope of transitioning not just to carbon-free economies but to collective, engaged societies that will benefit from and maintain these gains in our effort to stabilize the Earth System. As we have shown by looking at a place where a remedy for the climate change aspect of the Anthropocene is contested, a purely technological "solution" to a problem conceived of as "global" will foster neither human life nor non-human life. The histories of colonialism and extractivism – two of the key phenomena that led to the Anthropocene in the first place – teach us to beware of top-down solutions. And we must acknowledge and resist how dispossessive colonialist relations continue to inform many energy development and transition projects, especially in the global South. In the global North, we must instead aim for a future where new energy forms generate a new collective politics and an ethical awareness missing from the age of oil.

CONCLUSION

Renewable energy transitions and responses to the Anthropocene make it increasingly clear that elemental forces – like wind, water, and sunlight – now have political, social, and economic value. It is vital that an energy transition occurs, yet it will not bring the needed benefits or attract widespread political support if the technological transition is not also accompanied by a transition in human systems. Our research in Mexico revealed that it is all too easy for renewable energy development to occur with little or no social, political, or economic "transition" attached to it. If old hierarchies of power and political access lead to the further marginalization of Indigenous peoples and small-scale farmers then truly, as Bettina puts it, there is no real transition at all. If, in our necessary and ongoing expansion of renewable energy globally, we do not give real voice and decision-making powers to local populations then we may simply recreate the extractive principles of profit that propelled much of the Anthropocene. A true understanding of the Anthropocene as not just one phenomenon – climate change – but as an Earth System shift involving every aspect of the way our planet functions and all the multitude of human hopes and values that engage our world – will lead us to understand the need for a democracy of voices. That democracy of voices must, in our opinion, include Indigenous voices long marginalized or excluded from settler colonial democracies across the world. Replicating the structure of the systems that originally generated global inequality and exploitation will replicate the devastation that they caused, even if they now bear a "green" label.

REFERENCES

Bebbington, Anthony. 2009. "The new extraction: re-writing the political ecology of the Andes?," *NACLA Report on the Americas* 42(5): 12–20.

Boyer, Dominic. 2019. *Energopolitics: Wind and Power in the Anthropocene*. Durham, NC: Duke University Press.

Callison, Candis. 2014. *How Climate Change Comes to Matter: The Communal Life of Facts*. Durham, NC: Duke University Press.

Eakin, Hallie. 2006. *Weathering Risk in Rural Mexico: Climatic, Institutional, and Economic Change*. Tucson, AZ: University of Arizona Press.

Galeano, Eduardo. 1997 [1972]. *Open Veins of Latin America: Five Centuries of Pillage of a Continent*. New York: Monthly Review Press.

Gardiner, Stephen. 2006. "A perfect moral storm: climate change, intergenerational ethics and the problem of moral corruption," *Environmental Values* 15: 397–413.

Gudynas, Eduardo. 2009. "Diez Tesis Urgentes Sobre El Nuevo Extractivismo: Contextos y Demandas Bajo el Progresismo," in *Extractivismo, Política y Sociedad*. Quito, Ecuador: CAAP y CLAES.

High, Mette and Jessica Smith. 2019. "Introduction: the ethical constitution of energy dilemmas," Special Issue on Energy Ethics, *Journal of the Royal Anthropological Institute*, 25(S1): 9–28.

Howe, Cymene. 2019. *Ecologics: Wind and Power in the Anthropocene*. Durham, NC: Duke University Press.

Howe, Cymene and Dominic Boyer. 2020. "Verdant optimism: on why capitalism will never save the world," Theorizing the Contemporary, *Fieldsights, March 24.* https://culanth.org/fieldsights/verdant-optimism-on-how-capitalism-will-never-save-the-world (accessed October 2021).

Howe, Cymene, Dominic Boyer and Edith Barrera. 2015. "Los márgenes del Estado al viento: autonomía y desarrollo de energías renovables en el sur de México," *Journal of Latin American and Caribbean Anthropology* 20(2): 1–23.

McNeish, John-Andrew and Owen Logan, eds. 2012. *Flammable Societies: Studies on the Socioeconomics of Oil and Gas.* London, UK: Pluto.

SENER. 2007. *Energía eólica y la política energética mexicana.* Monterrey, México: Ing. Alma Santa Rita Feregrino Subdirectora de Energía y Medio Ambiente, SENER.

Steffen, Will, Johan Rockström, Katherine Richardson, et al. 2018. "Trajectories of the Earth System in the Anthropocene," *PNAS* 115(33): 8252–8259.

Whyte, Kyle P. 2018. "Indigenous science (fiction) for the Anthropocene: Ancestral dystopias and fantasies of climate change crises." *Environment and Planning E: Nature and Space* 1(1–2): 224–242.

CHAPTER 6

The Ascent of the Anthropoi: A Story

Amitav Ghosh

It was my book club buddy, Maansi, who introduced me to the word 'Anthropocene'.

Maansi and I had an odd relationship: in all the years we had known each other we had never spoken in person or seen each other face to face. All our interactions were online, and not very frequent either. But somehow, over time, these meetings had become very important to both of us.

We had met through an online book club that Maansi had started, after growing sick of all her other reading groups. 'People talk about themselves too much,' she said. So her club had one cardinal rule: 'It's not about you or me; it's about the book.' Few indeed were those to whom this appealed, so members rarely lasted very long. I, however, found that the rule perfectly fitted my temperament; since this was the case with Maansi as well, we rarely talked about ourselves, even when there was no one left in the group but the two of us. As a result, pretty much all I knew about Maansi was that she had grown up in Nepal but now lived in New York, where she worked as a sales manager for Anthropologaïa, an up-and-coming line of designer clothing.

Every New Year's Day, we would take it in turns to choose a subject to explore for the next twelve months. We were quite eclectic in our choices – one year it was 'Nautical Fiction'; another year it was 'Explorers' – but we were disciplined about sticking to whatever it was that we had chosen.

This year it was Maansi's turn to choose. 'I've got a little surprise for you,' she announced. 'You and I are going to read about the Anthropocene.'

I had been out late on New Year's Eve and was not at my sharpest. 'What was the word?' I said. 'I didn't quite catch it.'

'Anthropocene.'

I rolled the word gingerly around my tongue. 'What on earth does it mean?'

'I don't know,' Maansi confessed. 'But I need to find out. My company's adopted it as its fashion theme for the year.'

'But Maansi,' I protested. 'It sounds like a made-up word. Do you even know how it's pronounced?'

'No,' she said, 'but we can easily find out.'

So we did a screen share and started a search on YouTube. The first clip featured a bearded professorial type who insisted that the proper pronunciation was: Anth-ROP-ocene.

We gagged, in unison. 'Horrible!' cried Maansi.

'Disgusting!' said I. 'We can't have a word like that on our lips through a whole year!'

So then we did another search, which led us to another bearded professor, except that this one said: 'AN-thropocene.'

'Much better,' I said.

'Not stomach-turning at least,' Maansi agreed. 'I can live with it for a year, I think.'

'But are you sure Maansi?' I said. 'Do you really want to do this?'

'Yes,' she said. 'Don't worry. I'll dig into it a bit and send you a reading list tomorrow morning.'

Next morning I woke up expecting to find a message from Maansi in my Inbox. But there was nothing that day or the next. It wasn't till a week had passed that a message from Maansi appeared on my screen.

'I'm sorry I've been slow to get back to you,' she said. 'I've had a terrible few days. I found a reading list online and picked out a book at random, thinking it would be nice and science-y, with lots of numbers and charts. But it was nothing of the sort: it was about some poor people on a remote island who suffer the most dreadful fate. It kept me up late into the night, and when I fell asleep I had the most horrible dream – except that I don't even know whether it's my own dream, or a memory of a story that I heard from my grandmother. I was so shaken I went to see my therapist and she insisted that I write it down. So I did – and I wonder if you would mind taking a look at it?'

In my dream I was a young girl, growing up in a valley that was home to a cluster of warring villages, high in the Himalaya. Overlooking our Valley was an immense, snowy mountain, whose peak was almost always wreathed in clouds. The mountain was called Mahaparbat, Great Mountain, and despite our differences all of us who lived in the Valley revered that mountain: our ancestors had told us that of all the world's mountains ours was the most alive; that it would protect us, and look after us – but only on condition that we told stories about it, and sang about it, and danced for it – but always from a distance. For one of the binding laws of the Valley, respected by all our warring villages, was that we were never, on any account, to set foot on the slopes of the Great Mountain.

We heeded our ancestors and kept away from this mountain: we knew in our hearts that our mountain was a living being that cared for us; we saw proof of this every day, all around us, in the form of a tree that grew along the streams that descended from its slopes. This tree, which grew only in our Valley and nowhere else, produced things that were so miraculous that we called it the Magic Tree. Its leaves kept insects away; its wood was impermeable to water; its roots nourished rare mushrooms; its flowers produced exquisitely scented honey; and its fruit was delicious to eat. But the most miraculous thing of all was the nut that lay within the fruit: its fragrance was incomparable, and it had so many medicinal uses that traders from the Lowlands would travel long distances in search for it.

Even though we Valley People fought over many things, we were all in agreement on one matter: strangers would never be allowed to enter our Valley. So those who came in search of our goods had to wait at a mountain pass that was defended by a great portcullis. There once every year, when the snows retreated, our Eldermen and Elderwomen would go to meet the visiting merchants. In that one week our Elderpeople would acquire all the trade goods that we needed, in exchange for the gifts of our Mountain – the miraculous nuts, rare mushrooms, fine honey, herbs, and the like. At the end of Trading Week, as it was known, the Elderpeople would see to it that all the visitors had departed, after which they would post a squad of sentries to guard the portcullis for the rest of the year. Then they would return to their homes, and each village in the Valley would host a ceremony of gratitude, to thank the Great Mountain. When the prayers had been chanted, and the offerings made, the whole Valley would feast and dance: for us, that was the happiest day of the year.

Life in our Valley was not easy – we had to work hard for our food, and when we were not doing that, we were fighting with our neighbours. But we knew no other life and we were content with what we had. And why would we not be? We loved to listen to stories about our Great Mountain and our amazing trees; we loved to sing our songs, and we loved, most of all, to dance. Our dances were always led by women, and the most skilled of them were known as Adepts; sometimes, when dancing they would go into a trance, and afterwards they would tell us that they had felt the mountain speaking to them, through the soles of their feet.

Oh, how we envied our Adepts!

So things went on, as ever they had, until one year when the Elderpeople returned from Trading Week with solemn, troubled faces. They told us that a stranger of a new kind had come to the pass that year, from a land very far away. His people, he said, were called the Anthropoi; their savants had heard about our nuts and he had been sent on a mission to learn about our Valley, and all that it contained.

The Elderpeople showed him their wares – mushrooms and herbs, nuts and honey – but that was not enough for the stranger: he wanted to come into the Valley and see it with his own eyes.

This was impossible, the Elderpeople told him; it was against the Law of the Valley; the Great Mountain did not wish it. This displeased the stranger mightily, but he smiled and said: 'Since I can't enter your Valley, I must learn about it from you. Tell me about your Valley and about all the other valuable trade goods that it produces.'

'The most important thing in our Valley,' the Elderpeople told him, 'is something that cannot be traded – our living mountain, Mahaparbat.'

'Oh really?' said the stranger, 'Tell me about your mountain then.' So our elders told him about our beloved Mahaparbat, and the wonderful streams that were fed by its snows. The stranger listened with great care, and wrote everything down, so diligently that some of our elders began to worry about his intentions. It was a great relief to them when, at the end of the week, he left with all the Lowland people. Although he went quietly enough, his last words had an ominous ring: 'I am sure we will see each other again.'

A year passed, and then another, and there was no sign of the stranger, which was a matter of no little satisfaction for the Elders. But then suddenly one morning the Great Mountain began to shake and heave; avalanches came roaring down its slopes and rifts opened up in the Valley.

Terror-struck, everyone turned to the Adepts: 'What is happening? What is our Mahaparbat telling us?'

The Adepts put their ears, and their feet, to the ground and listened as they had never listened before. Then they turned to us, ashen-faced: 'A cycle of time has ended,' they said, 'and another one has begun: the Cycle of Tribulation. Strangers are coming from afar, a horde of them, armed with terrible weapons...'

Sure enough, not long after, a lone sentry came racing down from the mountain pass: an army of Anthropoi had arrived, he said. They were not many in number but they had very powerful weapons and were skilled in the art of war. They had stormed the portcullis and taken all the sentries captive. He alone had been set free, to bring a message to the Valley, to let us know that the Anthropoi had decided to conquer the Great Mountain! Their savants had studied all that was told to their envoy, and they were convinced that unbeknownst to us, great riches – minerals, metals and the like – were hidden within the mountain. We were unaware of this because we were a credulous and benighted people, who believed that our Mountain was alive. The savants of the Anthropoi were unmatched in their wisdom, and they had decided that since we were not making use of the Mountain's riches, they were fully justified in seizing them and taking whatever they wished.

A stunned silence spread through the Valley. 'Impossible,' we said, with one voice. 'We can't let them do that.'

'If we try to stop them,' said the sentry, 'they say they will fight us. We have no choice, they say, but to let them climb and conquer the Great Mountain. Not only that, we must help them do it, or else they will kill or enslave us.'

Of course such an ultimatum could not be accepted. It was decided that we would fight, and so we did, all of us, men and women, young and old. We fought valiantly, but our efforts were unavailing – some of our villages were defeated in battle, some were tricked into attacking their neighbours, and others were reduced to quiescence with drugs that sent them into dream-like trances.

Once we had been subjugated, the Anthropoi herded us together and told us that from now on we would be ruled by some of their most ferocious soldiers – they called them Kraani, or the 'Helmeted Ones'. They were to be our guards and overseers, to make sure that we did all the work that had been assigned to us. They were small in number, the Kraani, but they made up for this by conjuring up terrifying illusions of omnipotence – they created such a distance between themselves and us that we came to accept that the Anthropoi were not like us, that they were a different species of being.

The first thing the Kraani did was to dismiss all our old Elderpeople and appoint new ones, whom they chose themselves. In the past, amongst our Elders, there had been women as well as men, but no more. The new ones were all men, and we soon learned to fear these Eldermen almost as much as we feared the Kraani.

Next they imprisoned our Adepts, and forbade all our ceremonies and songs, stories and dances. They were all worthless, they said; our ancestral lore, they said, had brought nothing but doom upon us, which was why we were now reduced to this state of degradation and despair.

Our state was indeed as terrible as it could be, yet we soon noticed that the Anthropoi could not do without us: we were essential for their assault on the Great Mountain. It was we who ensured that they had the provisions and porters that they needed to climb its slopes – without the supplies that we provided the ascent would have been impossible. And so it happened that we became the suppliers who made it possible for the Anthropoi to conquer our own sacred mountain – under the Kraani's watchful eyes we toiled in the fields to produce the materials they needed for the assault. This was our place, the Kraani told us, this was where we belonged. Our bodies were not suited to the climb, we were not strong enough, our diets were enfeebling, our habits degenerate, our beliefs perverse, our minds weak, and our hearts lacking in courage. We were nothing but Varvaroi (which was what they called us).

Many of us came to believe all these things, and our eyes were drawn inexorably to the Anthropoi as they ascended Mahaparbat's mysterious, glistening snows. We watched spellbound as they rapelled upwards; we saw that their eagerness to ascend was such that they often fought amongst themselves; we saw that many among them were mutinous, unwilling to continue the climb, and we saw, to our horror, that these rebels were often hurled off the slopes – and all these dramatic and murderous episodes made the spectacle even more compelling. The lives of the Anthropoi seemed infinitely more exciting than our own wretched existences, down in the Valley – and in no small measure was the attraction enhanced by the fact that the Kraani were always telling us not to look in that direction: our job was to toil in our fields so the climbers never ran short of supplies.

As time went by, our attitude towards the mountain began to change – our reverence slowly shifted away from the mountain and attached itself instead, to the spectacle of the climb. Gradually, as the spectacle took the place that the mountain had once occupied in our hearts, we burned with the desire to ascend those slopes ourselves.

Some of us Varvaroi witnessed the ascent more closely than the rest – they were the porters, the muleteers, the sherpas, all from the families of the chosen Eldermen. The stories they told us about the ascent of the Anthropoi further inflamed our appetites. In our Valley wisdom had always resided with the women, and since they no longer had any place amongst our Elders, our leadership passed into the hands of those who least understood our Mountain – strong, covetous men, who were ruthless in enforcing their will. The Kraani, who were dwindling in number, came to trust them more and more, until at last our Eldermen began to think that the time had come for them to usurp their place.

Slowly, at the urging of our Eldermen, we began to defy the Kraani, timidly at first, but then with increasing determination. As time went by our confidence grew and the balance began to shift in our direction. We realized that we were many and they were few; we learnt that we could seriously hinder the climbers by downing our tools and refusing to do what was expected of us. We even won a few skirmishes and battles. And at last a day came, when it became clear to the Kraani that it would be impossible for them to sustain the illusion of omnipotence for much longer. Nor did they need the toilers of the Valley as much as they once had, because by this time the Anthropoi had indeed found great stocks of riches on the mountain's slopes – more than enough for them to sustain themselves. So one night the Kraani melted away and went racing off to join the other Anthropoi.

Now began a tumultuous, headlong race towards the mountain, and only after we Varvaroi had flung ourselves on it, in a mad breathless rush, did it become clear that we could not all attempt the climb together. No less than the Anthropoi would we need toilers to labour in the Valley, patiently sending up supplies to those of us who were to attempt the ascent. This realization set in motion a great upheaval in the Valley, with some villages attacking others, in the hope of turning them into drones and drudges; other villages were torn apart, with neighbours killing each other, in the hope of getting ahead. A great orgy of bloodletting filled our Valley, bringing slaughter and destruction on a scale far beyond that which the Anthropoi had inflicted on us in the past. So it went on until some kind of order came about and a great number of the Valley's inhabitants were successfully confined to the bottom of the slope, under the guns of newly formed legions of armed guards, picked from our own villages. These were the Kraani of the Varvaroi.

And now began another assault upon Mahaparbat, more carefully planned than those that had preceded it. The climb was much harder now because the Anthropoi had dirtied the slopes and covered them with wastes. But despite the difficulties, we persisted and it soon became evident that we were by no means unequal to the task ahead: our bodies were strong and our minds sharp; our hearts were full of courage and our resolve was steadfast. Faster and faster we climbed, while down in the Valley the toilers worked harder and harder too – for we had promised them that if they worked hard enough, they too would be allowed to join the ascent: this was the hope that sustained them. Soon the word spread, all the way down to the Lowlands, and more and more people came rushing up to the Valley to join us.

Our ascent was spectacular, performed in a much shorter time than the Anthropoi had taken. Much sooner than we had expected the higher slopes came into view, and we now realized, to our astonishment, that the Anthropoi were faltering, and hadn't yet reached the mountain's cloud-wrapped summit. We understood also that if we continued at the pace we had set so far, we might achieve something we had never allowed ourselves to contemplate – some of us might be among the first to set foot on the summit of our once-sacred mountain.

A great upsurge of euphoria seized us now, and for a moment, exhilarated and exhausted, we paused to catch our breath before launching the final assault. And as we stood there, thumping each other on the back and beating our chests with joy, it came to our notice that some of the Anthropoi – their savants – were signalling desperately in our direction, urging us to look down, at the foot of the mountain.

Turning our heads we beheld a sight that took us utterly by surprise. We saw that the combined weight of all the climbers had unsettled the snow on the lower slopes of the mountain. As a result, a series of devastating land-slides and avalanches had swept through our Valley, killing vast numbers of our fellow villagers. We stood there aghast, watching in horror, but there was nothing to be done – to turn back was impossible now. Nor would the villagers below have allowed us to turn back, even if we had been so inclined, for their only hope of survival was to follow us up the mountain.

We put our dead kin out of our minds – they were poor anyway, and there were so many of them that a few would not be missed. We gathered our resolve once again and threw ourselves on the slopes with redoubled fury, climbing ever harder and faster. And as we ascended we noticed that the Anthropoi's savants were signalling again, not pointing downwards this time, but towards the mountain itself. This puzzled us and we began to tap and probe as we climbed; we saw that strange crevasses were opening up everywhere, that each step was setting off a mudslide, some of which were sweeping even the Anthropoi away. But still we kept going, faster and faster.

Now, because of these ordeals, there was a change of heart among the Anthropoi, especially the savants, many of whom began to visit us, and talk with us. No longer did they call us Varvaroi; they became friendly to the point where they began to give us some of the Mountain's riches. From time to time they would even share their knowledge. This was how we learnt that the savants had now determined that our Mountain could support only a small number of climbers. If that number increased beyond a certain point then the ice would begin to melt – as it was melting now. Soon it would drown the Valley below and sweep everything away.

This astounded us. The Anthropoi had always told us that one of the reasons why they were so much stronger than us, was that their ideas were universal – unlike the false, local beliefs that circulated amongst us Valley-folk. They had laughed at our inherited ideas of the mountain's sacredness: that was all ignorant, pagan superstition, they said. All mountains were the same, they could all be climbed if only the climbers were strong enough, intelligent enough, resolute enough. That was what 'universal' meant, did it not? That all people everywhere could – and should – do the same thing?

How could one refute something so self-evident? How indeed, except in the way the mountain had done it, without words, without reasoning aloud? Could it be true then, we began to wonder, that our Mountain's mode of reasoning could only be understood, as our Adepts had always said, by listening carefully, and using, not our brains but the soles of our feet?

What to do now? As we were scratching our heads, we saw that the Anthropoi had dispatched a group of emissaries to consult with us. Even though we could see that some of the old Kraani were in this group, we decided to meet with them, to see if they could offer a solution to the problem that we were now all faced with. A long palaver was held, but in the end nothing came of it. To our astonishment, the former Kraani placed the blame for our common predicament squarely on *our* shoulders. It was because of us, they said, that this catastrophe had come about – there were simply too many of us to attempt a climb like this one. We were the latecomers they said, so it was up to us to leave the mountain and return to our Valley. This was the Age of the Anthropoi, and we had no place in it.

But it was you, we protested, who said that all people everywhere must attempt to climb the mountain. It was your savants who told us that you were the model we must emulate. All we did was to follow in your tracks – and it's a miracle that we have succeeded in coming as far as we have, for by the time we started climbing you had used up most of the mountain's riches.

They shrugged this off: that's all in the past, said the Kraani; why dwell on it? Let's talk about now, about the Age of the Anthropoi. Look at us, we are the Anthropoi, we always know best; you Varvaroi need to copy us even more closely than you did before. If you observe us carefully enough you will see that we are learning new ways to climb, so that we tread lightly on the mountain. This is what you must do – you must stop climbing in the old, bad way. You must learn to tread lightly, like us.

But there's no time for us to do that, we cried. Our people in the villages below are depending on us to climb as high as possible, in as short a time as possible, so that they too can begin their ascent. You and your people are already much safer than us, because you're higher up on the slope – even if you tread lightly, you are sure to set off avalanches that will sweep us away. We and our people will be doomed.

But that's your fault, they said, if you hadn't been so slow in starting the climb, if you hadn't let the foolish ways of your ancestors hold you back, you too would have been higher up. There's nothing for you to do now but accept your lot.

And then we understood that there was no point in bargaining with them. We understood that the climbers who were leading them did not, in their hearts, care about the Great Mountain at all; it had never held any meaning for them. The only thing they really cared about was being higher on the slope than we were; all that really mattered to them was to prove that they were always right and we were always wrong. Nor could they stop climbing even if they had wanted to – climbing was like a drug to them; their bodies could not do without it. And how in any case, could they bring themselves to turn back? Their pride, which was very great, would not allow it, for it would have meant disowning their past and their ways of thinking and climbing: it would have meant accepting that their savants knew a lot about how things work, but nothing about what they mean; they would have had to acknowledge that their stories were false, because their storytellers could not see that trees and mountains were living beings; they would have had to admit that it was not the manner of the climb that was to blame for our troubles – it was the climb itself. To hope for such a change was futile.

And what of us? Could we have turned back ourselves? No – that too was impossible now, for our bodies too had grown used to this drug, and to the thin air that we had risen to, and to all the excitement that accompanied our ascent. Nor would our kinsfolk, down in the Valley, have allowed us to turn back, for they were more desperate than ever, and were urging us to climb still faster. There was nothing to be done, but to keep on climbing. And so we did, but with heavy hearts now, for we could not forget that with every step we took we were advancing towards our doom.

But once again we forged on, even more frantically, and the gap between us and the climbers ahead began to dwindle rapidly. Soon we were so close that we could see their camps with the naked eye.

And now, at this long-awaited moment, when we had almost drawn abreast, we encountered another shock – we saw why the gap between us and the Anthropoi had closed so rapidly. It was because most of them had stopped climbing: the Kraani had turned on them, and were now forcing them, just as they had once forced us, to dig up the riches of the mountain so that they could build machines to carry them off the Mountain. But these machines were small, with room only for their leaders and the Kraani, and perhaps even a few of our own Eldermen. The other Anthropoi, most of them, would be left behind, even the savants (who, we now discovered, had always been secretly despised by the Kraani).

Now suddenly everything changed. Hordes of the Anthropoi came running towards us, crying out in despair, just as we had done for so long. Brought together by our shared foreboding we joined hands and embraced: no longer were we Anthropoi and Varvaroi – we were one.

'Maybe,' said their savants, 'there was some wisdom in your beliefs after all. Can you please tell us your old stories, sing us your old songs, and show us your dances so that we can determine whether your Mountain really is alive or not?'

Now, to our dismay, we found that we had forgotten the old stories and songs and dances. We too had come to believe that they were foolish and fantastical and had no place in the Age of the Anthropoi. So then began a frantic search to find someone, anyone, who remembered anything at all about our old ways.

After much searching we finally chanced upon an old woman who had once been an Adept, but had kept it secret for fear of the Kraani. It wasn't easy to persuade her to dance, but in the end she did agree to perform. And once she hit her stride, a strange, miraculous thing happened: we could feel the Mountain reverberating under our feet as though in answer to the dance.

We were all amazed but none more so than the savants of the Anthropoi, who cried out: 'You were right! The Mountain *is* alive! We can feel its heartbeat under our feet. This means we must look after the poor, dear Mountain; we must tend to it; we must care for it.'

At this the Adept ceased her whirling and came to a stop, her eyes blazing with anger.

'How dare you?' she cried. 'How dare you speak of the Mountain as though *you* were its masters, and it were your plaything, your child? Have you understood *nothing* of what it has been trying to teach you? Nothing at all?'

CHAPTER 7

Politics in the Anthropocene

Manuel Arias-Maldonado

COMING TO TERMS WITH OURSELVES

There is a new political actor in the Anthropocene: humanity as a whole. This entity must learn to act collectively to preserve itself, or collectively it will push the Earth System into an uninhabitable state. While the Anthropocene was not produced intentionally by political decisions, politics in all its many aspects (governing systems, relations of power among classes, values and ideology, and economic systems) will be crucial to mitigating its effects. In other words, politics and the Anthropocene, despite their different scales and framing, now need to converge if we are to ensure the conditions necessary to support the best of what it means to be civilized. This will take collective, conscious effort; the unintentional needs to become intentional. Our inadvertent destruction of the Holocene must become the deliberate management of the Anthropocene to prevent the demise of all political possibilities. In this hope, political scientists agree with Earth System scientists such as Will Steffen who call for a reorientation of politics, economics, behavior, and values (Steffen et al., 2018, see discussion in Chapter 2). The Anthropocene, as John Dryzek and Jonathan Pickering put it, is now "for better or worse humanity's chronic condition, a constant presence" (Dryzek and Pickering 2019: 11). It is for us to decide what to do about it.

The accidental quality of the Anthropocene is usually overlooked. While a few scientists such as the Italian Antonio Stoppani and the Russians Alexei Pavlov and Vladimir Vernadsky had some inkling of the consequences of human activities on the components of the planet, particularly the atmosphere, and there have been warnings about the impact of humanity on nature since at least the beginning of the Industrial Age (Bonneuil and Fressoz 2013: xiii), these were not only largely ignored, they were almost inconceivable before the concept of the Earth System. People certainly noticed the human impact on land-scapes or other animal species, but this is not the same as being aware of disrupting the way the planet as an integrated whole functions. In fact, as Will Steffen shows in Chapter 3, the very idea of the planet as a single system did not exist until the 1970s and this concept has only gradually emerged as the organizing principle behind much of the science central to the Anthropocene. In short, the Anthropocene is the result of a cumulated impact whose goal was not to cause the Anthropocene.

Recognizing this accidental quality is important because it provides us with a valuable resource for energizing moral engagement and political action. It allows us to excuse decisions made in a state of ignorance and avoid wasting time on mutual accusations regarding past sins in order to address the looming crisis. The late Tony deBrum, who acted as ambas-sador on climate change for the Marshall Islands, insisted on the need to shift from admonition to action and pushed for it at the Paris climate change negotiations in 2015 by convening a group of about 100 nations that called themselves the High Ambition Coalition. Rather than quar-reling about past injustices, our focus must be on preventing further damage to the Earth System. Justice, as Zoltán Boldizar Simon (2019) has argued, must be reoriented in this emergency not to adjudicate the wrongs of the past but to ensure the survival of everyone in the future. That is why politics must be reconfigured (Chakrabarty 2018: 29). Now that contemporary human beings realize the true extent of their environmental impact, we are the first generation with the responsibility to become "stewards of the Earth System" (Steffen et al. 2007).

It is time to focus on the future of the Earth System: the collective, unconscious agency we displayed in the past needs to turn into an intentional force that is directed towards keeping the planet hospitable as well as inhabitable for ourselves and other species. The Anthropocene has been produced by the *anthropos*, that is, the aggregation of human actions across time and space. In spite of radically different individual, social, and national contributions to it, this Earth-altering force is a product of collective activity and only the collective action of humanity as a whole can mitigate it. Admittedly, to stop arguing about past wrongs and reorient our efforts to the future is not easy now that the future has been turned into a scary place we do not wish to visit – partly out of fear of an ecological collapse. Two moves are required. First, a general pardon for past injustices should be agreed upon in which wrongdoers assume their responsibility and move to focus on the future. Second, in order to facilitate the pivot towards the future, we need a hopeful game plan. If the Anthropocene is perceived only as a threat, people will avert their eyes from it. Without downplaying the dangers, the Anthropocene must be presented as an opportunity to build a better future for human societies.

As Thomas suggests in Chapter 2, the main difficulty lies in agreeing at the global level that there is a biogeophysical threat, and yet once this "singular story" is widely embraced and the overall goal of Earth System stabilization is established, a diversity of means and some kind of a "democracy of voices" can be harnessed towards that goal. To assert that humanity must act collectively is not the same as suggesting that it can act *in unison* anytime soon, because there is no collective governing body with any real power. This situation means that individual, local, and national actions remain essential, even while we move slowly towards implementing international agreements and creating functioning global governance bodies.

THE HUMAN SPECIES AS A NEW AGENT OF POLITICS

Emphasizing our shared biological condition can be a powerful mobilizing force (although not invariably.) While recourse to biology as a tool for classification is not free of racist associations, as the practice of eugenics in the early twentieth century demonstrates, the opposite can also be true: declaring that all human beings are biological agents, with an impact on the environment that is newly aggregated at the level of the species, is a way of affirming our common belonging to the latter. This trait is shared by all individuals, regardless of their social position. I am not suggesting that social, economic, and national differences do not matter, since they most definitely do: privileged people weather difficulties better than others. However, we should be sophisticated enough to separate these two dimensions: on the one hand, all humans are members of a species that is destabilizing the Earth System (Thomas's "Singular Story" in Chapter 2); on the other, we are differentiated members of particular societies that bear different responsibilities and carry disparate burdens and potentials (Thomas's "Democracy of Voices" in Chapter 2) in relation to the Anthropocene.

While in the short run and locally, our vulnerabilities are radically different, in the long run and globally, we are all equally vulnerable. An Earth System gone awry spares nobody. Such is the inescapable conundrum of the Anthropocene: it emerges in a world of great inequality without global political institutions capable of coping with the planetary emergency, yet it puts human beings at the center of the stage (as a driver for planetary changes) and requires us to act collectively to save ourselves. Reflecting on the problem of scale, Aysem Mert (2019: 143) has pointed out that the only way to describe "a people" without bias and exclusion is to include all the planet's population – something that the concept of the Anthropocene has made possible. Acknowledging that it is the human species as a whole, irrespective of nationality, ethnicity, or moral and religious beliefs, that has driven the disruption of the Earth System, should be a first step towards facilitating global political cooperation.

The concept of humanity as a global agent has several dimensions. One is spatial: everybody on the planet makes up the collective, since we all contribute to some extent to the making of the Anthropocene. Translating this description of our shared plight into a normative argument will not be easy, as it will require new forms of global political representation and/or a widespread individual assumption of ecological duties that goes far beyond what is required by current laws. But there is also a temporal dimension, as people across generations should be included (see Kyle Harper's essay in Chapter 4) insofar as their agency and their needs will matter as much as ours. For now, however, the focus should be on living people, as they are the ones who bear the responsibility to start acting as a global collective.

Yet how to foster this sense of planetary belonging? How to create a global community of stewards of the Earth? As a matter of fact, the Anthropocene itself can help – the problem is part of the solution.

In particular, it is this concept's connection to deep time and planetary events that drives home the awareness that humanity is endangered, and it can contribute to the realization that we are all members of the same, troubled species.

On the one hand, the story of the Anthropocene has the capacity to connect people's perceptions with the particular "spatio-temporal vertigo" that we feel in the face of our geological past (see Milligan 2013). While an abstract idea, geological time is also something embodied in the Earth's landscapes. Humanity does not stand apart from geohistory, but is a part of it. If current planetary changes are set into this geological context, they do not look so unfamiliar and may be more easily understandable. On the other hand, there is also the question of size. Humanity has become colossal, reaching proportions that are almost impossible to understand or represent (Raffnsøe 2016: 12). And the same goes for the phenomena that surround humans and interact with them: hurricanes, wild fires, heat waves, the climate system itself, plastic debris, etc. As Will Steffen and Jan Zalasiewicz make clear in this book, we are learning that the very Earth System that we took for granted is a precarious home for humanity.

The Anthropocene thus invites a particular viewpoint: that of being at the end of the world. It places us at the juncture of two temporalities – the continuity of a planet on which we made an appearance only recently, and at the same time the rupture with the conditions that have prevailed over the last 12,000 years. In this context, human civilization is a rare event, an achievement to be preserved, and improved upon. As much as the stabilization of the Earth System is an end in itself, it is also a means – a means to the political goal of living meaningful individual lives in just societies on a new basis of planetary stewardship.

POLITICS FOR THE ANTHROPOCENE: THREE APPROACHES

The Anthropocene, then, can be told as the story of a species that comes to realize how powerful it is, and that acknowledges the urgent need to mend its ways. We are at the beginning of that process, but it may be that we are too late; progress, such as it is, does not seem fast enough. Adapting to the Anthropocene is difficult for individuals, groups, and countries because planetary pressures will constrain the range of permissible human behaviors. For the Earth to remain hospitable, anthropogenic impacts on natural systems must be reduced. Instead of accelerating, we need to decelerate. The Anthropocene is thus a collective action problem that requires meaningful social change to reorient our systems away from business-as-usual. Our future depends on political action at different levels – from the individual and the local to the national and the global. The question is how this should be achieved. Three main approaches can be distinguished: liberal democracy, eco-authoritarianism, and green communitarianism. Each tells its own story about humans in the Anthropocene. As I have mentioned, none of them has been adopted globally and hence there is no global political system dedicated to the task of realizing the general will of the human species. While any of them might yet become global, it is more likely that they will keep on coexisting and influencing each other. As there are no international governance structures capable of enforcing international law, we have to turn our attention to nation states, regional structures like the EU, and local efforts.

LIBERAL DEMOCRACY. Despite the belief that democracy is the government *by* the people *for* the people, Western democracies are actually representative governments in which the popular will is not the direct source of political decisions. They are mixed regimes in which citizens elect their representatives, whose decision-making ability is in turn limited by the rule of law, the separation of powers, and the operation of counter majoritarian institutions such as central banks or high courts. Thus they combine democratic elements (popular vote) with liberal ones (limits to state power, individual liberties). And while they prize individual freedom, managing the Anthropocene seems to require limitations on that freedom. So, tensions are naturally bound to emerge. Liberal democracies need to rein in environmentally harmful behavior and enforce structural changes. At the same time, they must avoid significantly curtailing individual freedoms or abandoning entirely the idea of economic growth, at least in some sectors, despite planetary limits. How can liberal democracies deal with this quandary?

A first source of tension is the liberal division between the private and the public sphere. Anthropogenic impact on the Earth System is caused by a massive aggregation of individual actions. These actions have two different lives: one is *episodic* and is associated with the private sphere, while the other is *systemic* and produces public consequences (Jamieson and Di Paola 2018). For instance, driving my car is a banal action, but the driving of 1,200 million cars is not. Likewise, buying a shirt seems no big deal, but clothing production doubled between 2000 and 2014 and, according to McKinsey, a kilogram of garments generates the equivalent of 23 kilograms of CO_2 (see The Economist 2017). From a democratic perspective, then, the problem lies in the unaccountability of private actions: I am not asked to justify taking the car or buying a shirt, yet I end up causing harm to people and beings that exist beyond my private sphere – including future generations of humans. The intricate causality of the Anthropocene also includes time lags, as both carbon dioxide emissions and plastic waste remain in the environment for a long time. Dealing with the Anthropocene thus seems to involve tampering with individual preferences in some way – a possibility that is not excluded by political liberalism, but which is still problematic.

The Anthropocene's conflicting temporalities clash with liberal democracy in other ways. On the one hand, most obviously, political and geological timescales have little to do with each other: electoral politics is defined by an almost exclusive focus on the short term, which is detrimental to the design and implementation of future-oriented policies. On the other, policy makers need to do more than just consider longer-term perspectives: they must also bear in mind that decisions made within the next decade or so are expected to have a strong planetary impact, not just for this century but far beyond (see Galaz 2019). The logic of electoral competition poses an additional problem for governing the Anthropocene. In order to gather popular support, political leaders and movements usually promise more because asking for sacrifices, or delivering bad news, is not a good strategy for delivering electoral success. In particular, the relation between candidates and their voters is grounded on the ability of the former to deliver new social, political, or economic goods. Dealing with the Anthropocene seems to require terminating, weakening, or changing the relation between human well-being and economic growth.

Hard questions follow: can progress be dissociated from economic growth? Can democracy work without offering material gains? Can the state retain its legitimacy if it does not materially improve people's lives? Growth should not be seen as an end in itself, but as a means to the fulfillment of emancipatory ends such as equality, freedom, autonomy, or wellbeing. Hence growth can be rightfully limited if it endangers these rights by steering the planet towards a dangerous state. But doing away with economic growth also endangers equality, autonomy, freedom, and wellbeing. In turn, this may lead to social unrest and political turmoil – hardly the best conditions for implementing radical environmental reform.

As Di Paola and Jamieson (2018) have pointed out, managing the problems of the Anthropocene puts liberal democracies in a bind. If they fail to address climate change, biodiversity loss, toxins, and other challenges associated with the new planetary state, their legitimacy can be challenged on account of their ineffectiveness. But if they pursue that goal too aggressively, their legitimacy may be challenged, too, on the grounds that such a preference has not been expressed by a majority of people. However, there is no reason why the pursuit of habitability in the Anthropocene cannot be accommodated within liberal democracy. It would obviously be preposterous to protect private liberty if the result was the elimination of the conditions that make the exercise of private liberty possible. As Helen Rosenblatt (2018) has demonstrated, there is a whole strain of the liberal tradition that emphasizes individual duties and the need to care for the political community. Private preferences, one might therefore argue, are legitimate only insofar as they are ecologically sustainable (Wissenburg 1998). In short, a liberal society cannot commit suicide in the name of freedom.

In fact, the assertion that individual freedom takes precedence over environmental protection is a caricature of how liberal democracies work. A whole number of behaviors are deemed impermissible, and are hence forbidden by public legislation – we cannot just do what we want regarding, for example, waste, pollution, or animals. While current applicable law is not enough to stabilize the Earth System, it is clear that liberal democracies are not oblivious to the need for action and already accept that, if necessary, individualism can lawfully be restrained in order to limit environmental harm. The goal of the liberal-democratic approach is to arrive at a point where free societies are compatible with the stabilization of the planet's trajectory.

Typical of the liberal-democratic approach, however, is an additional factor: the belief that market forces can be harnessed to solve the problems that they themselves generate. If they are steered in the right direction, the theory goes, firms and consumers will deliver social and technological innovations that – together with public regulation – will end up reducing the stress on the Earth System. According to this view, habitability cannot be achieved by the state alone: the ingenuity of firms and individuals is necessary. A key step is to ensure that producers and consumers face the environmental costs of their decisions, for instance by charging polluters – firms and individuals – in a way that hurts them. It is essential that the environmental costs of production be born by the producers, not passed along to the public.

Economic incentives and curbs are a means to increase the environmental effectiveness of everyday decisions without the need to resort to regulation. Think of the benefits that come from eliminating subsidies for unsustainable activities or sectors – from destructive timber sales to coal mining and oil drilling. There is now a wide recognition of the need to reduce fishing subsidies: they are estimated to be as high as $35 billion worldwide, 20 billion of which are thought to contribute directly to overfishing. While there is a clear commitment to reduce these, as reflected in the UN's Sustainable Development Goal number 14, an agreement has not been reached – though it is getting closer. Farming is another sector where huge sums go to large-scale agribusinesses that destroy soil and water health and reduce biodiversity through the heavy use of artificial pesticides and fertilizers. Another example is the reduced VAT rate (or sales tax) on meat common in many countries, which can be considered a subsidy of a product that is currently over-consumed as well as polluting. Germany, so far, is the one country in which increasing the price of meat has been more seriously discussed.

Incentives are frequently provided via state regulation. More often, however, public involvement is part of a larger governance scheme in which the state, markets, and the third sector operate together. In the Dutch livestock industry, for example, a virtuous interaction of government, markets, and ever more demanding consumers has led to a commitment to sustainability (Poppe 2013). Governments can use innovative programs to steer markets in a particular direction, or to facilitate the relations between NGOs and businesses. Consumers for their part can promote sustainability through their purchases, and NGOs can shame food manufacturers. Sometimes, NGOs and firms cooperate without the need for state intervention: UNICEF works with Procter & Gamble on disaster relief, and the Nature Conservancy partnered with PepsiCo to improve water supplies for communities wherever they operate. The Netherlands provide yet another example of market transformation in which the state has played a minor role: three-fourths of the coffee consumed in the country is now being produced in a sustainable way (see Ingenbleek and Reinders 2013). Interestingly, the driving forces of this market segment have not been consumers either, but coffee roasters and supermarkets, which were able to create a new demand by offering and branding sustainable coffee. In the US, there is also the possibility of major donors taking the initiative: Ted Turner's Endangered Species Fund was established in 1997 and supports a number of preserves to protect wildlife.

In any Anthropocene politics, the energy sector is key, as it contributes directly to climate change. The liberal-democratic approach rests on a combination of instruments that range from public regulation to market incentives, subsidies, and sanctions, as well as technological innovation. While a global carbon tax has not yet been implemented, a number of carbon markets have been created. The rationale behind them is to make carbon so expensive that firms will be forced to look for renewable alternatives. The European Union Emission Trading Scheme was launched in 2005 and remains the biggest scheme of its kind, having reduced CO_2 emissions in Europe by more than 1 billion tons between 2008 and 2016 (3.8 per cent of total EU-wide emissions). Germany launched a national emission trading scheme for heating and transport fuels in 2021, thus pushing most of its major sectors to face a CO_2 price. The UK is following a contrasting yet successful approach to decarbonization: with firms allowed to play a crucial role in the energy transition, market forces have been prevalent. In the US, over the past twenty-five years, there have been substantial investments in clean energy technologies, with the result that US energy markets have changed dramatically: utility-scale solar costs have declined by 86 per cent and wind energy prices have fallen by 67 per cent, opening up the possibility that renewable energy resources will drive coal out of business (see Ritter 2018). Whether this change goes far enough or is quick enough is a different matter. To complicate matters further, green energy efforts impede biodiversity protection efforts. This is a problem that only a low-population and low-impact social system might solve, provided that you can get a low-population and low-impact social system in the first place.

The liberal-democratic approach to the Anthropocene, in sum, is not limited to the reorientation of market forces – even though this strategy is central to it. For liberals, democracy can successfully respond to planetary challenges through a mixture of public regulation, market competition, private–public cooperation, and consumer pressure. They argue that there is no need to give up on democracy. In fact, without the resources provided by an open society, from new ideas and technologies to voluntary cooperation and spontaneous coordination, there is no way to stabilize the Earth System.

ECO-AUTHORITARIANISM. A different approach to the Anthropocene is eco-authoritarianism: the pursuit of sustainability by other than democratic means. Supporters of eco-authoritarianism argue that it is the only way to prevent planetary collapse – whether we like it or not. By this account, democracies are doomed to fail and must be replaced with strong authoritarian powers that devote their efforts to dealing with the challenges of the Anthropocene. We have to choose security over freedom, sacrificing individual wellbeing in order to achieve collective survival.

The authoritarian model has tempted environmentalism in the past. In the aftermath of the oil crisis back in the 1970s, a current of green thought argued that sustainability could only be achieved if the culprits of the ecological crisis – market capitalism and liberal democracy – were replaced with a non-democratic, ecologically enlightened technocracy[1]. There was a Malthusian echo in the arguments of these eco-authoritarian thinkers. According to them, scarce collective resources must be protected and regulated to avoid an ecological calamity, a protection that could only be enacted by political institutions exerting a strong degree of coercion. What is distinctive about such a state is that it is ruled by "a class of ecological mandarins who possess the esoteric knowledge needed to run it well" (Ophuls 1977: 163). In a world where the rise of populism has led to experts being regarded with suspicion, it is very unlikely that the bureaucrats of eco-authoritarianism could implement their rules without widespread resistance.

Most Western environmentalists abandoned this idea long ago. However, the pressures exerted by the Anthropocene, foremost among them climate change, have revived this thinking – and not just among environmentalists. The sense of urgency communicated by planetary destabilization suggests that perhaps liberal democracy is too slow or too compromised by the market economy to preserve habitability. It should, however, be noted that authoritarian solutions are typical of historical moments where public fears are high. At this present moment, as planetary pressures are increasingly coming to be felt in our daily lives, some may believe that democracy is a luxury of the Holocene. Global warming has already produced this effect: the prominent scientist James Lovelock has compared it to a war and suggested that democratic procedures be suspended while we wage it (Lovelock 2010). Others envision the rise of a "Climate Leviathan", namely an authoritarian eco-state that provides environmental security while restricting civic liberties and free enterprise (see Mann and Wainwright 2018). In short, eco-authoritarianism deems democracy incapable of implementing the structural changes necessary for stabilizing the Earth System.

---

[1] The influence of the "tragedy of the commons" (Hardin, 1977) is evident: collective resources must be protected to avoid an ecological collapse. This protection can only be enacted by coercive political institutions (Ophuls, 1977: 152; Heilbroner 1975: 86–90). A green Leviathan is advised: "Only a government possessing great powers to regulate individual behavior in the ecological common interest can deal effectively with the tragedy of the commons" (Ophuls 1977: 154). Such a centralized state is ruled by ecological experts – a green enlightened despotism.

China embodies the authoritarian route towards securing habitability. Led by a ruling class in which scientists and engineers abound, the Chinese regime is a one-party autocracy in which a great deal of power is held by the president. The American journalist Thomas Friedman (2009) once commented on the environmental benefits of such a system, suggesting that an autocracy that is led "by a reasonably enlightened group of people" had the great advantage of being able to impose politically difficult policies without fearing the reaction of the people. It can pay off, certainly: China has become a world leader in installed capacity of hydropower, solar photovoltaic, and wind energy. In particular, it has increased its renewable energy supply at an average annual rate of 12 per cent since the beginning of this century, all while sustaining strong economic growth over the past 30 years. Sustainability is not the only reason for this, as the Chinese government is also interested in expanding the renewable energy sector with the aim of creating new jobs and increasing exports (see Dell'Aquila, Atzori and Stroe 2020). This goal has been achieved through an aggressive industrial policy that includes preferential land policies, as well as the use of taxation and fiscal instruments that benefit manufacturers. However, it would be naive to believe that an authoritarian government can simply rule by direct command. On the contrary, incentives are needed – a tax targeting large vehicles with inefficient energy consumption, for instance, was introduced in 2008.

There are disadvantages, too. On the biodiversity front, the official call to advance towards a "beautiful China" has been backed by a significant increase in scientific research and the creation of more than 11,800 protected areas covering 18 per cent of its land and 4.6 per cent of its sea area (see Wang et al. 2020). Yet meeting the official goal of achieving "harmony between human and nature" is not easy when economic development is being pursued at the same time. Colossal infrastructure projects such as the Three Gorges Dam, the size of which is eight times that of the Hoover Dam, provide abundant hydroelectric power while inflicting severe damage to local biodiversity.

The Chinese pledge to protect biodiversity and to find a balance between economic growth and environmental protection writ large looks less credible when its rising ecological footprint outside the country's borders is taken into account. China imports huge volumes of products such as palm oil, which contributes to deforestation in tropical countries. It is also presumed to be responsible for much of the world's illicit wildlife trade – the demand for wild animals, both for private consumption and medical use, being a suspected driver of zoonosis infection, which, as we have seen with SARS-CoV-2, may cause a global pandemic. In the past two decades, China has been stripping the world of resources by closing deals with different countries: Chile for copper, Australia for iron ore, Angola for oil, Congo for cobalt, and so forth. Chinese state-owned companies assume a primary role in the acquisition of commodities in Latin America and Africa (see Economy and Levi 2014: 46–67). In the case of emerging countries, debt relief and financial assistance are provided in exchange for access to their resources. Often, much-needed infrastructure is also offered. The latter is in fact a key element of the Belt and Road Initiative, a project that aims to connect China to many regions of the world. In developing countries, there is a major risk that road and rail lines will be built without the necessary oversight to prevent serious damage to biodiversity.

Whether China is pursuing an imperial agenda or just trying to increase the material standards of life for its almost 1.5 billion inhabitants, the fact remains that its eco-authoritarian stance has clear limitations. British diplomat Crispin Tickell's (2011) assertion that China's actions display "the need to control market forces within a framework of the public interest" is not wholly convincing. If China were committed to a mitigated Anthropocene, it would behave differently beyond its borders. China's example, of course, does not necessarily ruin the case for eco-authoritarianism *tout court*. The Chinese model is not the only possibility: other forms of eco-authoritarianism are conceivable.

A more modest version of eco-authoritarianism is imaginable, one in which the stabilization of the Earth System is not compromised by the pursuit of economic growth, but this might well face problems of legitimacy. In a top-down approach, people must be led to accept "the rule of experts," otherwise they may resist their commands. That is precisely what the Chinese government tries to avoid by raising living standards. A state that gives up growth in the quest for sustainability will have to persuade people that this is the right thing to do. Yet the people's willingness to cooperate will depend on their perception of the state's legitimacy – something that is harder to come by when they do not have a say in the decisions that affect them. In countries where a democratic public culture has taken root, this problem is also acute, but there, public institutions allow input and negotiations to take place, unlike in eco-authoritarian states. Moreover, the experts do not know everything that is necessary to stabilize Earth. If a large-scale project goes wrong, a government may not be able to alter course because of sunk costs. Large dams all over Asia, for instance, are plagued by considerable financial risks, as well as environmental uncertainties regarding the tension between fresh water and clean energy (see Pomeranz 2009).

Finally, figuring out workable solutions to the challenges of the Anthropocene seems to require the free exchange of ideas and the social testing of innovations, not to mention the operation of a vibrant civil society from which new values and social practices can emerge. In other words, an authoritarian regime does not guarantee sustainable outcomes. Supporters of eco-authoritarianism will reply that democracy does not guarantee sustainable outcomes either. In their story, there is no time left for trying: human beings must be forced to reduce their impact on the planet and only a coercive state can do that fast enough.

GREEN COMMUNITARIANISM. Green communitarianism provides another way forward to mitigate the damage of our destabilized Earth System. This approach seeks to decrease the human impact on natural systems by reducing the size and scale of social systems without giving up democratic values. Instead of a global capitalist economy, communitarianism relies on self-organizing communities that embrace new social values and protect the commons. Politically, it leans towards democratic republicanism – a tradition that emphasizes direct participation, public deliberation, and the involvement of all members of the community in the defense of the common good. Neither individual freedom nor state coercion play a significant role in this approach, which heavily depends on public trust and civic engagement. The ideal held up by communitarianism is one of social harmony, collective effort, and voluntary self-limitation. In its telling, human beings learn to coexist with the planet

POLITICS IN THE ANTHROPOCENE

and with the non-human world while rediscovering the intrinsic value of social bonds.

As progress in the modern sense is contaminated by the pursuit of economic growth and the exploitation of nature, communitarians champion a different understanding of emancipation. Rather than looking for increasing standards of living through mass consumption and individualistic fulfillment, communitarians suggest that a life rooted in the community is more rewarding, providing the benefits of wellbeing that are to some degree unquantifiable. We are to live in a simpler way, finding prosperity in different places and activities: enjoying more spare time, assigning a greater role to individual creativity, doing more meaningful jobs. The emphasis on human flourishing is neatly summarized in John Barry's motto: "low-carbon, high quality of life" (Barry 2012: 11). It is not just that indefinite growth is ecologically untenable – it is also morally undesirable and spiritually unfulfilling.

Unlike the liberal-democratic approach, which tries to render capitalism sustainable, communitarians usually advocate the shift towards a degrowth society. Degrowth is the sustainable and equitable reduction of society's throughput – a significant decrease in the materials and energy used by human societies (see Kallis 2011). For all the benefits of wind and solar power, for instance, they are not "zero carbon" and nor can they by themselves sustain a globalized economy whose aim is indefinite economic growth. Therefore, a low-energy society is the only path towards avoiding global inhabitability: small is not just beautiful, but a matter of survival. We get to produce, trade, travel, and consume less, so that social life can be more local and less mobile. Economist Dietrich Vollrath argues that advanced capitalist economies are already moving in this direction, even without "green" imperatives, and that a stagnant economy may be a sign of success (Vollrath, 2020). The shift to renewable energies, strong redistribution schemes and the creation of economic value outside the market – these are the kind of structural changes that degrowth advances. For this change to take place in a democratic manner, thus avoiding the resort to authoritarian forms of governance, people must be recruited for the cause: simple ways of living need to become attractive, so that the "voluntary simplicity" (Alexander, 2013) of communal life is embraced by sufficient numbers of people.

In the meantime, there are places in which degrowth strategies and communal forms of self-organization are being attempted. They lead by example, highlighting the kind of response that local communities should give to the Anthropocene. Take the Transition Towns movement, which started back in 2005 and encourages communities to address planetary challenges at the local level. Initiatives of this kind have been set up in 50 countries – stories abound. There is the partnership between Granja Viana and Brasilândia, two Transition groups rooted in Sâo Paulo that have learnt how to store and filter rainwater from the roofs in a city where droughts are frequent. Or the successful Million Miles project launched in the Black Isle, Scotland, which aimed to cut car travel on the peninsula by a million miles in three years through promoting alternatives such as walking and cycling, the use of public transport, and car-sharing schemes. Another example is Pasadena's Repair Café, in which people exchange their time repairing for Time Dollars registered by a local Time Bank – an initiative that signals the rise of local money schemes such as the Bristol Pound. These currencies are conceived as tools for empowering local communities, as they encourage transparent economies based on local ownership. Community gardens have also bloomed across the world in recent years. This is a venerable tradition that goes back to the early nineteenth century, when the British government allocated plots of land to the poor to grow vegetables and flowers. In their current understanding, they are places where people grow food, cultivate local communities, and adopt sustainable practices. All these strategies can be seen as means towards building up the "mutualistic city" (presented by Mark Williams in Chapter 12 of this volume) – a city that coevolves with its environment in a harmonious manner and which also tries to prevent the amplification of existing social inequalities.

Sometimes, self-organization involves acts of resistance against decay or commodification. An inspiring story is that of Portpatrick, a beautiful Scottish seaside village whose port fell into disrepair after the loss of its two piers meant that the crossing to Northern Ireland got moved to another town. Villagers knew that the port had to be improved, lest vital tourist revenue should be lost to neighboring harbors. Yet they did not like the plan designed by the harbor's private owners and looked for a way to buy it back. They came up with the idea of a trust, which over five years led to the acquisition of the place for £350,000. Shares in the harbor were sold for a minimum of £25, yet each shareholder had one vote irrespective of the number of shares they bought. This ownership structure prevents large investors from taking over control and increases the sense of local belonging. Schemes of this kind have since become more common as community businesses have resorted to them across the UK – local pubs, renewable energy schemes, and woodland recovery initiatives have been funded through them.

As these examples make clear, the movement towards greater self-reliance and more democratic forms of local governance does not mark a clean break with capitalism: villagers from Portpatrick were afraid that touristic revenue would disappear, and local enterprises financed through community shares still engage in business. Degrowth is not the absence of growth, though, and a greater problem may lie in the distance between local change and structural transformation. In the current context of Earth destabilization, this piecemeal approach may not yield significant results fast enough. However, perhaps it makes more sense to see green communitarianism as an expression of moral and political pluralism within liberal society – an emergent, alternative way of doing things that supplements larger processes of transform-ation while contributing to cultural change and the spreading of sustainable values.

Degrowth is not without problems. It is not clear how pluralism can be reconciled with a less dynamic, less mobile society – there is the risk of cultural stagnation as well as the difficulty of restraining the human impulse towards innovation, discovery, and exploration. In other words, while minorities can certainly adopt a communitarian way of life, it is unclear whether majorities will follow suit. In emerging and poor coun-tries, degrowth can be expected to be unappealing. And even if capital-ism were to end, people will still have material needs such as energy, clothing, and food. The effects of degrowth on population trends are also hard to foresee – a communitarian way of life, for example, may end up increasing the birth rate. For its advocates, however, green commu-nitarianism is the only means for stabilizing the Earth System without sacrificing democracy on the way.

CONCLUSION: TOWARDS UNITY OF PURPOSE

Reducing the human impact on natural systems in order to stabilize the Earth System and veer away from the dangerous business-as-usual trajectory is the unequivocal goal of a politics for the Anthropocene – how exactly it should be done, however, needs to be negotiated among different social actors and countries. No matter how urgent the task may be, the workings of politics cannot be suspended: people must be persuaded, laws have to be passed, policies need to be implemented. Might human beings fail in stabilizing the Earth System just because they are unable to act in time? This scenario should not be ruled out, and it would certainly be a bitter testimony to the pettiness and unreason of our species. Nevertheless, I have argued that humanity has just enough room to maneuver, provided that it recognizes the magnitude of the challenge ahead. Ultimately, the most important driver of politics *in* the Anthropocene is the willingness of individuals, institutions, and countries across the globe to implement an ambitious politics *for* the Anthropocene. Unity of purpose, however, is compatible with a multiplicity of approaches. In turn, as Thomas cautions, the reality of the Anthropocene imposes limits to the kind of stories that we can tell ourselves.

In this chapter, I have given an account of the main responses to the Anthropocene – those provided by liberal democracy, eco-authoritarianism, and green communitarianism. They differ in many respects, including the role they assign to economic growth and the priority they grant to the fight against poverty or inequality: while political liberalism and eco-authoritarianism seem more interested in keeping a high level of growth and feel more concerned with poverty than with inequality, communitarianism emphasizes the common good and the need for equality even if that means lowering material standards. And while the latter supports degrowth as the means to achieve sustainability, liberal democracy and eco-authoritarianism pursue the greening of growth in the belief that political stability and greater global equality cannot be secured without it. Whether enough greening can be achieved in time to avert irreversible planetary change remains to be seen. Then again, the communitarian model is unlikely to be adopted around the world at the necessary speed, even if it expands its role as a generator of innovative solutions and sustainable lifestyles that also address the question of social justice.

Be that as it may, the problem is apparent: none of these approaches have been implemented at a global level. So far, they are nation-based or even just local-based. In the real world, they all coexist: China is an emerging superpower that leans towards eco-authoritarianism, while the UK is a liberal democracy in which Transition Towns and other communitarian initiatives have flourished. They can all be said to express an emergent common will, that of confronting the destabilization of the Earth System, albeit by different means. Ideally, stronger global institutions should be developed, so that cooperation among states is significantly increased. And while geopolitical competition hinders the creation of global political bodies, the recognition of humanity as an Earth System agent may push in the opposite direction.

The prospects for creating collective global agency are not propitious: China is on the rise; populism and heightened nationalism resist surrendering any aspect of national sovereignty; and fierce ideological and religious disagreements do not make things any easier. Besides, there is no clear answer as to whether a centralized system or a polyarchy best serves the goal of achieving global sustainability (see Biermann and Dryzek 2016). Hence it looks as though the key role in keeping our planet habitable will be played by international agreements in which different countries adhere to a common goal, such as the Paris Agreement on climate change or the Sustainable Development Goals launched by the United Nations.

Arguably, the Anthropocene should be governed in a democratic manner. Planetary challenges might even reinvigorate actually existing liberal democracies by giving them a unifying motive, a collective goal shared by everyone, irrespective of their ideology, gender, class, or ethnicity. This shared emergency may also strengthen cooperation between democracies and autocracies. Much, however, remains to be seen. For now, the most urgent task is to foster the widespread recognition that stabilizing the Earth System cannot wait – we are now inhabitants of the Anthropocene and we must act accordingly.

REFERENCES

Alexander S (2013) Voluntary simplicity and the social reconstruction of law: Degrowth from the grassroots up. *Environmental Values* 22(2): 287–308.

Barry J (2012) *The Politics of Actually Existing Unsustainability.* Oxford: Oxford University Press.

Biermann F, Dryzek J (2016) Critical dialogue. *Perspectives on Politics* 14(1): 174–178.

Bonneuil C, Fressoz J (2013) *The Shock of the Anthropocene: The Earth, History and Us.* London & New York: Verso.

Chakrabarty D (2018) Anthropocene time. *History and Theory* 57(1): 5–32.

Dell'Aquila M, Atzori D, Stroe OR (2020) The role of policy design and market forces to achieve an effective energy transition: a comparative analysis between the UK and Chinese models. In: M. Hafner and S. Tagliapietra (eds.), *The Geopolitics of the Global Energy Transition: Lecture Notes in Energy,* vol 73 (227–255). Cham, Switzerland: Springer.

Di Paola M, Jamieson D (2018) Climate change and the challenges to democracy. *University of Miami Law Review* 72: 369.

Dryzek J, Pickering J (2019) *The Politics of the Anthropocene.* Oxford: Oxford University Press.

Economy E, Levi M (2014) *By All Means Necessary: How China's Resource Quest is Changing the World.* Cambridge: Cambridge University Press.

Friedman T (2009) Our one-party democracy. *The New York Times,* 8th September: 29.

Galaz V (2019) Time and politics in the Anthropocene: Too fast, too slow? In: F. Biermann and E. Lövbrand (eds.), *Anthropocene Encounters: New Directions in Green Political Thinking* (109–127). Cambridge: Cambridge University Press.

Hardin G (1977) The Tragedy of the Commons. In: G. Hardin and J. Baden (eds.), *Managing the Commons* (16–30). San Francisco: W. H. Freeman and Company.

Heilbroner R (1975) *An Inquiry into The Human Prospect.* London: Calder & Boyars.

Ingenbleek P, Reinders M (2013) The development of a market for sustainable coffee in the Netherlands: rethinking the contribution of fair trade. *Journal of Business Ethics,* 113: 461–474.

Jamieson D, Di Paola M (2016) Political theory for the Anthropocene. In: D. Held and P. Maffettone (eds.), *Global Political Theory* (254–280). Cambridge: Polity.

Kallis G (2011) In defence of degrowth. *Ecological Economics* 70: 873–880.

Lovelock J (2010) Humans are too stupid to prevent climate change. *The Guardian,* 29th March.

Mann G, Wainwright J (2018) *Climate Leviathan*. London: Verso Books.

Mert A (2019) Democracy in the Anthropocene: a new scale. In: F. Biermann and E. Lövbrand (eds.), *Anthropocene Encounters: New Directions in Green Political Thinking* (128–149). Cambridge: Cambridge University Press.

Milligan B (2013) Space-time vertigo. In: E. Ellsworth and J. Kruse (eds.), *Making the Geologic Now: Responses to Material Conditions of Contemporary Life* (123–130). Brooklyn: Punctum Books.

Ophuls W (1977) *Ecology and the Politics of Scarcity*. San Francisco: W. H. Freeman and Company.

Pomeranz K (2009) The great Himalayan watershed. *New Left Review*, 58: 5–39.

Poppe K (2013) On markets and government: property rights to promote sustainability with market forces. *NJAS – Wageningen Journal of Life Sciences*, 66: 33–37.

Raffnsøe S (2016) *Philosophy of the Anthropocene: The Human Turn*. New York: Palgrave Macmillan.

Ritter B (2018) Market forces are driving a clean energy revolution in the US. *The Conversation*, 28th April.

Rosenblatt H (2018) *The Lost History of Liberalism: From Ancient Rome to the Twenty-First Century*. Princeton: Princeton University Press.

Simon ZB (2019) *History in Times of Unprecedented Change: A Theory for the 21st Century*. London: Bloomsbury.

Steffen W, Crutzen P, McNeill J (2007) The Anthropocene: are humans now overwhelming the great forces of nature? *Ambio* 36(8): 614–621.

Steffen W, Röckstrom J, Richardson K, et al. (2018) Trajectories of the Earth System in the Anthropocene. *PNAS* 115 (33): 8252–8259.

The Economist (2017) Green is the new black, 8th April: 62.

Tickell C (2011) Societal responses to the Anthropocene. *Philosophical Transactions of the Royal Society A*, 369, 926–932.

Vollrath, D. (2020) *Fully Grown: Why a Stagnant Economy is a Sign of Success*. Chicago: University of Chicago Press.

Wang W, Feng C, Liu F, Li J (2020) Biodiversity conservation in China: a review of recent studies and practices, *Environmental Science and Ecotechnology*, 2: 100025.

Wissenburg M (1998) *Green Liberalism: The Free and the Green Society*. London: UCL Press.

CHAPTER 8

Very Recent History and the Nuclear Anthropocene

Kate Brown

The Anthropocene Working Group voted in 2019 to use human-made radioactive contaminants as one of the key markers of the proposed new epoch.[1] After the first explosion of a uranium bomb at the Trinity test site in New Mexico in July 1945, new anthropogenic radioactive contaminants circulated the globe, saturating soils, flora, and fauna. Most fallout landed in the northern hemisphere. Climate change history often (and rightly) highlights the plight of the Global South and poorer countries, but zeroing in on the nuclear Anthropocene shows how ubiquitous radioactive toxins are especially in the wealthier northern hemisphere. This story has been mostly missed because, as military leaders detonated 520 nuclear bombs into the atmosphere from 1945–1963, the fallout that settled down became part of "background" or "natural" radiation. Cancers, which also rose steadily in the northern hemisphere after 1950, became part of a new normal as well. In the same decades that radioactive isotopes from atomic bomb testing began to circle the globe, so too did new classes of pesticides, herbicides, and chemical pollutants from new industries producing plastics, aluminum, and a host of goods that contaminated landscapes. In short, the blanketing of the Earth with anthropogenic toxins was so encompassing, the scale so grand, that this major change to the Earth System has been hard to discern. The increasingly lethal landscape of the last 70 years was often mistaken for the natural world. As we experience a death-dealing speed-up of changes to the planetary system, it helps to reflect on the ways radioactive

---

[1] Meera Subramanian, "Anthropocene now: influential panel votes to recognize Earth's new epoch," *Nature*, May 21, 2019.

contaminants changed biological time and transformed our understanding of human health. A focus on the nuclear Anthropocene reconfigures our sense of scale, and with it, time and human agency.

I came across the troubling global history of the nuclear Anthropocene, as I researched the more localized history of the environmental and health consequences of the Chernobyl accident. As Julia Adeney Thomas points out in Chapter 2, localizing the global is one way to sort the complex and confusing record of anthropogenic change on human health. What is the nuclear Anthropocene? Geologists use the layer of radioactive isotopes laid down after 1945 as a component in tracking and dating the new geological epoch. As medical doctors working with radiation for diagnostics well know, decaying isotopes show themselves readily.[2] There are two features of the Anthropocene debates that often get conflated: geologists are concerned with how to date the Anthropocene, while many other scholars, including those in the humanities, are concerned with the impact of the Anthropocene on human and non-human life. In these debates, scientists and pundits have focused a great deal of attention on climate change, but that is just one outgrowth of anthropogenic disturbances. In his essay, Will Steffen describes fossil fuels as an "external" factor in contributing to a warming Earth. If humans did not dig them out, he argues, they would still be locked away. A similar line of reasoning goes for anthropogenic radioactive isotopes. They existed, mostly buried until the late nineteenth century, when humans invented technologies to create new isotopes and to produce existing isotopes in increasingly impressive volumes. If one takes the horizontal line showing carbon dioxide emissions which Jan Zalasiewicz describes in his essay (Chapter 1), and places it alongside emissions of radioactive isotopes generated in producing and detonating nuclear bombs, then one would also see a horizontal line shooting vertical at nearly the same mid-century point as for carbon dioxide emissions.

Specialists in radiation medicine and radio-ecology debate the impact of these isotopes. For the last half century, two camps of scientists faced each other, feuding. One group claimed that the saturation of ecologies

---

[2] See, for instance, Angela N. H. Creager, *Atomic Tracings: Radioisotopes in Biology and Medicine* (Cambridge, MA: The MIT Press, 2014), Chapter 2.

with radioactive fallout was of little concern. The other camp argued that the historical novelty of massive radioactive contaminants had major implications for human and environmental health. The public tends to prefer the good news story that nature in the Chernobyl Zone is "thriving." "Nature will right itself" is the comforting message of a minority of scientists working on Chernobyl ecologies. Other scientists – and I myself – found this doubtful. Trying to see if Chernobyl archival records could shed light on this debate, I went to Kyiv.

Historians tend to rely on archival texts as our primary maps of human action, just as geologists might read rocks. But my experience with the Chernobyl story made me realize that I needed to expand my sense of where history lies hidden. My research began with paper documents – words imprinted on felled and processed trees – but ended with the trees themselves.

It happened like this. First I tapped into the records of the Soviet Ministry of Health and State Committee for Industrial Agriculture. I found thousands of documents in Kyiv, and with the help of two research assistants continued to search in Moscow, then Minsk, and finally down to the province and county level in Ukraine and Belarus. Bringing the documents home, I laid them out and sorted. That is when I saw I had a problem. The records were created during a period when Chernobyl was a censored topic in the USSR. Soviet leaders told the public that they had measured and found levels of radioactivity to be safe. That was good news, but I observed that public health officials were strongly encouraged to report just such wholesome news in their quarterly health accounts to back up the contention that the Soviet populace was getting happier and healthier every day. Some officials from territories contaminated with Chernobyl radioactivity dutifully sent charts supporting this narrative, but most officials strayed from this general line and recorded increasing frequencies of health problems. Two years after the accident, many, but not all, public health officials sent classified reports that showed troubling disease patterns rising each year after 1986.[3] In 1989, some doctors in contaminated territories pointed directly

---

[3] For more details and records, see Kate Brown, *Manual for Survival: A Chernobyl Guide to the Future*, (New York: W.W. Norton & Company, 2019).

to Chernobyl as a possible source for the elevated frequencies of disorders of the thyroid, cardiac, GI tract, and endocrine systems, plus growing numbers of cancers, and increases in fertility problems, infant death, and birth defects. In 1990, the Belarusian Minister of Health proclaimed that Belarus, where a large portion of Chernobyl fallout settled, was experiencing a public health disaster.[4] Experts in radiation medicine in Moscow and abroad refuted these claims. They insisted that the increased frequency of disease could not be from Chernobyl radioactivity because the doses were too low, compared to past instances of mass exposure in Hiroshima and Nagasaki. The local doctors were not specialists in radiation medicine; the Moscow and international experts were. The evidence of the first group screamed "disaster"; the evidence of the second said "all is well." I puzzled over these inconsistencies. Clearly, Soviet experts were having an argument that played out before me in the archives and continues to this day. How was a historian to decide who was right?

I sought a way to cross-check the records. The Anthropocene teaches us to focus on how natural systems and human systems interact, inseparably part of an integrated cycle. With this concept, the cycling of toxins out of industries and bombing sites into ecologies, from ecologies into bodies, and from bodies back to environments comes into focus as an important anthropogenic feature of the global metabolism.[5] The impossibly long lives of chemical and radioactive toxins gives historians new time scales to deal with and new sources to use. As toxins become part of

---

[4] V. S. Ulashchik, "Some medical aspects of the consequences of the accident at the Chernobyl, based on Byelorussian data," as reported in John Willis to Doug Mulhall, David McTaggart, August 14, 1990, GreenPeace Archive 1625, Amsterdam; and Ministerstvo zdravookhranennia Belorusskoi SSR v Ministerstva zdravookhranennia UkSSR, August 30, 1990, TsDAVO, 342/17/5220, 47–48.

[5] Following Rachel Carson, historians Linda Nash, Nancy Langston and Michelle Murphy, among others, have contributed to our understanding of the reciprocal nature of toxins humans spread in the environment which return to bodies. Linda Nash, *Inescapable Ecologies: A History of Environment, Disease, and Knowledge* (Berkeley: University of California Press, 2006); Michelle Murphy, *Sick Building Syndrome and the Problem of Uncertainty: Environmental Politics, Technoscience, and Women Workers* (Durham [N.C.]: Duke University Press, 2006); Nancy Langston, *Toxic Bodies: Hormone Disruptors and the Legacy of DES* (New Haven, CT: Yale University Press, 2010).

the environment, they also have an imprint on human bodies and ecologies that a historian can follow. And, while archives may fib, exaggerate, or outright lie, trees most likely do not. Historians of climate and Anthropocene histories draw on traces left in trees as archives to map the epoch. Could they not also help resolve disputes in nuclear history?

With that question, I decided to get a different kind of education to see if I could learn to read forests surrounding the blown Chernobyl plant like I read archives. I asked two biologists who regularly visit the Chernobyl Zone if I could join them. Tim Mousseau and Anders Møller invited me along on their twice annual trips. I learned a lot from them. I learned in a visceral way that timelines and periodization, that time itself – at the heart of most histories – makes much less sense in the Chernobyl context.

With the biologists, we went to the Red Forest, a ten square kilometer stretch of scotch pine that took the hardest hit of fallout from the burning Chernobyl reactor. After the accident, the trees turned red and died. Foresters cut them down and buried some, then thought better of it, and left the rest on the ground. Normally, when a tree dies, a horde of bacteria, fungi, larvae, and beetles swarm in to break down cellulose, resins, and polymers. This happens fast. In less than ten years a big tree is reduced to earth. But at levels of radiation of the Red Forest, microbes and invertebrates became seriously perturbed, and few larvae and beetles survived. Without their work, the process of decomposition slowed to the point that Mousseau and Møller found that the pines of the Red Forest, trees felled a quarter century before, which should have turned to dust, remained in place, fallen giants, 25 years after the accident.[6]

That fact astounded me. If Rumpelstiltskin woke up after a long nap in the Red Forest, he would have had trouble figuring out how much time had passed. Time is measured in things, and judging from nature, time in the Red Forest perceptively slowed. Historians try to glimpse time freeze-framed in the past, but finally finding a place where time stopped

---

[6] Timothy A. Mousseau, Gennadi Milinevsky, Jane Kenney-Hunt, Anders Møller, "Highly reduced mass loss rates and increased litter layer in radioactively contaminated areas," *Oecologia*, 2014, 175(1): 429–437; and "Chernobyl Trees Barely Decomposed, Study Finds," *NBC News*, March 26, 2014.

filled me with dread. The eerie stillness of the Red Forest underlined the lesson that decay, entropy, and expiration are essential for living.[7] Without the rich infusion of minerals into the soil by decaying trees, the living plants lag behind. The ground cover was brown and stunted. New pine trees did not grow tall and board-straight, but in short, shrubby balls.

Just as confusing, in other places in the greater Chernobyl Zone the reverse occurred. Time sped up. People and animals exposed to Chernobyl radioactivity experienced a rapid aging. Radioactive decay causes arteries to harden, vision to cloud with cataracts, and bone density to drop. Gastro-intestinal tracts slow. Men lose testosterone and sperm. Women's estrogen levels dwindle and eggs wither. These natural aspects of aging occurred prematurely in children and young adults who absorbed radioactive isotopes after the Chernobyl accident. Rather than the braking of time as in the Red Forest, residents of contaminated zones experienced an acceleration that hurtled them toward a premature old age. The Anthropocene fiddles with our understanding of time, some things slow down, others speed up. This problem is biological and chemical and also spiritual, philosophical, and historical.

Scale presents another problem when thinking of nuclear issues. The 1986 Chernobyl explosions released from 50 to 200 million curies of radioactivity. A year later in Goiania, Brazil, a couple of scavengers broke into an abandoned oncology ward and pried open a cobalt source that emitted 1,000 curies of radioactivity. In Goiania, four people died, two hundred people were hospitalized and two villages were bulldozed.[8] The International Atomic Energy Agency (IAEA) rated Goiania a level five accident and Chernobyl a level seven. The jump from 1,000 to 200,000,000 curies emitted into the environment ranked only a two-point difference on the IAEA scale. The work of bringing disparate events on the globe into the same frame by means of scale is a modernist project which geologists tracking and scaling the Anthropocene use. But, in the IAEA's case, what do those numbers, five and seven, mean? The

---

[7] On time, see Julian Barbour, *The End of Time: The Next Revolution in Physics* (New York: Oxford University Press, 2001): 11–15.

[8] Author interview with José Goldemberg, Saõ Paolo, Brazil, August 9, 2017.

certainties they seem to present quickly fade away on the ground. I found as I worked in the archives, that Soviet officials quickly lost track of radioactive contaminants spreading through the food chain.

These wrinkles in time and scale were unnerving. They belonged in science fiction, not in my history. Historians are used to thinking of time occurring with almost metronomic regularity over days, years, and decades. Historical timelines cannot speed up and slow down. Physicists puzzling over Schrodinger's cat, both dead and alive, would recognize my quandary. Time, they have argued for the last hundred years, expands and contracts in unpredictable ways, and that was the impression I had researching the Chernobyl accident. Most everywhere I looked, time was somersaulting around the clock. And it wasn't just happening in my research material. I read in the newspaper about cascades of extinctions and rising planetary temperatures that occurred over decades, not, as before, across millennia. On the other end of the spectrum, scientists explained that some inorganic chemicals, such as common plastics, can't be broken down; that they are, for all intents and purposes, eternal. These are the new challenges the Anthropocene presents historians, as we try to periodize and plot change over time, even as time is now elongated, foreshortened, and jumbled in the Anthropocene.

Following Mousseau and Møller, I learned on an elementary level to recognize the imprint of radioactive contaminants on the forests and swamps of Northern Ukraine and Southern Belarus. I came to notice in areas with high levels of radioactivity the twisting mutations of pines, their stunted, bonsai growth patterns, the paucity of birds, and absence of forest smells. After that education, I wanted to know more about the ecosystem when it is healthy.

The Chernobyl Plant is located in the Pripyat Marshes, Europe's largest swamp. In the sixties, Soviet hydrologists drained large portions of the swamp for agriculture and construction of what was projected to be Europe's largest nuclear power plant, while another segment of the swamp was turned into an Air Force bombing range. In 1961, soldiers resettled ten villages from the O'lmany swamp, about 300 kilometers from what later became the Chernobyl plant, to make room for the pilots' bomb paths. I asked a local forester, Ivan Gusin, to show me around the abandoned military site.

Gusin drove me in his jeep to the area where a village had once been. The cemetery was the only thing left, standing on a raised knoll, the highest ground for a mile. Gusin pointed out large cavities where fighter pilots had taken aim at the modest graves. I noticed a spindly pine tree growing from a bomb crater. It didn't look right. The pine needles were disorganized, curling in rounds rather than straight from the branch. A number of factors, including some viruses or fungi, can cause trees to mutate, but pines are especially vulnerable to radioactive decay.[9] I'd seen plenty of pines like this one inside the Chernobyl Zone. I asked Grusin how old he thought the tree was. About 40 years, he estimated. Pointing out that was ten years before Chernobyl, I asked Grusin if he saw many trees like this. Gusin shook his head, looking a bit disturbed. There were a lot of other pines around. None were growing out of a crater. None had mutations.

The sickly pine told me something. In the early nineties, after the USSR collapsed, people revealed secrets they had closely guarded for decades. In 1991, the politically well-connected Belarusian writer, Ales' Adamovich jotted in his diary that the Soviet army tested strategic nuclear weapons, the small battlefield variety, in the O'lmany bombing range.[10] I could not confirm that fact in the archives because the records of Soviet nuclear weapons development, stored in Moscow, are off-limits to researchers. That is the nature of state power. It can make the past go away as it is constituted in archives, if it so deems. But the sickly tree was a clue. I placed a photo of it in a file with other unverified accounts about nuclear tests in the ecologically sensitive marshes, much as Americans tested in Nevada, Mississippi, and the Marshall Islands.[11] The sacrifice zones of the Anthropocene are enormous. In the file, I had a note from an interview with a Belarusian doctor, Valentina Drozd, who told me she noticed an unusually high number of birth defects in the regions bordering the bombing range. The strange thing, she said, is the big

---

[9] B. V. Sorochinsky, "Molecular-biological nature of morphological abnormalities induced by chronic irradiation in coniferous plants from the Chernobyl exclusion zone: emphasis on a possible role of the cytoskeleton," *Cytology and Genetics*, 2003, 37: 49–55.

[10] Ales' Adamovich, *Imia sei zvesde Chernobyl'*, (Minsk: Kovcheg, 2006): 73.

[11] Greenpeace recorded "rumors" of testing in the marshes. VT to Science Unit, April 7, 1993, GPA 1002.

spike occurred among people born *before* the Chernobyl accident.[12] The file also contained a document detailing how the Belarusian government paid compensation to "veterans who took part in military exercises using atomic weapons."[13] I found a book called "Global Fallout of Radioactive Cesium" published in 1974 by the Russian Atomic Energy industry. The book described a four-year study that the biophysicist A. N. Marei carried out in the Pripyat Marshes in the 1960s. Marei showed up everywhere in the USSR where a clandestine nuclear accident occurred. Marei's team found that radioactive cesium had saturated the boggy, mineral-poor soils of the Marshes. He reported that plants, animals, mushrooms, and berries efficiently drank up radioactive cesium into their organisms and that human swamp-dwellers, who farmed and foraged for their food, had ten to thirty times more radioactive cesium in their bodies than residents of Kiev and Minsk. The book, censored before publication, attributed the swamp's radioactivity to fallout from U.S. nuclear weapons' tests.[14]

More generally, thinking about that crooked tree, I was struck by the persistence of radioactive contaminants in this part of the world. In the late 1980s, Soviet propagandists honed a public information campaign that repeatedly insisted "the danger was over," that the Chernobyl accident had ended. International agencies rallied to this message and reiterated it in the 1990s. But after Chernobyl, as before Chernobyl, the drumbeat of accidents continued at the two dozen Ukrainian nuclear power installations and missile sites. Sixty-six accidents and excursions at nuclear reactors in Ukraine occurred alone in the year after Chernobyl. In October 1991, reactor no. 2 of the Chernobyl plant blew a hole in the roof of the machine room. Footage showed another explosion, another

---

[12] Author telephone interview with Valentina Drozd, February 12, 2016. For evidence of abnormally high rates of birth defects, see "Spravka po pediatricheskoi sluzhbe Dobrusheskogo riaona," 1988, Natsionalnyi arkhiv respubliki Belarus (NARB) Minsk, Belarus 46/14/1261:134–136. On testing in the US, see Howard Ball, *Justice Downwind: America's Atomic Testing Program in the 1950's* (New York: Oxford University Press, 1986); and Sarah Alisabeth Fox, *Downwind: A People's History of the Nuclear West* (Lincoln, NE: Bison Books, 2014).

[13] "Protokol zasedaniia soveta po voprosu," January 16, 1992: Natsionalnyi arkhiv respubliki Belarus (NARB), Minsk, Belarus 507/1/12: 2–4.

[14] A. N. Marei, R. M. Barkhudarov, N. Ia. Novikova, *Global'nye vypadeniia Cs 137 i chelovek*, (Atomizdat: Moscow, 1974).

hole, another film crew exposed while capturing images of twisted rebar on celluloid. More mishaps occurred elsewhere in a quickening drumbeat as the Soviet political economy dissolved into fragments.[15] As the pace of accidents accelerated, they became mundane, no longer worthy of international media attention. The banality of catastrophe is another feature of the Anthropocene.[16]

After the 1986 accident, KGB officers counted over 600 unregulated nuclear waste depositories leaking into Ukrainian aquifers. Ukrainian KGB officers were also worried about chemical exposures at industrial sites, smog-filled cities located amidst belching factories, and poisoned water in communities peppered with uranium mine tailings.[17]

Every territory on Earth is the site of some former ecosystem and of contaminants produced in the Anthropocene, but there, in the midst of the Pripyat Marshes where I stood in rubber boots, which I did not need because of the unusually hot, dry spring in a succession of hot, dry springs, I grasped the dramatic changes in this place.[18] For nearly a

[15] "Informational Communiqué," November 30, December 6, and December, 1987, SBU 16/1/1256: 273–274, 303–304; February 11, February 17, April 8, May 10, and October 22, 1988, Haluzevyi derzhavnyi arkhiv Sluzhby bezpeky Ukrainy (SBU), Kyiv, Ukraine 16/1/1262: 61, 76, 151, 192–193; "Informational Communiqué," October 22, 1988, SBU 16/1/1266: 179; January 19, 1989, SBU 16/1/1273: 31–33; October 13 and October 24, 1989, SBU 16/1/1279: 112, 139; "Informational Communiqué," September 8, 1988, SBU 16/1/1266: 96–97; "Some Problems of Safety at NPP," August 6, 1990, 16/1/1288, 127–129; "Results of Safey Inspection at Rivne NPP with IAEA Methods," April 17 to May 18, 1987, RGAE 859/1/592: 118–127.

[16] Joseph Masco, "The crisis in crisis," *Current Anthropology*, 2017, 58(S15): S65–S76.

[17] "Informational Communiqué," November 23, December 6, and December 14, 1987, SBU 16/1/1256: 273–274, 303–304, 307–308; February 11, February 17, April 8 and May 10, 1988, SBU 16/1/1262: 61, 76, 151, 192–193; January 19, 1989, SBU 16/1/1273: 31–33; October 13 and October 24, 1989, SBU 16/1/1279: 111–112, 139; "Informational Communiqué," October 22, 1988, SBU 16/1/1266: 179; "To V.A. Ivashko from N. Holushko on Problems with Raising Safety at ChAES," SBU 16/1/1279: 111–112, 139, 178–180; and "Some Problems with Liquidating Consequences of ChAES Accident," November 14, 1990, SBU 16/1/1289: 43–48. On accidents at Soviet- built plants in Bulgaria, see "Circumstances at the Bulgarian NPP," November 13, 1990, SBU 16/1/1289: 41– 42.

[18] For two distinct versions of this narrative, see Martin Bürgener, *Pripet-Polessie: Das Bild Einer Polnischen Ostraum-Landschaft*, (Gotha, Germany: Justus Perthes, 1939); and Joice M. Mankivell, Sydney Loch, *The River of a Hundred Ways: Life in the War-Devastated Areas of Eastern Poland*, (London, UK: George Allen and Unwin Ltd, 1924). For commentary, see

century, Tsars, Polish, and German reformers planned to dry up the marshes and make them useful for human beings. In the mid-sixties, Soviet bulldozers accomplished that goal. In just a few decades, what had been a repository filtering and storing flood water and a massive carbon sink as well as a rich ecosystem held small farms and industries. Then, even more quickly, they turned the Pripyat "wasteland" into a true chemical and biological wasteland.

Staring at the crippled pine, I realized that the perforations of radioactive isotopes into the cellular structures of organisms of the swamp long pre-dated the day of the Chernobyl explosions. With that understanding, I saw that Chernobyl might better be conceived of as an acceleration than a one-off accident.[19] That is another insight of the Anthropocene; historians usually represent wars, emergencies, and disasters as if they have clear, chronological end points. As Julia Adeney Thomas points out in Chapter 2, we now grasp the open-ended quality of the Anthropocene. If, for example, a scientist graphed radioactive emissions around the Pripyat Marshes, it would show a point that starts in the late forties and rises upward in small jumps as Soviet and American generals detonated nuclear bombs in the Marshall Islands, Kazakhstan, Nevada, and Novaia Zemlia; the fallout from these tests circulating mostly in the northern hemisphere. In the early sixties the line would surge in greater and greater leaps as new nuclear powers tested bombs to reach a crescendo at the end of 1962 as the superpowers raced to test massive hydrogen bombs before the 1963 Atmospheric Nuclear Test Ban treaty.[20] After the test ban, the tracks on the graph would slip downward

---

David Blackbourn, *The Conquest of Nature: Water, Landscape, and the Making of Modern Germany* (New York: Norton, 2006). On the drying of the peat bogs, see "Rekomendatsii," April 14, 1990, Gosudarstvennyi arkhiv Mogilevskoi oblasti (GAMO), Mogilev, Belarus 7/5/4126: 84.

[19] John McNeill, Peter Engelke, *The Great Acceleration*, (Cambridge, MA: Harvard University Press, 2016).

[20] Nuclear weapons tests make up the primary man-made contribution of radioactive exposures to the world's population. Globally, atmospheric tests released at least 20 billion curies of radioactive iodine alone. Chernobyl issued far less at 45 million curies of iodine 131. Three-quarters of fallout from nuclear testing landed in the Northern Hemisphere. F. Owen Hoffman, A. Iulian Apostoaei, Brian A. Thomas. "A perspective on public concerns about exposure to fallout from the production and testing of nuclear

only to again flare up in 1986 and again in 1991 when reactor #1 blew and yet again when forest fires funneled through the Chernobyl Zone in 2017 and 2020 releasing radioactive gases stored in leaf litter and trees. A plan to dredge a large shipping canal called the E-40 through the Pripyat Marshes will pass within a few kilometers of the blown plant. If the canal is built, dredging could release radioactive isotopes in the swamp bottom, while the canal will dry the marshes causing the likelihood of fires to increase.[21] This graph would show how Chernobyl sits on a timeline of events involving a tangle of high-modernist plans of the twentieth century; a timeline in which war, preparation for war, reconstruction, commerce, production, nuclear emergencies, and accidents continued apace, war and peace entwining indistinguishably. The threat presented by the next "emergency" or the opportunity afforded by the next technology justified ever more radical and Earth-defying solutions.

One could also create other graphs of the same period to see the damage of a half century of nuclear bomb testing and nuclear-powered

weapons," *Health Physics*, 2002: 736–749; Gary J. Hancock, Stephen G. Tims, L. Keith Fifield, Ian T. Webster. "The release and persistence of radioactive anthropogenic nuclides," in *A Stratigraphical Basis for the Anthropocene*, ed. C. N. Waters (London: Geological Society, 2014), 265–281; John R. Cooper, Keith Randle, Ranjeet S. Sokhi, *Radioactive Releases in the Environment: Impact and Assessment* (New York: Wiley, 2003), 17; Australian Mission to the United Nations, November 26, 1974, and R. H. Wyndham to Dr. S. Sella, November 15, 1973, UN NY S- 0446– 0106- 09; and "Study of the Radiological Situation at the Atolls of Mururoa and Fangataufa," IAEA Board of Governors, Technical Cooperation Report for 1997, April 30, 1998, IAEA Board Of Governors, Box 33054. "Report of the United Nations Scientific Committee on the Effect of Atomic Radiation to the General Assembly," 2000, www.unscear.org/docs/reports/gareport.pdf (accessed October 2021). On equivalency with Hiroshima bombs, see "General Overview of the Effects of Nuclear Testing," CTBTO, www.ctbto.org/nuclear-testing/the-effects-of-nuclear-testing/general-overview-of-the-effects-of-nuclear-testing/ (accessed October 2021). Testimony of Owen Hoffman, "National Cancer Institute's Management of Radiation Studies," Hearing before the Permanent Subcommittee on Investigations, U.S. Senate, September 16, 1998, 48.

[21] Phoebe Weston, "Chernobyl Fears Resurface as River Dredging Begins in Exclusion Zone," *The Guardian*, December 23, 2020, sec. Environment, www.theguardian.com/environment/2020/dec/23/chernobyl-fears-resurface-over-contract-to-dredge-river-in-exclusion-zone-aoe (accessed October 2021).

"progress" on human health. As global fallout sifted down, mostly in the Northern Hemisphere, thyroid cancer frequencies grew exponentially. Human thyroids take up radioactive iodine which can cause cancer or thyroid disease. Rates of thyroid cancer in the United States tripled between 1974 and 2013, and better detection did not account for all the increases.[22] In Europe and North America, childhood leukemia, also radiogenic and which used to be a medical rarity, increased in incidence year by year after 1950.[23] Australia, hit by fallout from British and French nuclear bomb tests, has the highest incidence of childhood cancer worldwide.[24] American researchers discovered decades ago that exposure to radiation greatly reduces human sperm. An analysis of 42,000 men showed sperm counts among men in North America, Europe, Australia, and New Zealand dropped 52 per cent between 1973 and 2011. No such dip was recorded in other countries of the southern hemisphere that have Western medicine.[25] These statistics show a correlation, not a causal link. Whether these changes have to do with the concurrent blanketing of the northern hemisphere with radioactive fallout from over 500 nuclear bombs detonated into the atmosphere in the second half

---

[22] Hyeyeun Lim Susan S. Devesa, Julie A. Sosa, David Check, Cari M. Kitahara, "Trends in thyroid cancer incidence and mortality in the United States, 1974–2013," *Journal of the American Medical Association* 2017, 317(13): 1338–1348; B. A. Kilfoy, Tongzhang Zheng, Theodore R. Holford, et al. "International patterns and trends in thyroid cancer incidence, 1973–2002," *Cancer Causes Control* 2009, 20: 525–531; and F. De Vathaire, V. Drozdovitch, P. Brindel, et al., "Thyroid cancer following nuclear tests in French Polynesia," *British Journal of Cancer* 2010, 103: 1115–1121.

[23] Peter Kaatsch, "Epidemiology of childhood cancer," *Cancer Treatment Reviews* 2010, 36 (4): 277–285; National Cancer Institute, "SEER Cancer Statistics Review, 1975–2013," https://seer.cancer.gov/archive/csr/1975_ 2013/#contents (accessed October 2021). Upward trends are not a given; in Brazil, for example, they declined. Arnaldo Cézar Couto, "Trends in childhood leukemia mortality over a 25-year period," *Jornal de Pediatria (Rio J)* 2010, 86(5): 405–410.

[24] Children's Leukemia and Cancer Research Foundation, https://childcancer research .com.au/ (accessed October 2021).

[25] Hagai Levine, Niels Jorgensen, Jaime Mendiola, Hagai Levine, Anderson Martino-Andrade, Irina Mindlis, Shanna H. Swan, et al., "Temporal Trends in Sperm Count: A Systematic Review and Meta- Regression Analysis," *Human Reproduction Update* 23, no. 6 (December 2017): 646– 59.

of the twentieth century, is a question few scientists have tackled.[26] That job is apparently a chore left to humanists.

How does the nuclear Anthropocene offer a window on understanding the large planetary changes of the past century? It gives pause to historians who have written the human past on a supposedly firm foundation of temporal struts and beams. Scientists have used scale in similar fashion to think across disparate events in order to equate and compare them. Much like solid ground quivering in an earthquake, the nuclear Anthropocene shows that, when perturbed, time liquifies and scale dissolves. With such realizations, arguments over a "starting point" for the Anthropocene and measuring a "baseline" for damage become political more than empirical exercises. The spread of radioactive fallout is so grand, has so saturated daily existence, that humans have had a hard time seeing it, even as it reconfigures ecologies and bodies.

---

[26] While a great deal of research has been done on a few outcomes of exposure to high levels of radiation (Japanese bomb survivor studies) – especially as related to thyroid cancer and leukemia, far less research has been carried out on low-level, chronic radiation among the general population. The epidemiologist, Ernest Sternglass, did take this problem seriously in his publications. He was greatly maligned for his research. See Ernest Sternglass, *Secret Fallout: Low Level Radiation from Hiroshima to Three Mile Island*, (McGraw Hill: New York, 1981). For repeated calls to use Chernobyl to study chronic low level radiation, see Ernest Sternglass, "Chernobyl: Mission to Russian Federation, Belarus, Ukraine," September 10–16, 1994, UN NY S-1082/46/5/ acc. 2007/0015; "For Information on United Nations, Press Conference Chernobyl," November 30, 1995, Archive of the United Nations, New York (UN NY) S-1082/46/5/ acc. 2007/0015; "A. M. Zlenko, A. N. Sychev, S. V. Lavrov to Mr. Boutros Boutros-Ghali," January 9, 1995, UN NY S-1082/46/5, acc. 2007/0015; "Strengthening of the Coordination of Humanitarian and Disaster Relief Assistance," September 8, 1995, UN NY S-1082/46/5/ acc. 2007/0015; "Strengthening of International Cooperation and Coordination of Efforts to Study, Mitigate and Minimize the Consequences of the Chernobyl Disaster," October 27, 1997, "Press Conference on Funding to Address Effects of Chernobyl Disaster," May 1, 1998, Sergio Vieira de Mello, May 18, 1999, "Note to the Secretary-General," April 23, 2001, UN NY S-1092/96/5, acc. 2006/0160. "Notes of the Secretary-General's meeting with the Minister of Foreign Affairs of Ukraine"; "Meeting of Jan Eliasson and Victor H. Batik," February 25, 1993; and "Meeting with Gennadi Buravkin, Belarus," March 4, 1993, WHO E16–445-11: 16.

CHAPTER 9

Stratigraphy: Finding Global Markers in a Small Canadian Lake

Francine McCarthy

Crawford Lake is small, but has many stories to tell through the sedimentary layers beneath its surface. This unique lake on the Niagara Escarpment of Ontario, Canada is so deep that its sedimentary record is undisturbed by wind or burrowing water-dwelling animals, and therefore razor-sharp. Little light filters down the nearly 24 metres to the lakebed, but geologists can see into the past by examining core samples made up of thin layers called varves, each recording sedimentation during a single year. One annual layer comprises light (inorganic calcite) and dark (organic) sediment that, like tree rings, allow scientists to read and date Earth's past going back almost 1000 years. For instance, the fossils of microscopic aquatic organisms and the chemical characteristics of the varved sediments trace impacts, human and otherwise. Ice sheets ripped the roof off a former limestone cave as they retreated about 12,000 years ago, creating the deep basin of Crawford Lake. Some stories recorded in the varves are local, such as evidence of ecosystem disruption by Iroquoians farming near its shores between the late thirteenth and fifteenth centuries, or by a lumber mill that operated on its south shore when Canada was still a very young country in the late nineteenth century. The most recent layers, however, tell a new story of human activities on a global scale that impacted even this small lake in a conservation area in a rural area of southern Ontario. These varves record the dramatic impact of the Nuclear Era and the Great Acceleration in the mid-twentieth century, the event chosen by the Anthropocene Working Group to define the base (or beginning) of our human-dominated epoch. Crawford Lake is now one of the places being investigated as a potential type section ('golden spike') to define the Anthropocene as a formal interval of geologic time. Under my leadership, 'Team Crawford' is part of this effort, working to demonstrate how the chemical and fossil component of the varves capture the essence of our altered planet since the early 1950s.

There have been many large-scale climatic changes over the last 12,000 years of the Holocene (Yu et al., 1997; Yu, 2000), but it is the activities of humans over the last seven centuries that most impacted the lake (Rybak and Dickman, 1988; Ekdahl et al., 2004, 2007; Turton and McAndrews, 2006; Krueger and McCarthy, 2016; McCarthy et al., 2018). No one can be sure when the first human saw Crawford Lake, but Iroquoian people decided to settle near its shores by the late thirteenth century, cultivating crops to supplement game hunted from the surrounding mixed forest in the Great Lakes region of what would eventually become Canada (Finlayson, 1998). In the 1970s, scientists studying the lake's sediments found pollen of such crops as maize and sunflower in varves dating back to the middle of the last millennium, alerting them to the presence of this Iroquoian settlement (Boyko, 1973; Boyko-Diakonow, 1979; McAndrews and Boyko-Diakonow, 1989). Archaeological excavations soon followed in the 1970s and 80s (Finlayson, 1998).

Today thousands of people who visit the reconstructed village annually get a good sense of how Iroquoian people lived over 500 years ago. Six cedar bark longhouses have been constructed on their original positions and contain artefacts, such as stone tools and pottery, that have been unearthed from the site during excavations (Park Details – Crawford Lake (conservationhalton.ca)). Each of the longhouses would have been occupied by several dozen members of an individual matrilineal clan, with two families living across from one another and sharing a hearth. Archaeological evidence suggests that the village was occupied for around 50 years in the fourteenth century, 35 years in the early fifteenth century, and perhaps an additional 25–30 years in the latest fifteenth–earliest sixteenth century (Finlayson et al., in prep.). A short, accessible boardwalk trail of only 1.4 km allows visitors to circle this small body of water, reading signs explaining the flora and fauna of the Niagara Escarpment and the unique characteristics of Crawford Lake.

In 1883, the Crawford family emigrated from Great Britain and George Crawford bought the lake and 100 acres of land surrounding it.

George and his son Murray began farming the land where the Iroquoian village had once stood, and they started logging huge white pines whose jagged-spired stumps can still be seen along the rocky shores of the lake. They operated a sawmill on the south shore of the lake in the latter decades of the nineteenth century, providing lumber for industry in the newly confederated Canada, and the lake was officially named Crawford Lake in 1898 (The Longhouse People of Crawford Lake | Hiking the GTA; Park Details - Crawford Lake (conservationhalton.ca)).

The increase in nutrients associated with these human activities (a phenomenon called cultural eutrophication) caused algae to bloom, allowing their consumers, such as water fleas and tiny rotifers or 'wheel animals', to thrive in the lake that had been nutrient-poor (oligotrophic) prior to human impact (Ekdahl et al., 2004, 2007; Turton and McAndrews, 2006; Krueger and McCarthy, 2016). While an increase in nutrients might sound like a good thing, the lake ecosystem was permanently altered, not only by the hundreds of people who inhabited the longhouses, but by animals attracted to the crops that would have included the 'three sisters' of maize, squash, and beans planted close together to help one another (like sisters). Nitrogen fixed by beans from the atmosphere was available to the nitrogen-requiring maize through their roots, the corn stalks providing the beans with a natural trellis to grow on, and the squash plants providing ground cover that controlled weeds and limited moisture loss through evaporation. Droppings, most of which DNA tests confirm were deposited by Canada geese, are common in sediments rich in spores produced by the pathogens that attack cultigens, such as corn smut, as well as pollen that are evidence of nearby cultivation (McAndrews and Turton, 2007, 2010). Although microfossils record improvement in water quality after the village was abandoned, the lake did not return to pre-disturbance conditions in the nearly 400 years between the late-fifteenth century and when the Crawfords started to clear the land. This demonstrates the long-lasting human impacts on ecosystems and the difficulty in fully restoring pristine conditions (McCarthy et al., 2018).

More significantly, all the additional biomass resulting from cultural eutrophication eventually sank to the lakebed of this naturally fishless lake (the Crawfords introduced sportfish to the lake in the late nineteenth century) causing oxygen to be depleted from bottom waters, as it was consumed by bacterial decomposition. This anoxia inhibited further decomposition, allowing exceptional preservation of rarely fossilized things, such as the cellulosic covering of dinoflagellates – the single-celled algae that produce 'red tides' (Krueger, 2012; McCarthy and Krueger, 2013). In fact, the resting cysts of several dinoflagellate species germinated when one of my graduate students let the test tubes containing sediment and water sit over the weekend instead of immediately continuing with acid treatment as planned. Imagine our surprise when the slurry she eventually mounted on microscope slides was found to contain abundant dinoflagellates representing all stages of algal development – including some actually undergoing cell division! Even more surprising was that the oldest sediments that contained viable cell contents were deposited before 1867 – the year Canada became a country (Krueger, 2012; Krueger and McCarthy, 2016).

We know exactly how old the cysts that germinated are because the light–dark sediment couplets accumulate annually in the deep basin of Crawford Lake, so that we can count back in time (Boyko-Diakonow, 1979). The varve-count ages have also been confirmed using 23 radiocarbon dates over a 78.8-cm freeze core collected in 2001 (Ekdahl et al., 2004). When sunlight warms the upper waters during the late spring and summer, calcium and carbonate dissolved from the 425-million-year-old limestone precipitates, and tiny crystals of light-coloured calcite (the mineral that chalk is made of) sink slowly and accumulate on the lakebed. Organic matter that accumulates during the rest of the year, but particularly during winter-kill of plankton in late fall and early winter, forms the dark layer of the varve (Dickman, 1985).

Now that geologists have decided to propose formalization of the interval of geologic time defined by pervasive human impact (Working Group on the 'Anthropocene' | Subcommission on Quaternary Stratigraphy), a geologic sequence must be designated as the type section to define the beginning of this geologic time interval. This decision was taken in 2019 and a formal proposal is expected in 2022. A Global Boundary Stratotype Section and Point (GSSP) is an internationally agreed stratigraphic section which serves as the reference for a boundary on the geologic time scale, identifying the beginning of an interval of geologic time (and thus, the end of the preceding interval). The GSSPs have earned the nickname 'golden spikes' with reference to the custom upon completing railway lines in the nineteenth century, and now small round golden plaques made of brass are typically embedded into rock sections to signify the precise position of a new geological time interval. There hasn't been enough time for cliffs of rock to form over the short period humans have substantially altered the Earth System (see Steffen Chapter 3), so possible candidate GSSPs that will literally define what it means to *be* Anthropocene include cave deposits, peat bogs, and coral reefs as well as lake and marine sediments (Anthropocene Working Group, 2020).

A clear majority of the 34 person Anthropocene Working Group panel (88%) voted in favour of looking for a potential GSSP to define the Anthropocene Epoch, with a starting date in the mid-twentieth century (Working Group on the 'Anthropocene' | Subcommission on Quaternary Stratigraphy). While there is much evidence of earlier anthropogenic impact (even on tiny, secluded Crawford Lake), stressors like agriculture and industrialization affected different parts of our planet at different times. This would lead to a multitude of 'local Anthropocenes', but the beginning of a formal interval of geologic time is, by definition, synchronous and globally correlatable. Fallout from early thermonuclear nuclear weapons testing during the Cold War is an anthropogenic marker that meets those criteria (Waters et al., 2015 and Brown, Chapter 8). The Great Acceleration of the post-war interval is recorded by atmospheric deposition of the byproducts of enormous consumption of energy around the world (Steffen et al., 2015; Syvitski et al., 2020). GSSPs are stratigraphic entities – as is the geologic time scale that they help formalize – so the stratigraphic studies at Crawford Lake and the other potential candidates for the golden spike are essential to the formal designation of the Anthropocene Epoch.

Small, very deep lakes are good potential GSSP candidates (Waters et al., 2018) because wind cannot mix the entire water column, allowing sediments to accumulate undisturbed. Such lakes are called 'meromictic' and waters below the depth to which wind can mix are effectively isolated from the atmosphere (Zadereev et al., 2017). (In Crawford Lake, the wind affects nothing below 15 metres, meaning that the bottom 9 metres rest in tomb-like stillness.) As a result, one of the other potential candidates being assessed by stratigraphers to formally define the beginning of the Anthropocene Epoch is another varved meromictic lake – Longwan Maar in China (Anthropocene Working Group, 2020). Varve counts allow the base of the Anthropocene to be dated (probably 1950 or 1952 CE), and any sediments above that varve containing the basal signal (such as the earliest traces of nuclear fallout) would be considered to have been deposited during the Anthropocene, while those just below would be said to have been deposited at the end of the Holocene Epoch. Even relatively remote idyllic lakes like Crawford Lake record evidence of major ecosystem changes resulting from the Great Acceleration in sediments deposited since the mid-twentieth century (Gushulak et al., 2021).

For many decades it was assumed that the annual laminae remained undisturbed in the deep basin of Crawford Lake because bottom waters lacked oxygen, preventing clams and other burrowing animals from inhabiting the deep basin of the lake. All publications about the deep basin of Crawford Lake described the water below the mixing zone as anoxic (Boyko, 1973; Boyko-Diakonow, 1979; Dickman, 1985; Rybak and Dickman, 1988; Ekdahl et al., 2004, 2007; Krueger and McCarthy, 2016), which is virtually always the case in meromictic lakes because oxygen bacterial decomposition of organic matter on the lakebed quickly consumes the available oxygen (Zadereev et al., 2017). This is what normally prevents animals from inhabiting and churning up the sediments in deep basins of meromictic lakes, allowing varves to accumulate undisturbed. However, Team Crawford's measurements of physical and chemical properties of the water column, when we collected freeze cores as part of the Anthropocene GSSP Project (funded by the Haus der Kulturen der Welt in Berlin), identified almost as much oxygen above the lakebed in the deep basin as at the surface (McCarthy, 2020). I initially thought the probe had not been calibrated correctly, but measurements through the 2020 water year revealed sufficient oxygen to allow survival of organisms with aerobic metabolisms (those who breathe oxygen – in other words, all life other than some bacteria; Gooday et al., 2009) throughout the water column (Heyde, 2021). In fact, we also routinely collected plankton samples through the water column in the deepest part of the basin and found that zooplankton were abundant above the lakebed through the winter months, migrating toward the surface in late spring and feeding on the abundant algae there through the warm months (Heyde, 2021)

Our one-year study of the water column demonstrated that the waters that dissolved the limestone basin (as well as many other sinkholes and caves in the Late Silurian-aged limestone; Priebe et al., 2018) continue to flow through groundwater flow zones called aquifers (Llew-Williams et al., 2020). The lower 9 metres of the deep basin contain highly conductive ('saline') water that is groundwater that flows out of the rock, and its density is another factor that isolates it from the fresh, low-density water above it that is primarily derived from rain and melting snow. The groundwater also transports enough dissolved oxygen into the deep basin of Crawford Lake to allow microscopic animals like water fleas to overwinter there, in waters that remain relatively warm (5–6 °C) when ice up to 1 metre thick builds up at the surface (this is the stable platform we prefer to use to collect sediment cores).

Despite the presence of oxygen, the varves remain undisturbed because burrowing animals tolerant of the high conductivity ('salinity') in the bottom waters were simply not able to colonize the deep basin of Crawford Lake. The largest animals below the mixing zone are tiny crustaceans called ostracods, whose calcareous shells that they shed when they moult are less than 1 mm in diameter, that are adapted to living in groundwater and known from caves worldwide (Karakaş and Külköylüoğlu, 2008; Özuluğ et al., 2018). These ostracods apparently migrated into the deep basin through groundwater flowing through aquifers because the species that occupy the deep basin are not found in the upper mixing zone of Crawford Lake. Our analysis of the micro-fossil record in the varved sediments revealed that aerobic (oxygen-breathing) organisms lived on and above the lakebed in the deep basin except for a few (geologically) short intervals when tiny moulted shells ceased to accumulate on the deep basin lakebed (Heyde, 2021). Only occasionally, when people inhabited the longhouses and for several decades during the late nineteenth–early twentieth century, when the lumber mill operated at the south end of the lake, did the influx of biomass exceed the oxygen available to decomposers (Chan et al., submitted). In other words, the small deep basin is a limestone cave environment hidden below a larger 'normal' lake has almost always had oxygenated water, even though it is completely isolated from the atmosphere.

While very unusual and interesting, why is the fact that water in the deep basin of this unique meromictic lake is *not* anoxic relevant to the quest for a GSSP? This is because the primary marker chosen by the Anthropocene Working Group to define the Anthropocene (and the reason for the mid-twentieth century designation) is plutonium-239 (^{239}Pu). This fissionable material used in nuclear weapons is very rare in nature, but sediments deposited during the Cold War contain relatively high concentrations, deposited as fallout from atmospheric tests (UNSCEAR, 2000). Because the half-life of ^{239}Pu is 24,110 years, its radioactivity will remain detectable for the next quarter of a million years (by comparison, the half-life of radiocarbon is only 5,730 years), making it useful as a chronostratigraphic marker for countless generations to come.

Because they represent one moment in time, markers that define the beginning of a geologic time unit such as the Anthropocene Epoch should be deposited world-wide and preserved in sediments, identifying them as having been deposited during that interval. Because plutonium fallout can be dated very precisely, it will be possible to place the base of the Anthropocene at a specific year – probably 1952 when a pronounced increase in nuclear testing occurred (Figure 9.1). Unfortunately, ^{239}Pu is readily mobilized in the reducing (anoxic) conditions that characterize most depositional environments that allow sediments to accumulate undisturbed (Kaplan et al., 2004). Crawford Lake has the very rare combination of varved sediments accumulating in a meromictic lake with oxygenated bottom waters, so the plutonium that accumulated in varves in 1952 will stay in place rather than 'bleeding' into the sediments and making the boundary less knife-sharp.

Although we have measured a strong radiocarbon 'bomb spike' between the sediments deposited between 1949 and 1950 and those whose varve count dates them between 1955 and 1957 CE (A.E. Lalonde AMS Laboratory report, March 13, 2020), as I write this, sediments from Crawford Lake have yet to be analyzed for ^{239}Pu. The reason for the lag may, ironically, have to do with the warming of our planet. The winter of 2019–20 wasn't cold enough to allow thick ice to form, and ice at least 30 cm thick is needed for Team Crawford to walk onto the

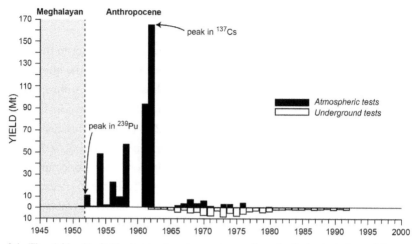

9.1. The yields of individual tests of nuclear weapons allow detailed calculations of the fallout of radionuclides from the atmosphere. The atomic bombs that brought an end to the Second World War are barely detectable, but there is a marked increase in 1952, essential to the proposed beginning of the Anthropocene, which would mark the end of the Holocene, and thus the boundary between the Late Holocene (Meghalayan) Age and the Anthropocene Epoch. The ban on nuclear testing between November 1959 and February 1960 is clearly visible, and the peak occurred in 1963. Modified from UNSCEAR (2000).

lake and collect cores from the lakebed. These are called 'freeze cores' because the samplers consist of a slurry of dry ice and ethanol in a hollow metallic sampler that freezes a rind of the lake onto it, allowing the varves to remain distinct, without compression. We need to collect enough sediments for all the required tests (including fuel ash and black carbon, ^{210}lead and ^{237}caesium, in addition to ^{239}Pu) that the Anthropocene Working Group needs to assess the suitability of the various potential GSSPs in order to choose the best one to propose to the International Commission on Stratigraphy. As I finish this essay in the winter of 2020–21, we are hoping for a long hard winter to allow for a successful freeze coring expedition. If the plutonium signature is strong, the varved sequence from Crawford Lake will be a strong candidate to define the Anthropocene Epoch.

If Crawford Lake is selected as the site for the Anthropocene GSSP, it would be impossible to install a 'golden spike' in situ. In any case, putting a brass plaque 15 cm into the sediment at the bottom of this very deep lake would be pointless since these sections have to be readily accessible. Instead, the GSSP would be in a freeze core collected from the deep basin and archived at a secure site. There is precedent, since the base of the Greenlandian and Northgrippian stages of the Holocene are both defined by GSSPs in ice cores archived at the University of Copenhagen (Walker et al., 2008, 2009). I think that it would be fitting to have the freeze core from Crawford Lake housed in a museum, given the centrality of human beings to this story. The core would probably be archived at the Royal Ontario Museum in Toronto, which has a long history of investigation of the varves, primarily out of the lab of then Curator of Botany John (Jock) McAndrews. Jock was my Masters thesis supervisor and he also supervised the MSc research of Maria Boyko, who is something of a hero in this story. By painstakingly examining microscope slides from all grasses in the museum's pollen reference collection, Boyko identified the abundant pollen in varves deposited between the thirteenth and fifteenth centuries as *Zea mays*, the cereal grain first domesticated in southern Mexico about 10,000 years ago. She inferred that the pollen of cultigens implied the existence of a nearby Iroquoian village, and – undeterred by the skepticism of her supervisor – she discovered from Thomas Howard that he had found several artefacts while tilling the fields where the village now stands. The Conservation Authority that bought the land from him funded the first archaeological excavation in 1971, resulting in the reconstructed village that stands there today. Team Crawford is using this unique meromictic lake to chart the distant past and recent human impacts, but without Bokyo's determination and scientific curiosity, the site might well be developed by now instead of providing insights into deep time and human culture. The varves in the deep basin of this readily accessible but protected conservation area may literally define the interval of geologic time in which we live.

REFERENCES

Anthropocene Working Group (2020) Newsletter, Volume 10: Report of activities 2020. http://quaternary.stratigraphy.org/wp-content/uploads/2021/03/AWG-Newsletter-2020-Vol-10.pdf (accessed October 2021).

Boyko M (1973) European impacts on the vegetation around Crawford Lake in Southern Ontario. Unpublished M.S. thesis, Department of Botany, University of Toronto, Ontario, 114pp.

Boyko-Diakonow M (1979) The laminated sediments of Crawford Lake, southern Ontario, Canada. In: Schluchter, C. (Ed.), *Moraines and Varves.* A. A. Balkema, Rotterdam, pp. 303–307.

Dickman MD (1985) Seasonal succession and microlamina formation in a meromictic lake displaying varved sediments. *Sedimentology* 32:109–118.

Ekdahl EJ, Teranes JL, Guilderson TP, et al. (2004) A prehistorical record of cultural eutrophication from Crawford Lake, Canada. *Geology* 32:745–748.

Ekdahl EJ, Teranes JL, Wittkop CA, et al. (2007) Diatom assemblage response to Iroquoian and Euro-Canadian eutrophication of Crawford Lake, Ontario, Canada. *J Paleolimnol* 37:233–246.

Finlayson WD (1998) *Iroquoian Peoples of the Land of Rocks and Water A.D. 1000 to 1650: A Study in Settlement Archaeology.* London Museum of Archaeology, London, UK, 448pp.

Gooday A, Jorissen F, Levin L, et al. (2009) Historical records of coastal eutrophication-induced hypoxia. *Biogeosci Discuss* 6:2567–2658.

Gushulak AC, Marshall M, Cumming BF, et al. (2021) Siliceous algae response to the 'Great Acceleration' of the mid-twentieth century in Crawford Lake (Ontario, Canada): a potential candidate for the Anthropocene GSSP. *Anthropocene Review* https://doi.org/10.1177/20530196211046036

Heyde A (2021) *Crawford Lake Consumers: Water Column and Palynological Studies.* MSc Thesis, Brock University, St. Catharines, Ontario, Canada, 147 pp.

Kaplan DI, Powell BA, Demirkanli DI, et al. (2004) Influence of oxidation states on plutonium mobility during long-term transport through an unsaturated subsurface environment. *Environ Sci Technol* 38:5053–5058.

Karakaş Sarı P, Külköylüoğlu O (2008). Comparative ecology of Ostracoda (Crustacea) in two rheocrene springs (Bolu, Turkey). *Ecol Res* 23:821–830.

Krueger AM (2012) Freshwater dinoflagellates as proxies of cultural eutrophication: a case study from Crawford Lake, Ontario. MSc thesis, Brock University, St Catharines, Ontario, 97pp.

Krueger AM, McCarthy FMG (2016) Great Canadian Lagerstätten 5: Crawford Lake – a Holocene lacustrine Konservat-Lagerstätte with two-century-old viable dinoflagellate cysts. *Geosci Canada* 43:123–132.

Llew-Williams BM, McCarthy FMG, Turner KW, et al. (2020) Limno-chemical mystery resolved for Crawford Lake, Ontario, Canada; GSSP candidate for the Anthropocene Epoch. Conference paper. Geological Society of America – Virtual Conference, October 2020.

McAndrews JH, Boyko-Diakonow M (1989) Pollen analysis of varved sediment at Crawford Lake, Ontario: evidence of Indian and European farming. In: Fulton, R.J. (Ed.), *Quaternary Geology of Canada and Greenland, Geology of Canada,* vol. 1. Geological Survey Canada, Boulder, CO, pp. 528–530.

McAndrews JH, Turton, CL (2007) Canada geese transported cultigen pollen grains to Crawford Lake from 14th and 15th century Iroquoian maize fields. *Palynol* 31:9–18.

McAndrews JH, Turton, CL (2010) Fungal spores record Iroquoian and Canadian agriculture in 2nd millennium A.D. sediment of Crawford Lake, Ontario, Canada. *Veg Hist Archaeobot* 19:495–501.

McCarthy FMG (2020) Crawford Lake – *NOT* anoxic??? *Canadian Assoc. Palynol Newsletter* 43:5–10.

McCarthy FMG, Krueger AM (2013) Freshwater dinoflagellates in paleolimnological studies: Peridinium cysts as proxies of cultural eutrophication in the southeastern Great Lakes region of Ontario, Canada. In: Lewis, J.M., Marret, F., Bradley, L. (Eds.) *Biological and Geological Perspectives of Dinoflagellates*. The Micropalaeontological Society, Special Publications. Geological Society, London, UK, pp. 133–139.

McCarthy FMG, Riddick NL, Volik O, Danesh DC, Krueger AM (2018) Algal palynomorphs as proxies of human impact on freshwater resources in the Great Lakes region. *Anthropocene* 21:16–31.

Özuluğ O, Kubanç SN, Kubanç C, Demirci GI (2018) Checklist of Quaternary and Recent Ostracoda (Crustacea) species from Turkey with information on habitat preferences. *Turkish J Biosci Coll* 2:51–100.

Priebe EH, Brunton FJ, Rudolph DL, Neville CJ (2018) Geologic controls on hydraulic conductivity in a karst-influenced carbonate bedrock groundwater system in southern Ontario, Canada. *Hydrogeol J* 27:1291–1308.

Rybak M, Dickman M (1988) Paleoecological reconstruction of changes in the productivity of a small, meromictic lake in Southern Ontario, Canada. *Hydrobiologia* 169:293–306.

Steffen W, Broadgate W, Deutsch L, Gaffney O, Ludwig C (2015) The trajectory of the Anthropocene: The Great Acceleration. *The Anthropocene Review* 2:81–98.

Syvitski J, Waters CN, Day J, et al. (2020) Extraordinary human energy consumption and resultant geological impacts beginning around 1950 CE initiated the proposed Anthropocene Epoch. *Commun Earth Environ* 1: 32.

Turton CL, McAndrews, JH (2006) Rotifer loricas in second millennium sediment of Crawford Lake, Ontario, Canada. *Rev Palaeobot Palynol* 141:1–6.

UNSCEAR (United Nations Scientific Committee on the Effects of Atomic Radiation) (2000) Sources and effects of ionizing radiation. *UNSCEAR 2000 Report to the General Assembly, with Scientific Annexes. Volume I: Sources.* United Nations, New York. www.unscear.org/docs/publications/2000/ UNSCEAR_2000_Report_Vol.I.pdf (accessed October 2021).

Walker M, Johnsen S, Rasmussen SO, et al. (2008) The Global Stratotype Section and Point (GSSP) for the base of the Holocene Series/Epoch (Quaternary System/Period) in the NGRIP ice core. *Episodes* 31:264–267.

Walker M, Johnsen S, Rasmussen SO, et al. (2009) Formal definition and dating of the GSSP (Global Stratotype Section and Point) for the base of the Holocene using the Greenland NGRIP ice core, and selected auxiliary records. *J Quaternary Sci* 24:3–17.

Waters CN, Syvitski JPM, Gałuszkaet A, et al. (2015) Can nuclear weapons fallout mark the beginning of the Anthropocene Epoch? *Bull Atomic Sci* 71:46–45.

Waters CN, Zalasiewicz J, Summerhayes C, et al. (2018) Global Boundary Stratotype Section and Point (GSSP) for the Anthropocene Series: where and how to look for potential candidates. *Earth-Science Reviews* 178:379–429.

Yu ZC (2000) Ecosystem responses to late-glacial and early-Holocene climate oscillations in the Great Lakes region of North America. *Quaternary Sci Rev* 19:1723–1747.

Yu ZC, McAndrews JH, Eicher U (1997) Middle Holocene dry climate caused by change in atmospheric circulation patterns: Evidence from lake levels and stable isotopes. *Geology* 25:251–254.

Zadereev ES, Boehrer B, Gulati RD (2017) Introduction: meromictic lakes, their terminology and geographic distribution. In R.D. Gulati et al. (Eds.), *Ecology of Meromictic Lakes*, Ecological Studies 228, Springer International Publishing, New York, 405pp.

CHAPTER 10

Curating the Anthropocene at Berlin's Haus der Kulturen der Welt

Bernd Scherer

Hurricanes, heat waves, droughts, wildfires, and floods – nowadays such natural disasters are not purely natural anymore, but heightened and sometimes even provoked by humankind. These changes destroy people's livelihoods, trigger mass migration, and destabilize entire societies in the process. It is increasingly evident that the promise of modernity – to subdue the Earth and its material processes to human control – is losing its plausibility.

In 2010, we at Haus der Kulturen der Welt (HKW, House of World Cultures) asked ourselves what a cultural institution should look like in the twenty-first century. Quickly, we realized that it was no longer a matter of showcasing world cultures in Berlin, which was the role originally assigned to the HKW. Rather, the deep social and cultural changes caused by planetary processes inevitably had to be in the spotlight. The accelerating speed at which our life-giving environments are being transformed generates an urgent need to not only understand these processes but to intervene in them, since the very existence of humanity and that of other species depends on them. Our "Welt" has changed dramatically, and thus the Haus der Kulturen der Welt has had to shift its focus and redefine itself to put this dangerous new world center stage.

In 2010, we decided to embark on a deep exploration of the fundamental social and planetary processes of transformation. Inspired and influenced by the 2009 climate summit in Copenhagen, we inaugurated the project "Über-Lebenskunst" (2011), sometimes translated as "the art of survival." Instead of understanding climate change, biodiversity loss, and all else as processes over which we have absolutely no control, the project's guiding principle was to place the focus on the agency of individuals, groups, and even entire societies. The project's title entailed a dual meaning, alluding on the one hand to the "art of survival" and on the other asking what might constitute a good life in the early twenty-first century. Berlin was and is home to a broad range of social, political, and cultural groups experimenting with new ways of life. With this in mind, we formulated a "call for future," to which an enormous number of local groups responded. The most significant among the proposed projects addressed mobility, housing, resources, and food. Out of approximately 800 applications we selected 30 projects and in addition invited artists and scientists to join us. After an intense period of collaboration lasting over a year, we presented many of these projects at the "Über-Lebenskunst-Festival." The artist collective known as "my villages" installed an infrastructure that could supply 10,000 people with local food for a period of eight days. The architects known as "fatkoehl" created multi-purpose, easily movable meeting spaces which were not only used at the festival, but reappeared in various contexts around Berlin in the following years. Finally, a handbook for sustainable art production was compiled and circulated throughout Germany with the help of our cooperation partner Kulturstiftung des Bundes.

"Über-Lebenskunst" put the spotlight on new forms of life practices, but it was a bottom-up project without any grand theoretical framework. However, during our research for the project, I came upon the Anthropocene hypothesis. Immediately it was clear to me that the concept of the Anthropocene was excellently suited as a thought framework for our treatment of the processes of transformation. We immediately contacted Jan Zalasiewicz (see Chapter 1) and Colin Waters of the Anthropocene Working Group (AWG), who, from the very beginning, expressed their willingness to collaborate with us. At the same time, we developed an intense working relationship with the Max-Planck-Institut für Wissenschaftsgeschichte (Max Planck Institute for the History of Science) in Berlin and one of its directors, Jürgen Renn (see Afterword).

The Anthropocene hypothesis, as we came to understand it at the HKW, can essentially be summarized as follows: the human being as a species is becoming the greatest force of nature. It is no longer merely interfering with nature; it is changing the entire planet. Thus, the history of humans is becoming planetary history. The exponential growth of the curves of the Great Acceleration, which illustrate essential parameters of the Earth System, from CO_2 emissions through the acidification of the oceans to the enormous growth of human populations, cities, and infrastructures, indicate something even more worrying: humankind is not just changing the planet, but destabilizing the Earth System, altering the planetary metabolism of the Holocene status quo that has been dominant since the end of the last ice age.

While the natural scientists who put forth the Anthropocene hypothesis and who are working on the scientific formalization of the term focus on the processes of material change on a planetary scale, we at the HKW see it as our task to highlight the Anthropocene's challenges to our cultural imagery, narratives, and systems of representation.

Since the nineteenth century, our understanding of external reality has been increasingly marked by natural-scientific findings replacing personal experience and religious teachings as the central frame of reference. At the beginning of the twenty-first century, scientists have come to the conclusion that their subject, nature, is now essentially a product manufactured by humankind; it is now a result of human activity and hence culture. When I heard of the Anthropocene for the first time, I was immediately fascinated by these implications, since the natural scientists were realizing that the object of their investigations has changed fundamentally, that it is an object in which natural and cultural processes are increasingly intertwined. This conjunction also reveals that the disciplinary boundaries between the natural sciences on the one hand and the humanities and cultural sciences on the other – a split that mainly developed in the nineteenth century – were proving inadequate for the purposes of addressing the phenomenon of the Anthropocene, a recognition central to the themes of this volume and of the work of the HKW. In short, the Anthropocene world demands new forms of knowledge production. For the HKW, this realization altered the course of our work. We as an institution would curate the Anthropocene, helping to conceive new forms of knowledge production.

In 2011, I presented two basic ideas to the budgetary committee of the Deutscher Bundestag (German Parliament). These ideas would become the foundation of a long-term intercultural project at the HKW. First, we are in an existential crisis caused by the destabilization of the Earth

System through human activity. Second, we need new forms of knowledge in order to develop suitable strategies of action to deal with this fundamental crisis. Rüdiger Kruse, a member of the Bundestag, immediately understood the significance of the Anthropocene hypothesis and the project we were proposing. He persuaded the budgetary committee, in cooperation with the Minister for Cultural and Media Affairs, to make available more than three million euro for long-term research. This money allowed us to develop a complex project that would do justice to the conceptual challenges posed by the Anthropocene.

In the years 2011 and 2012, we held a series of workshops during which we and the Max Planck Institute for the History of Science formulated central questions and project approaches. In charge of this and all that followed was the curatorial team of Katrin Klingan, head of the Department of Literature and Humanities at the HKW, and her research associate Christoph Rosol, who is also a research scholar at the Max Planck Institute for the History of Science in Berlin.

In January 2013, we launched The Anthropocene Project, which was originally scheduled for a period of only two years. At the opening conference a range of artistic interventions and scientific papers were developed, highlighting that the concept of the Anthropocene concerns not only scientific questions but also new ways of thinking and acting as individuals and societies. Additionally, we invited representatives from important research institutes to a forum at the opening, asking them to develop strategies for the future. The forum was attended by, among others, scientists of the Potsdam-Institut für Klimafolgenforschung (Potsdam Institute for Climate Impact Research), the Environmental Humanities Lab of the KTH Stockholm, the Institut Michel Serres and the Complex Systems Institute IXXI of the École Normal Supérieure de Lyon, the Centre for Research Architecture, Goldsmiths, the "Inquiry into the Modes of Existence" project of Sciences Po and the Institute for Advanced Sustainability Studies in Potsdam.

The most important result of this forum from the point of view of the HKW Anthropocene Project was that the need for new forms of knowledge production and education was widely recognized. Everyone seemed on board with this paradigm-shifting realization. This insight led directly to the "Anthropocene Curriculum" project of the HKW, in which the collaborative and trans-disciplinary exploration of new teaching materials and approaches opens up new forms of knowledge and new ways of representing it. The concept was originally proposed by Christoph Rosol.

All these HKW projects were and remain focused on generating new forms of knowledge in which scientific strategies merge with artistic and social forms of creativity. This approach can be described as "curating ideas in the making." In other words, it is about an experimental, exploratory approach in which new ideas, perspectives, and terminologies are developed. Curating, in this context, literally becomes a continuous process attending to emergent esthetic and cultural forms, and caring for them, so that gradually there might be a stabilization of new points of view.

These novel forms of knowledge arise both from the critical analysis of the emerging scientific findings concerning the Anthropocene and from developments in artistic production. First, to the sciences: science and its technological offshoots were not on the sidelines during the "Great Acceleration" from around 1950. Rather, scientific research and its technological applications drove the acceleration of human-made impacts on the Earth. The knowledge generated by the sciences changed from being knowledge *about* the world to being knowledge that *generated* a new techno-scientific world that some have termed the technosphere. The creation of this techno-scientific world and hence the transformation of our social world has accelerated to such a degree in recent decades that ultimately only a handful of experts in science and industry have true insight into its inner workings. This move had repercussions for democracy.

In Germany, essential decision-making procedures were switched to expert committees, circumventing democratic processes of social participation in the decision regarding what developments were even desirable for a society. The mere fact that scientific recommendations could be implemented superseded the question whether they were of any benefit to society. Against this background, a fundamental change of perspective is called for, one that recognizes that all people are affected, either directly or indirectly, by this development. At the same time, we have to acknowledge that the people directly affected by the Anthropocene and its repercussions, be they people whose crops have failed due to drought, or people whose land is contaminated by chemicals, or people whose existence is threatened by rising sea levels, are experts in their own way of life. As a consequence, the knowledge possessed by these social players must be included in the development of new forms of knowledge. Julia Adeney Thomas explores this idea of a "democracy of voices" in Chapter 2.

At the same time, the Anthropocene world, which is changing ever-faster due to increasing knowledge and increasing human impacts on the planet, also represents a major challenge for the scientific world, divided as it is by disciplines. Since whole technologies now expire in five-to ten-year cycles, reality is changing more quickly than ever. To comprehend the burgeoning reality of the Anthropocene world, new holistic conceptual approaches are required. The arts play an important role in this context. For many artists such as The Otolith Group, Andreas Siekmann, Alice Creischer, Lawrence Abu Hamdan, Nabil Ahmed, Jennifer Colten, Ravi Agarwal, and Andrew Young, to name but a few we have worked with, the art canon represented by museums is increasingly losing its significance. They criticize what they see as ossified structures in the museum-based art business. But their practice is not restricted to esthetic strategies that ask critical questions about art institutions and their strategies and mechanisms. They also consciously abandon the well-defined spaces of art museums to make art outside museums, creating new realities and exploring new esthetic languages. Artists and artist collectives such as Armin Linke, Pinar Yoldas, Territorial Agency, Dani Ploeger, Clarissa Thieme, Bouchra Khalili, Harun Farocki, and Omer Fast are developing documentary strategies that address the impact of environmental destruction on the oceans, the storage and global movement of consumer trash, migration in the Mediterranean region or at the border between Mexico and the US, or the latest wars. In order to release the imaginative potential hidden in our encounters with reality, they quite often blur the borderline between reality and fiction in their esthetic language.

Artistic strategies complement scientific approaches. Essentially, the aim is to see the world anew. Scientists, as Will Steffen shows in Chapter 3, use visual images, charts, and diagrams in their endeavor to grasp the magnitude of Earth's transformation. Artistic strategies enable sensual access to Anthropocene phenomena, rendering visible (or, in some cases, audible or tactile) how local developments are interwoven with planetary processes, thereby revealing the scaling processes of the Anthropocene. And finally, artists make the abstract, destructive processes of the Great Acceleration concrete by tracing their links back to particular individual and social experiences. This combination of scientific with esthetic and social scientific research methods became the central mission of the HKW. Its building, originally constructed in 1957 as the Congress Hall, symbolizing the reconciliation of the US and the Federal Republic of Germany, became a public forum in which these planetary processes of change could be discussed.

On this basis, the team led by Katrin Klingan and Christoph Rosol continued, in cooperation with the Max Planck Institute for the History of Science, to develop the Anthropocene Curriculum project into an international platform for more than 300 artists, scientists, scholars, and social activists. In the form of co-learning and co-producing, accompanied by a reflexive methodology, the network tackles fundamental problems of the Anthropocene. The project has a dual structure, comprising a digital platform (www.anthropocene-curriculum.org) and a series of events, each lasting several days (Anthropocene Campus) and exploring local environments within the planetary context. The first Anthropocene Campus was held in 2014 in Berlin: an intensive, nine-day HKW event featuring seminars, discussions, and public forums involving 140 young researchers, educators, artists, and activists from more than 30 countries. From the "geo-political" interdependencies between desertification and armed conflict to the mediatization of the Anthropocene to urban metabolisms or socioeconomic modeling studies, the campus consisted of concrete case studies and cross-disciplinary research endeavors. A second campus followed in 2016 in Berlin, focusing on the dazzling concept of the technosphere: that manmade Earth sphere of technology – analogous to a biosphere or hydrosphere – which plays a decisive role in driving forward the rapid development of the Anthropocene. This campus format has now been further refined and extended to locations around the world.

Although Berlin provided an important hub for the project in its first years, the project then expanded to engage other contexts. A series of globally dispersed initiatives emerged at varying scales – full-scale campuses, co-learning hubs, field trips, and workshops – all dealing with local concerns around the world. Taken together, these partner projects create a heterogeneous network of situated knowledge topographies, each of which relate to and engage differently with the Anthropocene concept. Working independently, according to their own approaches and capacities, these satellite initiatives all find a common space under the umbrella of the Anthropocene Curriculum.

Reflecting this new focus on diverse Anthropocene topographies, the project reoriented itself towards more situated and field-based inquiries. This approach is based on the recognition that the Anthropocene is a planetary phenomenon that expresses itself differently in different parts of the world. A case in point was the large-scale "Mississippi" project which the HKW realized in 2018 and 2019 in cooperation with the Max Planck Institute for the History of Science and together with hundreds of local and regional artists, activists, and scientists along that American river. Participants experienced how the technological interventions associated with the Anthropocene had transformed the Mighty Mississippi into a "Water Highway" and considered how new arts of survival might combine social and political battles with far-reaching industrial and economic transformation. The sites visited during the course of the project ranged from the northern source of the river, where the indigenous population is fighting to conserve the natural resources essential to its existence from a threatening pipeline, all the way to the delta, where the descendants of slaves living in the notorious "Cancer Alley" are fighting against the contamination of air and groundwater by the globally networked petro-chemicals industry on the sites of former plantations.

In addition to the Anthropocene Curriculum and Campus structure, the HKW developed a range of projects that addressed, in various formats, fundamental problems brought forth by the Anthropocene. One example is the exhibition "The Whole Earth," curated by Anselm Franke and Diedrich Diederichsen. It explored the cultural processes which formed the basis for a set of planetary technological developments ultimately manifesting themselves in today's digital networks. The exhibition turned the spotlight on California, where the counterculture movement established itself in the 1960s and 1970s, and struggled against, for example, the military-industrial complex and the Vietnam War. Inspired by ideas from Asian religions and European Romanticism, the counter-culture celebrated the idea that every individual is connected to the cosmos. The movement experimented widely with mind-altering drugs and communal living. A medium of key importance for this group was Stewart Brand's *The Whole Earth Catalog*, showcasing tools for alternative lifestyles which ranged from instructions for growing crops to advanced technologies such as those capable of creating hypnotic group experiences at rock concerts through lighting and sound effects. When most communes imploded in the 1970s, the people around *The Whole Earth Catalog* began trying to implement the social ideas of the counterculture movement in technological fields. They influenced Steve Jobs, the founder of Apple, as well as later tech entrepreneurs who created large social media platforms. The Apple computer transformed the counter-cultural idea of individual creative agency into a corporate technological strategy. Social media platforms transferred the idea of community to the technological world of social networking. The idea that technology can manipulate the world to such an extent that natural human worlds are being replaced by an entirely artificial one – this idea, in its essence, is what the Anthropocene entails. The apparent winners of the Anthropocene, many of them tech billionaires, are already dreaming of new worlds to master, launching space programs that allow them to consider outer space as an alternative to a desecrated Planet Earth (see Clive Hamilton's story in Chapter 11).

Other projects such as the exhibition "Ape Culture" (2013), curated by Anselm Franke and Hila Peleg, and the music project "Unhuman Music: Compositions by machines, by animals and by accident" (2015), curated by Detlef Diedrichsen, explored the emergence of the separation between nature and culture and investigated how humankind relates to other species whose very existence is now threatened by human actions.

For me, the most important aspect of the HKW's work over the past decade has been showcasing and, more importantly, enabling the sciences involved in conceptualizing the Anthropocene. We have created a space where scientists can reflect on their role in producing knowledge about the Anthropocene as a phenomenon that can be described, measured, and ultimately articulated as the overarching framework for understanding Earth's transformation. The group central to this endeavor is, of course, the Anthropocene Working Group (AWG). As described by Francine McCarthy in Chapter 9, they are tasked with doing the meticulous scientific research necessary for formalizing this new geological time interval. An essential part of gathering this evidence is taking core samples from various locations around the globe (including McCarthy's Crawford Lake) and measuring a range of biological and chemical indicators. This evidence will then be used to determine the GSSP (global stratotype section and point) or "Golden Spike" of the Anthropocene which marks the beginning of the new geological epoch. However, this research is extremely expensive, and the AWG has no funding.

It was at this juncture that I envisioned an important – and unusual – role for the HKW. Our cultural institution could support this crucial scientific endeavor financially. To this end, after consulting with the AWG, I raised the sum of one million euro. The HKW's support for the AWG's research was ultimately supplied by the German government through a special appropriation by the Deutscher Bundestag in 2019. The AWG, in return for this funding, agreed to allow the HKW access to the core samples and the results of their analysis for the development of a cultural project. Rarely, if ever, have cultural institutions and scientific bodies collaborated in quite this way.

This collaboration with the AWG enables the HKW to play two crucial roles in bringing the Anthropocene to public awareness. First, our aim is to communicate to the widest audience possible how scientists are constructing an evidence-based understanding of this new epoch. Since it is challenging for everyone to grasp the enormity of the Anthropocene and since the science behind it is difficult, the arts have the unique opportunity to expand public understanding through esthetic strategies, some of them quite experimental as described above. Second, by introducing "nature," in the form of core samples, into the collection of an institution dedicated to "culture," we underscore how these two categories have collapsed in the Anthropocene. These core samples are Earth's Anthropocene Archive, capturing the moment when human activity overwhelmed fundamental planetary metabolisms. They are the material evidence of our impact and as such are cultural objects as much as natural ones. Such core samples reveal the historical development of humanity's relationship with Earth and are fitting objects in any museum of the Anthropocene. The work of the HKW realigns our understanding of culture and nature as inseparable under Anthropocene conditions. In short, the House of World Cultures has also become the House of World Nature.

The year of this volume's publication, 2022, is a turning point in the development of the Anthropocene concept in several ways, and the HKW is a focal point in this Earth-redefining process. Cooperating with the Anthropocene Working Group, we plan to present the AWG's core samples to the public for the first time. This exhibition will explain the processes of drilling and analysis. In May 2022, the HKW will host leading scientists for a forum on their research to determine the Golden Spike, helping to facilitate their conversation under the auspices of our cultural institution. By the end of 2022, the AWG, now led by its second chair Colin Waters, plans to complete the proposal supporting the formalization of the Anthropocene as an epoch; it will use research that the HKW has funded. By early 2023, the Quaternary Subcommission of the International Commission on Stratigraphy, the next bureaucratic level of stratigraphers, may well have incontrovertible evidence of the Anthropocene in their hands.

PART THREE

FUTURE HABITATIONS

CHAPTER 11

Anthropocene Ethics, as Seen From a Mars Mission: A Story

Clive Hamilton

She adjusted the telescope to bring the Earth into sharper focus. Pearl found it comforting, but also melancholy, to sit in the glass Observatory at the stern of the spaceship. She could make out an eerie orange glow on the dark side of the planet. Her mother had told her the Amazon is burning, 'all of it'.

It was a month now since the Alset P85D had blasted off from Arizona carrying its 805 passengers and crew on a one-way journey to Mars. It was 2042 though Pearl knew she would have to forget about Earth years and get used to Mars years, twice as long. Would she therefore die young, she wondered? The year 2042 had been on target to be the hottest ever, hotter than the previous record in 2041, which had scorched land surfaces everywhere.

Ever since the ship had escaped the Earth's gravity, Captain Elon had been jubilant. 'We leave behind a tragedy on Earth', he told them at their first Convocation, 'but we will build a new paradise on Mars. That is our duty, it's our destiny.'

There was a rumble of approval from some. Pearl felt uneasy; it was those eyes, staring into the middle distance. She noticed others looking at the floor and, sitting next to her, a shadow crossed her mother's face.

Her mother, Doris, had been included among the Elect because there is nothing about the workings of a spaceship she doesn't know. When Captain Elon asked her to be Chief Engineer, Doris agreed on the proviso that her daughter could come too. The Captain agreed. 'Her genetic profile is excellent,' he noted, adding with a chuckle: 'Perhaps, in the new colony she will make little Martians!'

Before blasting off, they'd all taken their places on the Alset knowing that few, if any, humans would survive on Earth beyond a decade, two at most. Extreme weather events were dislocating the systems cities relied on – food supplies, electricity, sewerage, water. Out in the countryside, the survivalists were realizing self-reliance was not so easy. They were running out of replacement solar panels, plastic piping, axes, matches, medicines and bullets. They were mounting raids on each other's compounds.

Pearl and Doris sat at their bench eating breakfast. Her face is pale, thought Pearl, and her sunny smile is gone. I know why. My heart aches too, because we left them behind. Her father said they must go, but the guilt is gnawing away at them. Leaving her brother left a sharp pain in her chest, but the rules say only healthy specimens can be pioneers.

'We should have stayed', she said to Doris as they tidied up. Tears welled in her mother's eyes.

'I wanted you to grow up and have a life,' she replied. 'If we perish on Mars at least we will have tried.' Pearl wondered about that. She guessed that most on board felt the shame of leaving loved ones behind and saving themselves. Wherever people gathered on the ship she could smell it, the smell of guilt.

*

The next day, as part of her study for her final high school exams, Pearl walked down to the spaceship's lower deck for a tour of the Storehouse of Civilization. She was pleased to see Denis at the back of the little group. He was the Captain's son. Captain Elon had named him Æ AW-12, but by age ten the boy was so distraught by the school-yard ridicule – the children called him 'Ee-aw' or just 'Whacko' – that he renamed himself Denis and would respond only to that.

She had first met Denis at the Orientation and Training Courses in the weeks before blast off. Pearl felt shy in his company, perhaps because at eighteen he was two years older and because of his father. She noticed that, although he acted very cool, Denis wanted to impress her. Sometimes she caught him looking at her. She liked that.

The Curator led them into the Storehouse, a vast cavern of racks reaching to the ceiling. The group followed the Curator down the aisles as she pointed to rows of old masters by Moroni, Rembrandt, van Gogh, they were all there. She showed them rows of paintings by impressionists, cubists and modernists, and at the end of one aisle stood a glass box containing the Mona Lisa.

'My father was over the moon when he bought it', Denis murmured, gesturing towards the mysterious smile. 'The art market had collapsed and he got it for $50,000. Who wants an old master when the world is about to end?'

The Curator could not contain her excitement. 'The next three rows store the great books of human civilization, beginning with the Etruscan Gold Book. Here are first editions of Chaucer, Isaac Newton, Shakespeare, Mark Twain ... all the greats are here. Captain Elon says it's our mission to save human civilization. And here it is. It's all in this Storehouse.'

Denis leant into her: 'Why should we save civilization? It couldn't save us.'

'And look what we did to the animals', Pearl whispered. 'Those that aren't already extinct soon will be. If human civilization couldn't save nature, does it deserve to be saved?'

*

Pearl and Denis belong to the same Pod. It meets each week, fifty of them if they all turn up. The Pod's convenor is Deputy Luke, Captain Elon's right-hand man. Always well-dressed, Luke begins each meeting with 'The Check-In'. Sitting nearby, with a Mona Lisa smile on her lips, is the Psychologist. Luke invites her to speak.

'How are we all doing?' She has a sing-song voice. 'We are all on a life-changing journey, but it can be tough at times. You know what they say, the most stressful life events are death of a loved one, divorce and moving house. Now we have to add a new one, changing planets!'

A titter ran around the room in response to her joke.

'Anyway, it's only human if things get you down. That's why I'm on this ship with you. If you have negative thoughts, you know where to find me. Studies show it's best to take your mind somewhere else, and for that I recommend you take these.'

She held up a bottle of pills. 'These are Lethe tablets. They make you think pleasant thoughts.'

Pearl had always been a quiet girl who kept to herself. But as she listened to the Psychologist's patter, something snapped inside her and she found herself on her feet and speaking passionately to Deputy Luke.

'The Earth is burning, everything is dying. We shouldn't just forget it. Who did it? Who is *responsible*?' She suddenly felt embarrassed and sat down. She glanced across at Denis. He was looking at her admiringly.

Deputy Luke turned his serious face to her and spoke as if she were a child. 'It's no one's fault, Pearl.' She felt people looking at her and tried to shrink into her chair. 'We miscalculated. We believed we were operating the global economy within the Earth's limits. But the planetary boundaries were not as flexible as we believed.'

Then the Economist spoke up. 'Yes. Calculations using our Dynamic Integrated DICE model clearly showed that, at the appropriate discount rate, the welfare benefits from an economy growing at 3.25 per cent each year outweighed the costs of allowing the world to warm by four degrees centigrade. We were not to know, however, that on the path to that amount of warming the Earth would cross tipping points and we would lose control of the system.'

Pearl was struck dumb. The Economist spoke with such authority. She felt crushed. Then she felt a movement next to her. Doris stood and said: 'That's not true. The Earth Scientists warned us repeatedly that the Earth System is unpredictable and tipping points were approaching. You only heard what you wanted to hear. You were interested only in what you could easily put into your damned model. Don't lie to us!'

Everyone looked shocked. Pearl found herself on her feet again.

'What about the animals? Were they in your model? And the poor people who have been dying in millions for years. How much did they count in your prize-winning model?' This time she did not sit down.

The Economist began stammering. 'You need to . . . if you understood the algorithm . . .'. But Deputy Luke cut him off.

'Now, now, let's calm down a little. I know it's stressful adjusting to a new home, a new future. Let's break now and have a good dinner.'

As the Pod dispersed, most wouldn't look at Doris and Pearl, although three or four passed them murmuring 'Well said' and 'I'm with you, it's a disgrace what we did'. The Psychologist approached and stroked Doris's arm. 'I understand', she said. 'Here, take one of these Lethe pills. It will keep your spirits up. You too Pearl. Come and see me, I have plenty more.'

*

Pearl did not take the Lethe pill. She couldn't get the confrontation with the Economist off her mind. She tried to study for her final exams, but while searching Omniscient, the spaceship's AI system that stored all of the information available on the world's Hypernet, she came across a document she'd never seen, *Declaration of the Rights of Animals*.

'All creatures on Earth have a right to exist', it began. 'Human beings have the power to shape the planet's future, but it's our planet too and we demand our voices be heard.'

Pearl remembered images of panicking kangaroos trying to outrun a wildfire and emaciated polar bears snuffling through rubbish dumps. She flushed with the shame of being human and began to cry. 'I'm only sixteen', she thought, 'but could I have done something? Or must young people leave it to adults?'

Pearl knew the answer: for decades adults were responsible for the care of the Earth and look what they did to it. The pictures of the dying animals stayed in her mind. She remembered that when leaving the Storehouse of Civilization in the ship's basement they passed a door marked 'Gene Repository'. The Curator said she didn't know much about it but it held DNA samples of more than a million species of plants and animals.

Pearl wondered what the point was of the Gene Repository if the Earth's life-forms were ripped from the planet on which they evolved. Even if some animals could be reconstituted, they would be kept in human zoos on an alien planet for our entertainment or benefit. Maybe Captain Elon keeps alive the possibility of resurrecting the animals because he likes the idea of playing God. Or perhaps underneath he feels guilty too?

Pearl walked to the Observatory at the back of the ship hoping that Denis would be there. When they sat alone in the Observatory gazing out into space, she felt he understood her. When they weren't together, he was increasingly in her thoughts. She guessed that after her outburst at the Pod he would need to be even more careful not to irritate his father, who disapproved of their friendship. Her mother, too, discouraged her from meeting Denis. Pearl tried to reassure her.

'He's not like his father.'

'I know Elon better than I care to admit', Doris said. 'Believe me, Denis can't escape his influence.'

Denis arrived. He seemed agitated. She wondered if he'd quarrelled with his father. They sat quietly together, then they took turns to study the Earth through the telescope. South America was invisible because of the smoke.

'Are we leaving the Earth', Denis said, 'or did the Earth expel us? I mean, who would blame the Earth if it turned against humans. I think the trouble began when we decided to separate ourselves from nature and told ourselves we could do without it. Then we fell in love with our machines.'

'Maybe', said Pearl. 'But technology is pretty cool. The invisibility cloak is amazing. And those artificial neurons implanted in your head make you smarter, don't they?'

'I can do without them', he replied.

"Well, what about Robo-Siri? She can do all kinds of things.'

Denis blushed. 'Okay, but were we unhappy before those things? When I was little, my grandmother told me that she and her brothers grew up before there were computers. Back then, the only phones were landlines and microwave ovens had not been invented. She said they were happier then. Everyone was.'

'You're right', said Pearl. 'And look where our obsession with technology has got us. Stuck in a hi-tech shipping container running for our lives.'

*

It was another month before the next Convocation. Everyone was there, except a skeleton crew flying the Alset. Captain Elon gave a report. He said they are making good progress on their journey to Mars, with five months to go. Four other spacecraft carrying Mars pioneers would arrive at around the same time as the Alset – one from Russia, one from Germany and two from China, although some believe there had been other secret launches from China. Following the Alset are two American ships, the Zucker B and the nuclear-powered USAF Mayflower II.

The Captain showed some slides of an artist's impression of the New City being built. They pictured the enormous domed city of Anla, with futuristic vehicles moving along clean avenues overflowing with abundant vegetation. He then asked the Chief Terraforma to speak.

'The Earth System was not well-behaved', he began. 'It was less predictable than we believed, and harder to master. We tried to engineer the climate system with a solar shield, by spraying sulphate particles into the stratosphere. The technology was sound but the climate feedback effects went haywire. We didn't anticipate that and, well … you all know what happened.'

A slide appeared showing the surface of Mars. 'As you can see, the Red Planet's surface is rocky and desolate. There's not much weather, which is good for us, as it makes planetary management easier. A well-behaved planet is best for humans.'

Captain Elon thanked the Chief Terraforma and introduced the Sociologist, Steve.

'The Earth experiment failed; the planet is now a no-go zone for human beings.' Steve looked out at us. 'But we've learned a lot and now we have the chance to start again. For some time now, Captain Elon and I have been making careful plans. With our blueprint, we will build a peaceful, co-operative and, yes, sustainable society on Mars. It will be a new civilization that will make us proud.'

Another slide appeared showing ten or twelve domed cities on Mars joined up by translucent passageways. 'It will take some time', the Sociologist explained, 'but we have the technology, including the social management technology. For our descendants, the Earth will be a distant memory, and we will be seen as the pioneers, pilgrims with AI.'

Pearl had decided a while ago, while watching the super-hurricane breach New York's dikes and destroy Manhattan, that she would not have children. It would be wrong to bring a child into a broken world where survival, let alone happiness, could not be guaranteed. When she thought about missing out on motherhood, a hollowness opened inside her. Then she burned with resentment that adults – well, some adults at least – had created a world with no future for young people like her.

As the Sociologist droned on, Pearl decided she would not bring a baby into his world either. Let it be populated with little Steves and little Elons.

*

The Alset was now only three weeks from its destination. Everyone was becoming nervous as they thought more about their new home on another planet. Even Captain Elon had been overheard snapping at his girlfriend, Kim. Denis stayed out of his way as much as he could.

Pearl and Denis were the only ones to visit the Observatory now. Unlike the others, they liked to look back on the Earth. They imagined it ridding itself of the human plague and then, after the ravages, ever-so-slowly healing itself and returning to something like its Holocene state. Although they knew it couldn't happen – the Earth of their ancestors has vanished forever – they dreamed of one day returning to an unspoiled Earth, just the two of them, to live in a verdant garden full of fruit trees.

As they sat quietly gazing towards the Earth, Pearl reached across and took Denis's hand. It was the first time they'd touched and she felt a warm energy pulsing through her.

At that moment the spaceship lurched and the lights flickered. They hurried back to the Refectory where people had gathered. There was a hubbub. The Alset had been hit by an asteroid, they were saying. A message came through the tannoy system. 'There is no cause for alarm. We have a minor technical problem but our technicians are working to fix it. Please resume normal activities.'

Pearl did not see her mother for two days, except when she came to their cabin to snatch a couple of hours sleep. Doris confided that they had flown into a rogue asteroid cloud and the navigation system was down. It was believed that other ships on the way to Mars had also been hit, with some more badly damaged.

On the third day, Captain Elon convened a Convocation. He wore his usual confident smile, but his skin was grey.

'We have been temporarily diverted from our course', he began, 'but I am confident our systems will be fully operational within a few days and we will arrive on Mars safely and on time. There's no need to worry but if you do feel anxious then please see the Psychologist.'

The Psychologist sat over to the side with a manic grin on her face. She had taken too many Lethe tablets, and who knows what else.

Pearl knew that Captain Elon was lying. Doris had told her that the navigation system was beyond repair. They had been knocked way off their course to Mars and the spaceship was now careening helplessly toward the black emptiness beyond the solar system. Uncannily, the asteroid cloud had rained upon all of the other spaceships, which were now space debris or hurtling into the star-spangled void like the Alset.

*

They had been sitting for some time, lost in the grand panorama beyond the window of the Observatory. They knew where to locate the Earth without the telescope and caught sight of the majestic Saturn and the golden haze of its moon, Titan. Pearl held Denis's hand. His touch was tender and his eyes sad.

'Doris says the mission has failed', said Pearl. 'We are heading into oblivion.'

'Yes. Elon has been running around like a crazy man. He saw himself as the Saviour and he can't cope with failure.'

'Whoever sent that asteroid shower made sure no humans will settle on Mars', said Pearl, 'so that's the end of us'.

Denis clasped her hand a little tighter. 'Yes, that's the end.'

They were silent for a moment, then Pearl said:

'I'm glad.'

'Me too.'

FURTHER READING

Although there are several books on climate change ethics, there are none on the ethics of the Anthropocene. However, some of the ethical dilemmas raised in this story are considered in *Defiant Earth: The Fate of Humans in the Anthropocene* (Polity Books, 2017) by Clive Hamilton. A careful deconstruction of the kind of vision represented by Captain Elon is presented by Lisa Sideris in *Consecrating Science: Wonder, Knowledge, and the Natural World* (University of California Press, 2017). The definitive work on the politics, ideology and practicalities of 'space expansionism' is *Dark Skies: Space Expansionism, Planetary Geopolitics, and the Ends of Humanity* (Oxford University Press, 2020) by Daniel Deudney. One of the best ways to grapple with the ethical issues raised in this story is to watch critically the animated motion picture *Wall-E* (2008), directed by Andrew Stanton.

CHAPTER 12

Mutualistic Cities of the Near Future

Mark Williams, Julia Adeney Thomas, Gavin Brown, Minal Pathak, Moya Burns, Will Steffen, John Clarkson, Jan Zalasiewicz

In what follows we imagine cities of the near future that will diffuse and blend into the countryside around them. Into a rejuvenated lowland beech ecosystem if you live in the London of the future, or a tropical broadleaf biome if you are an inhabitant of future Jakarta. From a distance these cities will be difficult to see. They will be green, their many surfaces of different shapes, textures, and materials designed to provide space for other animals and plants, capture water and energy, and regulate the local climate. Buildings will not seek straight lines but will contour with the landscape and be recycled back into it at the end of their lives. The many products used in these cities, from furniture to clothes, will all be recyclable. Life is thriving in these cities, both human and nonhuman. Indeed, mimicking the cyclical flows and intimate connections of a natural ecosystem, mutualistic cities will pulsate with birth and growth, and reincorporate all that decays and dies. This vision is far removed from even the most sustainable or smart city of the early twenty-first century. Here we describe in detail what such a place would be like.

First a few definitions. How does a mutualistic city differ from sustainable cities or smart cities that people are currently discussing? Both of the latter are useful ideas, but they fail to emphasize the regenerative cycles of birth and death, use and reuse at the heart of our vision of mutualism. Sustainable cities seek to provide a safe and equitable environment for all of their human inhabitants,[1] which is important, but the focus is often on lessening resource demands while continuing to grow the economy. Smart cities, on the other hand, seek to use energy and infrastructure more

---

[1] https://unstats.un.org/sdgs/report/2020/goal-11/

efficiently through sophisticated data collection and targeted technologies. While those ideas are also important, they tend to bolster top-down, undemocratic "rule by experts" regimes without community involvement and fail to consider the full life cycle of the materials, such as rare earth metals necessary for sophisticated technologies. Sometimes, top-down solutions – however well intentioned – can also have unforeseen and negative consequences.[2] They also, because of the emphasis on efficiency and high-tech, tend to be less nimble in unpredictable emergency situations. Neither sustainable nor smart cities solve the problem of human over-consumption. For cities to survive and develop over long timeframes they must fully emulate natural ecosystems that have co-evolved with the available mineral, biological, water, and energy resources of their environment.

Today better cities are crucial for human thriving, but for most of human history we did not live within built settlements but were hunter-gatherers. That lifestyle can support about 10 million people,[3] roughly the population 10,000 years ago. Permanent built settlements are a recent innovation tied to the development of farming.[4] They first appear in the eastern Mediterranean and Near East between about 12,000 and 11,000 years ago. Eventually, between 6000 and 4000 years ago, cities began to emerge, first in Mesopotamia, and then in regions such as Peru, Egypt, and the Indus Valley. Despite the local rise and fall of towns and cities, ever since their beginning, at some place on Earth, people have lived an urban lifestyle.

[2] Sterman, J.D. 2012. Sustaining sustainability: Creating a systems science in a fragmented academy and polarized world. In: M.P. Weinstein and R.E. Turner (eds.), *Sustainability Science: The Emerging Paradigm 21 and the Urban Environment*, Springer, New York. DOI 10.1007/978-1-4614-3188-6_2.

[3] Burger, J.R., Fritsoe, T.S. 2018. Hunter-gatherer populations inform modern ecology. *PNAS* 115, 1137–1139.

[4] By permanent built settlements we are referring to such as Çatalhöyük and Jericho, regarded as some of the proto-urban settlements. We are not referring to the semi-permanent settlements made by Pleistocene hunter-gatherers, such as documented by Wojtal, P., Wilczyniski, J., Wertz, K., Svoboda, J.A. 2016. The scene of a spectacular feast (part II): animal remains from Dolní Vestonice II, the Czech Republic. *Quaternary International* 406, 129–143.

Over time, at first slowly and tentatively, and then decisively, cities[5] emerged as one of the great engines transforming the Earth. Although covering only about 3% of the land,[6] more than 4 billion of us (out of almost 8 billion) live in them, more than 1.7 billion of us live in cities of more than 1 million people, and 33 have more than 10 million inhabitants. As human population has grown, the urban population has expanded even more rapidly and by 2050 will likely account for 68% of us,[7] including in rapidly industrializing and urbanizing nations where energy use is increasing.[8] Without intervention, towns and cities will continue to consume voraciously and at increasing rates.[9] They will also disgorge ever more waste into the air, water, and land around them.

Cities have evolved to consume beyond what is available locally, to source materials globally, and to waste materials without recycling, all of which will impact on their long-term survival by damaging their immediate surroundings and the entire Earth. Land use change towards urbanization often results in a decline in biodiversity within and beyond the city. Cities account for as much as three-quarters of human energy consumption and carbon emissions.[10] This is why the European

---

[5] There are a variety of definitions of urban, see: www.un.org/en/development/desa/population/events/pdf/expert/27/papers/II/paper-Moreno-final.pdf (accessed October 2021); also, McDonald, R.I., Mansur, A.V., Ascensão, F., et al. 2020. Research gaps in knowledge of the impact of urban growth on biodiversity. *Nature Sustainability*, 3, 16–24.

[6] Shwartz, A., Turbé, A., Simon, L., Julliard, R. 2014. Enhancing urban biodiversity and its influence on city dwellers: an experiment. *Biological Conservation* 171, 82–90.

[7] UN, Department of Economic and Social Affairs, Population Division 2019. World Urbanization Prospects 2018: Highlights (ST/ESA/SER.A/421).

[8] Dhakal, S. 2009. Urban energy use and carbon emissions from cities in China and policy implications. *Energy Policy* 37, 4208–4219.

[9] Energy consumption may reach the equivalent of using 17,435 million tonnes of oil by the mid to late twenty-first century: Creutzig, F., Baiocchi, G., Bierkandt, R., Pichler, P.-P., Seto, K.C. 2014. Global typology of urban energy use and potentials for an urbanization mitigation wedge. *PNAS* 112, 6283–6288.

[10] Seto, K.C., Dhakal, S., et al. 2014 Human settlements, infrastructure and spatial planning. In: O. Edenhofer, R. Pichs-Madruga, Y. Sokona, et al. (eds.) *Climate Change 2014: Mitigation of Climate Change*. Contribution of Working Group III to the Fifth Assessment Report of the Intergovernmental Panel on Climate Change. Cambridge University Press, Cambridge, UK and New York, USA; Güneralp, B., Zhou, Y., Ürge-Vorsatz, D., et al. 2017. Global scenarios of urban density and its impacts on building energy use through 2050. *PNAS* 114, 8945–8950.

Commission has said that "the future of cities will determine the well-being of future generations,"[11] and the Deputy Secretary-General of the United Nations has said that the "battle for sustainability will be won or lost in cities."[12]

Some scholars draw comparisons between the present environmental crisis and disintegration of past civilizations,[13] although earlier collapses were local and specific. Today we face a global challenge. Over-use of resources, divisions within society, invasion and conquest, disease, a lack of adaptability to environmental change, and complex interactions between these and other factors have all been suggested as mechanisms of urban decay.[14] In order to address the role of cities in the current environmental crisis, we must bring together many forms of knowledge, from a deep understanding of the Earth's functioning natural systems[15] to an understanding of how communities create trust. Much of this book has focused on describing the dangers we face; here we discuss what might be done to avoid, in the words of historian and activist Mike Davis, "a moral failure on a scale unparalleled in history."[16]

[11] European Commission - Joint Research Centre. "The future of cities." European Commission, January 2, 2019. https://urban.jrc.ec.europa.eu/thefutureofcities/introduction.

[12] United Nations. "Battle for sustainability will be won or lost in cities, Deputy Secretary-General tells high-level general assembly meeting on new urban agenda, UN-Habitat | Meetings coverage and press releases." https://www.un.org/press/en/2017/dsgsm1080.doc.htm. (accessed October, 2021).

[13] See Diamond, J. 2005/2011. *Collapse: How Societies Choose to Fail or to Succeed.* Penguin Books, New York, London; Kemp, L. 2019. www.bbc.com/future/article/20190218-are-we-on-the-road-to-civilisation-collapse (accessed October 2021).

[14] e.g., Janssen, M.A., Kohler, T.A., Scheffer, M. 2003. Sunk-cost effects and vulnerability to collapse in ancient societies. *Current Anthropology* 44, 722–728; Larsen, C.S. Knüsel, C.J., Haddow, S.D., et al. 2019. Bioarchaeology of Neolithic Catalhöyük reveals fundamental transitions in health, mobility and lifestyle in early farmers. *PNAS* 116, 12615–12623; Middleton, G.D. 2012. Nothing lasts forever: environmental discourses on the collapse of past societies. *Journal of Archaeological Research* 20, 257–307; Robbins Schug, G, Blevins, K.E., Cox, B., Gray, K., Mushrif-Tripathy, V. 2013. Infection, disease, and biosocial processes at the end of the Indus Civilization. *PLoS ONE* 8(12), e84814.

[15] The way that air, earth, sea and life co-evolve and interact.

[16] Davis, M. 2010. Who will build the ark? *New Left Review* 61, 29–46, here 46 quoting the *UN Human Development Report* 2007/2008, pp. 6, 2.

THE MUTUALISTIC CITY

A *mutualistic city* co-evolves with its environment, actively fostering virtuous feedback loops[17] that avoid waste and depletion, and encourage renewable energy sources, promote biodiversity, clean water and air, and recycling, and create the equitable, trust-building social, economic, and political relations that will allow us to respond to myriad challenges of the Anthropocene. For cities of the global North, the emphasis must be on lessening per capita demands while for cities of the global South, building decent lives within regenerative systems will take top priority. We use "mutualistic" in the sense of its biological meaning, where co-habiting organisms function in a way that is beneficial to each other. This applies to cities because they resemble biological organisms or whole ecosystems in the way they grow, work, and produce waste.[18] Our focus on cities is because they consume most of the energy in human ecologies. But mutualistic relationships need to be developed for all human-modified ecologies – not just the urban – and the characteristics we describe apply to agricultural, pastoral, and managed forest contexts. This vision is not dissimilar from Kate Raworth's view of thriving cities using her "green doughnut" model,[19] has parallels in the transformative approach to cities that Paul Chatterton elaborates in his book *Unlocking Sustainable Cities*,[20] builds upon the recent scholarly interests in nature-based solutions in cities,[21] and pays homage to those scholars who have

---

[17] An example here would be a city that captures and recycles its water, limiting its use of a local aquifer. This is a self-limiting or balancing feedback, which allows the aquifer to be replenished, thus providing a water source to the city in times of drought.

[18] Barragán, A., Terrados, J. 2017. Sustainable cities: an analysis of the contribution made by renewable energy under the umbrella of urban metabolism. *International Journal of Sustainable Development Planning* 12, 416–424.

[19] Creating city portraits_Methodological Guide_v.1, available at www.kateraworth.com/2020/07/16/so-you-want-to-create-a-city-doughnut/ (accessed October 2021).

[20] Chatterton, P. 2019. *Unlocking Sustainable Cities. A Manifesto for Real Change.* Pluto Press, London.

[21] Lafortezza, R., Chen, J.-Q., Konijnendijkvan den Bosch, C., Randrup, T.B. 2018. Nature-based solutions for resilient landscapes and cities. *Environmental Research* 165, 431–441; Nature-based Solutions (NbS) are defined by IUCN as "actions to protect, sustainably manage, and restore natural or modified ecosystems, that address societal challenges effectively and adaptively, simultaneously providing human well-being and biodiversity benefits."

argued for more mutualistic relationships between cities and the biosphere.[22]

Currently no city is mutualistic. But those which try to emulate or work with natural ecologies will have greater resilience to environmental change, and therefore an advantage as humanity's negative impact on the Earth becomes more and more tangible. In turn, mutualistic cities could actively mitigate the worst consequences of human interaction with the Earth and actually enrich the environment, regenerating eco-systems that support healthy human lives, greater biodiversity, cleaner air and water, and strengthened community ties. Such cities would look and feel very different from the ones we know today. They would have a slower pace, a quieter soundscape, and a lusher sense of life. Here we explore the relationships a mutualistic city builds between its people, water, energy, earth, life, and air to evolve a better future.

PEOPLE. The metabolism of a city is its economy. Currently cities are like massive, wasteful gluttons bent on indulging without restraint, sucking in resources and people, and spewing out detritus. The metabolism of a mutualistic city would function very differently. A better economy means, first and foremost, one that rejects infinite growth and is redirected toward a steady-state economy or even degrowth. One of the first steps in realizing what a mutualistic economy would look like is recognizing all the different types of activities that already go in to making societies hum happily. Currently, the mainstream economic system focuses relentlessly on wage labor and GDP (gross domestic product) along with financial services that organize allocation of capital and debt. But as the work of economic geographers J.K. Gibson-Graham and her collaborators[23] shows, there's a whole

[22] Ozer, E. 2014. Mutualistic relationships versus hyper-efficiencies in the sustainable building and city. *Urban Ecosystems* 17, 195–204.

[23] Gibson-Graham, J.K, 2006, *A Post-Capitalist Politics*, University of Minnesota Press, Minneapolis; Gibson-Graham, J.K., 2008 Diverse economies: performative practices for other worlds. *Progress in Human Geography* 32(5), 613–632. Gibson-Graham, J.K., Cameron, J., Healy, S. 2013 *Take Back the Economy: An Ethical Guide for Transforming our Communities*, University of Minnesota Press, Minneapolis; Gibson-Graham, J.K., Hill, A., Law, L. 2016, Re-embedding economies in ecologies: resilience building in more than human communities. *Building Research Information* 44(7), 703–736.

world of diverse practices that are actually part of the economy, even if they fall out of the official definition. Lots of crucial work is unpaid and under-valued in contemporary societies – such as caring for children, the sick, and the elderly, forming neighborly associations, creating art, and improving the natural environment in small ways like bird feeders and in big ways like political action.[24] Mutualistic economies in mutualistic cities will recognize these efforts as valuable and find ways to support the people behind them. Especially important will be the work to expand self-provisioning and urban agriculture in spaces that are held in common, rather than privatized. There are many examples of ways in which communities have self-organised to provide collective care, mutual aid, and engage in environmental repair in crisis moments, whether those are economic crises,[25] the aftermath of "nat-ural disasters,"[26] or pandemics.[27] The challenge is to translate these commu-nity responses into more visible and sustained components of the economy outside of crisis moments. To do so would involve something very difficult indeed, rearticulating our values so that "success" is not about high-paying jobs, let alone massive wealth, but is defined in terms of dense circles of friendship and honor within communities.

For this reason, a mutualistic city fosters the bottom-up creation of sustainable cycles that draw people away from their consumer roles to producer roles: growing food, building and repairing dwellings and furniture, and fostering other species in a host of ways such as planting milkweed for monarch butterflies. Private ownership with a big premium on the newest consumer product can be replaced by sharing cars, bicycles, clothing, and the implements used in households and gardens among friends and neighbors. In societies where the market has become the usual matrix for most interaction with others beyond work and home, such efforts may be awkward initially. Purchasing status is simpler than

---

[24] Bhattacharya, T. 2017. *Social Reproduction Theory: Remapping Class, Recentering Oppression.* Pluto Press, London.

[25] Sitrin, M. (ed.) 2006. *Horizontalism: Voices of Popular Power in Argentina.* AK Press, London.

[26] Conroy, W. 2019. The (Im)mobilities of mutual aid: Occupy Sandy, Racial Liberalism, and the making of Insurgent Infrastructures. *ACME: An International E-Journal for Critical Geographies* 18(4).

[27] Springer, S. 2020. Caring geographies: the COVID-19 interregnum and a return to mutual aid. *Dialogues in Human Geography* 10(2), 112–115.

building a reputation for frugality, but it's no great stretch of the historical imagination to remember the many communities where thrift and frugality, home canning, and parents building steps for the school were admired. A true sharing economy (as opposed to a monetized sharing through companies like Uber and Airbnb) requires time, energy, and often the spark of a particularly charismatic and determined individual, plus government and private grants.[28] Unlike smart city initiatives which herald their streamlined efficiency and can work anywhere, true sharing economies foster resilience through overlapping, redundant, local networks of conversations, knowledge, and lending a helping hand. While a smart city model would elevate the one, best way to solve a problem, the mutualistic city model, like nature itself, evolves several alternatives so as to cope when circumstances change – just as happens in biological systems.

Mutualistic cities are about slowing time, not ramping up the warp speed of capitalist development in new technologies.[29] Knitting together communities while producing virtuous cycles for human well-being has been shown to work in, for instance, Detroit which now boasts 1400 community gardens in a city that used to be marked by "food deserts".[30] The USDA estimates there to be 65,000 food deserts across America, with 23.5 million inhabitants, 11.5 million of which are impoverished.[31] Enabling people to help themselves can be done by initiatives that enhance social bonds and environmental justice. As Mike Davis says, the mutual attraction between communal ethos and greener urbanism is "magnetic, if not inevitable."[32] These local bonds are particularly important in emergency situations when state powers and technologies fail. A case in point is the March 2011 Fukushima disaster on Japan's northeastern shore. As the

[28] Schor, J.B. 2020. *After the Gig: How the Sharing Economy Got Hijacked and How to Win it Back.* University of California Press, Los Angeles and Berkeley.

[29] Dorling, D. 2020. *Slowdown: The End of The Great Acceleration—and Why it's Good for the Planet, the Economy, and Our Lives.* Yale University Press, New Haven.

[30] A food desert is defined by the US Department of Agriculture (USDA) as low-income areas where fresh food is hard to access. USDA Economic Research Service, https://www .ers.usda.gov/data-products/food-access-research-atlas/documentation/#definitions (accessed October 2021).

[31] Dutko, P. 2012. Characteristics and influential factors of food deserts, ERR-140, U.S. Department of Agriculture, Economic Research Service, August 2012.

[32] Davis, M. 2010. Who will build the ark? *New Left Review* 61, 29–46, here 42.

tsunami rolled into local communities, those which suffered the least loss of life were not characterized by better sea walls or more efficient texts with official instructions to take care of oneself first and foremost. Instead, they were the ones where neighbors sought one another out to ensure that people survived.[33] Since the current and future economic crises might compel us to default on our public commitments, disasters may become so severe that emergency services fail. We cannot afford to leave the low-tech bride at the altar.[34]

Along with streets and public spaces that nurture wildlife and recycle resources, a mutualistic city encourages people to interact more with each other so that they can pass along information about an older person's fall and help one another out with, say, a plumbing problem. After decades in which supposedly "public" spaces have been progressively privatized in both use and ownership, we need to consider how urban design can rebuild spaces as urban commons open to everyone. The *City Repair Project*[35] in Portland, Oregon has worked with localized communities to redesign intersections in residential neighborhoods in ways that build attachment to place, encourage residents to socialize with each other in public space, and foster forms of sharing and mutual exchange. Crucially, these experiments have not been delivered from above by the local government but developed with the active participation of local residents, thereby helping to change the relationship of those residents with the spaces around them. The social foundation of a mutualistic city is trust. When a city is riven by differences in wealth and dangerous crime, accessible, attractive public spaces have been shown to help heal the wounds.[36]

While the central ambition of mutualistic cities is directed at enriching their immediate environments, we are not arguing for absolute autarky. Trade and exchange in goods, resources, and services will need

[33] Aldrich, D.P. 2019. *Black Wave: How Networks and Governance Shaped Japan's 3/11 Disasters.* University of Chicago Press, Chicago.
[34] Davis, M. 2010. Who will build the ark? *New Left Review* 61, 29–46, here 36.
[35] https://cityrepair.org/
[36] Chatterton, P. 2019. *Unlocking Sustainable Cities* (see especially Chapter 4 "The common city") Pluto Press, London; Groenewegen, P. P., van den Berg, A. E., de Vries, S., Verheij, R.A. 2006 Vitamin G: effects of green space on health, well-being, and social safety. *BMC Public Health* 6, 149.

to continue beyond the immediate locality of the city, even if these flows are much reduced and subject to new priorities. This localism will take some getting used to. Maybe Bolivian bananas aren't necessary in Bristol in February, but what about medical supplies? Questions like these are currently answered through market mechanisms. In a mutualistic city, these are environmental, ethical, and political questions. Answering them must always bear in mind the imperative not to amplify existing social inequalities or create new ones.

To create trust and greater equity, we need to add education as a key factor in creating a mutualistic city. Only when all are equipped to understand the goals of mutualism, the roles that everyone can play, and the pleasures to be had of living in a society where burdens and rewards are shared, will it be possible to realize mutualism. While mutualistic systems emerge in nature without conscious guidance, the mutualism we envision here must be directed and self-aware.

WATER. Nobody and no society can function without fresh water. But water is a scarce commodity,[37,38] and our consumption of it has increased rapidly in the twentieth century (Figures 12.1 and 12.2), exceeding what is sustainable.[39] Water demand will exceed what is available by as much as 40% by 2030.[40]

Currently, much of the water used in cities is captured remotely in reservoirs, then chemically treated before being distributed to people. Large cities (>750,000 inhabitants) alone move something like 184 km^3 of water per year (25 times the volume of Loch Ness), over a distance of approximately 27,000 km, drawing this from over two-fifths of the global

---

[37] The hydrosphere comprises 1340 million km^3 of water, but only 3% is fresh. Only about 0.013% of this is lakes and rivers. Arndt, N. 2015. Hydrosphere. DOI: https://doi.org/10.1007/978-3-642-27833-4_757-3 (accessed October 2021).

[38] www.worldwildlife.org/threats/water-scarcity (accessed October 2021).

[39] Jaramillo, F., Destoumi, G. 2015. Local flow regulation and irrigation raise global human water consumption and footprint. *Science* 350, 1248–1251; Steffen, W., Richardson, K., Rockström, J., et al. 2015. Planetary boundaries: guiding human development on a changing planet. *Science* 347, 6223.

[40] Saurí, D. 2013. Water conservation: theory and evidence in developed parts of the world. *Annual Review of Environment and Resources* 38, 227–248.

Sector	Global fresh-water use (km³)	Urban fresh-water use (km³)	
		Embedded water in agriculture scaled to urban population	Embedded water in agriculture scaled to urban energy consumption
Agriculture	2710	1490	1897
Industrial	723	723	723
Municipal	429	236	236
TOTAL	3862	2449	2856

12.1. Consumption of freshwater in urban areas: Since 2010 human fresh-water consumption plateaued at around 4000 km³ per year. In that year, 2710 km³ is estimated to have been used by agriculture, 723 km³ in industry and 429 km³ in households. For agriculture, we assign fractions for urban areas assuming that 55% of the human population is urban (column 3) and that urban areas account for 70% of energy consumption (column 4).[41] We assume the bulk of water consumption for industry is urban (columns 3 and 4). We scale municipal water consumption to the percentage of urban population (columns 3 and 4). By these calculations urban areas may use nearly 3000 km³ of freshwater a year.

land surface.[42] After use, "wastewater" is delivered to sewage plants, where solid materials are neutralized by microbes, before the water is

---

[41] Global fresh-water use that can be assigned to urban areas is in the range of 63–74% of the total, depending on whether the scaling is done by population or energy use. For agriculture, although water is consumed almost entirely outside of cities, we consider "embedded water" as that needed to grow and process the food consumed in cities. We could make two different assumptions here: (i) "embedded water" is proportional to the urban population (55%), assuming that city dwellers consume, on average, the same amount of food as rural dwellers, (ii) "embedded water" is proportional to the energy consumed by the urban population (we take a mid-range estimate of 70% for this, see Seto, K.C., Dhakal, S., et al. 2014. Human settlements, infrastructure and spatial planning. In: O. Edenhofer, R. Pichs-Madruga, Y. Sokona, et al. (eds.) *Climate Change 2014: Mitigation of Climate Change.* Contribution of Working Group III to the Fifth Assessment Report of the Intergovernmental Panel on Climate Change. Cambridge University Press, Cambridge, UK and New York, USA; Güneralp, B., Zhou, Y., Ürge-Vorsatz, D., et al. 2017. Global scenarios of urban density and its impacts on building energy use through 2050. *PNAS* 114, 8945–8950), based on the extra energy needed to process the food before it can be shipped to cities compared to rural dwellers and, more importantly, that more of the food wastage occurs in cities, and in the processes needed to transport, distribute, and market food to cities. Assumption (ii) thus leads to a higher per capita consumption of fresh water for cities. For industry we assume that the vast majority of industrial processes are located in or adjacent to cities. For households we assume that consumption is proportional to population.

[42] McDonald, R.I., Weber, K., Padowski, J., et al. 2014. Water on an urban planet: urbanization and the reach of urban water infrastructure. *Global Environmental Change* 27, 96–105.

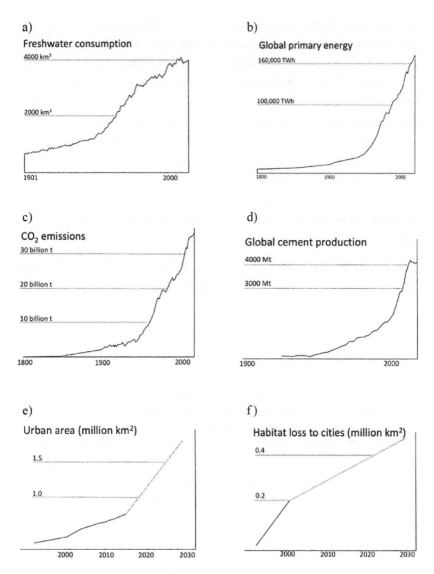

12.2. Increasing global consumption: (a) Humanity's increasing consumption of freshwater[43]: perhaps as much as 70% of this occurs in cities (Figure 12.1). (b, c) Consumption of energy (in TWh[44]) and emissions of carbon dioxide

---

[43] Simplified from: Ritchie, H., Roser, M. 2017. Water use and stress. https://ourworldindata.org/water-use-stress (accessed October 2021).

[44] 1 TWh = 85984.5 tonnes of oil equivalent.

released back to the environment and by-products used in energy production, land spread, or dumped. Overall, water distribution and treatment are energy intensive,[45] and much simply leaks away.[46]

In natural environments plants and animals conserve water in
various ways, especially where it is scarce, including storing it within
their bodies, reducing the amount of water expended in feces and urine,
and making habitats underground that protect from heat. A mutualistic
city emulates this, whilst also maintaining a clean and safe supply of water
for its inhabitants, recycling the water it captures for reuse, including the
materials within so-called yellow, brown, black, or gray water.[47]
Citizens think of the water they flush away as "reusable," rather
than "waste."[48] This means that used water can be recycled for

---

12.2. (*cont.*) since 1800[49]: cities may be responsible for as much as three-quarters of energy
consumption and emissions.[50] (d) Global cement use[51]: about 2800 million tonnes may be
used to build urban structures each year. (e, f) The growing area of land covered by towns
and cities and the cumulative habitat loss to cities since 1992: graphs redrawn from,[52]
dotted lines are projections.

[45] Elías-Maxil, J.A., van der Hoek, J.P., Hofman, J., Rietveld, L. 2014. Energy in the urban
water cycle: actions to reduce the total expenditure of fossil fuels with emphasis on heat
reclamation from urban water. *Renewable and Sustainable Energy Review* 30, 808–820.

[46] www.un.org/waterforlifedecade/swm_cities_zaragoza_2010/pdf/facts_and_figures_
long_final_eng.pdf (accessed October 2021).

[47] Euphemisms for water containing urine, feces, both of these, and the products of
detergent, respectively: Verstaete, W., Vlaeminck, S.E. 2011. ZeroWasteWater: short-
cycling of wastewater resources for sustainable cities of the future. *International Journal of
Sustainable Development & World Ecology* 18, 253–264.

[48] Verstaete, W., Vlaeminck, S.E. 2011. ZeroWasteWater: short-cycling of wastewater
resources for sustainable cities of the future. *International Journal of Sustainable
Development & World Ecology* 18, 253–264.

[49] Simplified from: Ritchie, H., Roser, M. 2020. Energy. https://ourworldindata.org/
energy (accessed December 2021); Ritchie, H. Roser, M. 2020. CO_2 and Greenhouse Gas
Emissions. https://ourworldindata.org/co2-and-other-greenhouse-gas-emissions
(accessed December 2021).

[50] Güneralp, B., Zhou, Y., Ürge-Vorsatz, D., et al. 2017. Global scenarios of urban density
and its impacts on building energy use through 2050. *PNAS* 114, 8945–8950.

[51] Simplified from: Andrew, R.M. 2019. Global CO_2 emissions from cement production
1928–2018. https://essd.copernicus.org/preprints/essd-2019-152/essd-2019-152.pdf
(accessed October 2021).

[52] Graphs simplified from McDonald, R.I., Mansur, A.V., Ascensão, F., et al. 2020. Research
gaps in knowledge of the impact of urban growth on biodiversity. *Nature Sustainability*, 3,
16–24.

drinking.[53] A mutualistic city seeks to capture its local influxes of rain and floodwater. These will become increasingly valuable as climate change makes water supplies precarious, as happened in Cape Town, South Africa in 2018, when its water supply was almost exhausted. In these ways a mutualistic city fosters feedbacks that conserve and recycle water, rather than depleting its natural resources.

The surfaces of most cities and towns are impervious and, together with storm management infrastructure, allow rainwater to be quickly lost. This water may also contain pollutants washed from urban surfaces and if discharged into rivers and lakes damages aquatic ecosystems downstream. Systems for capturing rain and storm water can remove contaminants – some of which are economically important – and purify water to be reused. Water capture can be facilitated through constructed wetlands,[54] green streets that are planted with vegetation borders that slow down and absorb the flow of storm water,[55] and by the development of infrastructure to divert water to spreading grounds, where water can seep through soil and replenish groundwater reservoirs.[56]

Most citizens of developed countries who casually waste gallons of water would never pour gallons of champagne down the drain. But in a mutualistic city, water would be more treasured than a fine vintage, since water bubbles fizz with the gift of life for people, animals, plants, and all the tiny microorganisms that weave the natural world together. A dry city is a dead city. A household in a mutualistic city, perhaps drawing inspiration from the systems designed to conserve water on space stations, would recycle yellow and gray water,[57] limit showers, and laundry, and

[53] https://www.bbc.com/future/article/20160105-why-we-will-all-one-day-drink-recycled-wastewater#:~:text=In%20some%20parts%20of%20the,drinking%20water%2C%20 20bottled%20or%20tap (accessed October 2021).

[54] Dou, T., Troesch, S., Petitjean, A., Gábor, P.T., Esser, D. 2017. Wastewater and rainwater management in urban areas: a role for constructed wetlands. *Procedia Environmental Sciences* 37, 535–541.

[55] See for e.g., http://nrcsolutions.org/green-streets/ (accessed October 2021).

[56] Garrison, N., Sahl, J., Dugger, A., Wilkinson, R.C. 2014. Stormwater capture potential in urban and suburban California. https://pacinst.org/wp-content/uploads/2014/06/ca-water-stormwater.pdf (accessed October 2021).

[57] Sullivan, K. 2019. How the ISS recycles its air and water. www.popsci.com/how-iss-recycles-air-and-water/ (accessed October 2021).

avoid gardens of non-native, overly thirsty plants. Water-efficient appliances like washing machines and dishwashers, especially in developed countries, can lower indoor water usage by up to 50%, and even retrofitted appliances have a significant but smaller impact (9–12%)[58] while also saving the embedded energy of replacing the machine (see below). And after household use, any remaining gray water could be recycled again, for use in office buildings.[59] The inhabitants of the mutualistic city will also seek to reduce their water consumption in food, not wishing to waste it, and reducing their intake of foodstuffs that require extensive water for production, like meat and dairy.[60]

How much water might be saved? Among the places that have implemented solutions to water use is Barcelona. It has installed a smart tele-management watering system for its parks and gardens. This uses sensors and weather stations to determine how much water the plants need daily. Gardeners can see the measurements and control watering. Joan Puigdollers, the Councillor for Environment and Urban Services says that the parks are learning from traditional Catalan farmers and using technology to make their use of water more efficient. As a result, the parks have lowered water usage by 25%.[61]

ENERGY. Most natural ecologies rely on the sun's energy. This dwarfs what is extracted by humans from oil, gas, coal, and nuclear sources.[62] Sunlight is everywhere at the surface and when converted by photosynthesis to plant mass, forms the basis of the food chain in the oceans and on the land. Cities and towns, in contrast to natural ecologies, find most of their

---

[58] Inman D., Jeffrey P. 2006. A review of residential water conservation tool performance and influences on implementation effectiveness. *Urban Water Journal* 3,127–143.

[59] Moslemi Sadeh, S., Hunt, D.V.L., Lombardi, D.R., Rogers, C.D.F. 2013. Shared urban greywater recycling systems: water resource savings and economic investment. *Sustainability* 5, 2887–2912.

[60] www.sustainablewaters.org/five-big-ways-to-conserve-water/ (accessed October 2021).

[61] Barcelona City Council "Smart Watering for Parks and Gardens" Info Barcelona, March 26, 2014, www.barcelona.cat/infobarcelona/en/my-new-post-1498_25404.html (accessed October 2021).

[62] The energy of sunlight delivers an average of 340 watts of energy for every square meter at the top of the Earth's atmosphere. Some of this energy is reflected back to space, and about 71% is absorbed by the atmosphere and Earth's surface. The energy received by the Earth is nearly four million exajoules a year.

energy from nonrenewable sources transported over long distances, and beyond the immediate connections of the local ecology. They consume the energy equivalent of more than 10,000 million tonnes of oil per year[63] and are responsible for up to three-quarters of global CO_2 emissions (Figure 12.2). Although more than 100 cities around the world find most of their energy from renewable sources and are developing technologies for its efficient use,[64] most are far from achieving a mutualistic relationship with the Earth, by which we mean that their energy must be sourced from renewables, and the materials that produce and transport the energy must be made from materials that are recyclable too. That's currently a tall order. Many "renewable" energy sources rely on distant supplies of rare Earth minerals or, as with hydroelectric dams, damage the surrounding ecosystem.

How cities consume energy is very complex, with flows of people, vehicles, food, building materials, power, commodities, and manufactured products into and out of the city, whilst waste materials like plastics, heat, and CO_2 are produced as by-products. Radical new technologies may greatly reduce consumption at whole building and city scales, such as air conditioning that mimics the funnel structures of termite nests,[65] concrete that mimics skin and self-repairs, prolonging the life of buildings,[66] and new forms of energy from sources as diverse as soil microbes, to fuel cells powered by hydrogen.[67,68] Many energy-efficient

---

[63] In 2018, total global energy consumption was the equivalent of 13,865 million tonnes of oil.

[64] Over 100 cities now get 70% of their energy from sustainable sources https://www.cdp.net/en/cities/world-renewable-energy-cities (accessed October 2021); www.theguardian.com/cities/2018/feb/27/cities-powered-clean-energy-renewable#:~: text=Burlington%2C%20Vermont%2C%20was%20the%20only,having%20fully% 20transitioned%20in%202015 (accessed October 2021).

[65] Bronsema, B., van Luijk, R., Swier, P., Veerman, J., Vermeer, J. 2018. Natural air conditioners: what are we waiting for? *REHVA Journal* April 2018, 21–25.

[66] e.g., Dade-Robertson, M., Keren-Paz, M.A., Zhang, M., Kolodkin-Gal, I. 2017. Architects of nature: growing buildings with bacterial biofilms. *Microbial Biotechnology* 10(5), 1157–1163; Heveran, C.M., Williams, S.L., Qiu, J., et al. 2020. Biomineralization and successive regeneration of engineered living building materials. *Matter* 2, 481–494.

[67] www.plant-e.com/en/ (accessed October 2021); www.sciencedaily.com/releases/2019/03/190326132712.htm (accessed October 2021).

[68] www.power-technology.com/comment/standing-at-the-precipice-of-the-hydrogen-economy/ (accessed October 2021).

technologies are emerging, but their full impact on sustainable consumption is not yet clear[69] and often just how these technologies will fit into communities and alter the relations of power is murky. Changing patterns of consumption in cities also begins at home by using technologies such as solar panels, solar heating systems, heat exchangers, and biomass boilers that improve energy efficiency,[70] and by using appliances for their full life, including repairing them, rather than replacing them with the latest new gadget, and recycling them at the end of their life. Some energy-saving technologies are already used. London has invested in smart lighting and has switched to LEDs, installed sensors, and all of the lights are connected to a central management system that sets the brightness and color depending on location, time, and how busy the area is.[71] This delivers 60% energy savings. But what happens to the old light bulbs? Would this masterful system work if the grid went down? These are the questions that mutualism puts: what is the entire life cycle of all materials used? Along with brilliant efficiency in predictable time, will the system respond to the unpredictable events more and more likely in this first century of the Anthropocene? *In a mutualistic city, systems are nimble.*

Equally important to technology are the responses of people to energy consumption. For example, driving cars, even with hydrogen fuel cells or electric batteries, will impact the environment. Low-energy systems of mass transit, and the redesign of cities to allow people to commute to work locally or share vehicles, may be much more significant solutions to excessive energy consumption. Similar solutions must be applied to a consumer market that encourages consumption of everything from clothing to mobile phones. The latter are part of a

---

[69] Edwards, P.P., Kuznetsova, V.L., David, W.I.F, Brandon, N.P. 2008. Hydrogen and fuel cells: towards a sustainable energy future. *Energy Policy* 36, 4356–4362; Iles, A., Martin, A.N. 2013. Expanding bioplastics production: sustainable business innovation in the chemical industry. *Journal of Cleaner Production* 45, 38–49.

[70] IRENA. 2016. Renewable energy in cities. International Renewable Energy Agency (IRENA), Abu Dhabi. www.irena.org/publications/2016/Oct/Renewable-Energy-in-Cities (accessed October 2021).

[71] Robinson, D. 2019. The Critical Role of Street Lighting in London's Smart City Project, NS Energy. www.nsenergybusiness.com/features/smart-city-street-lighting/ (accessed October 2021).

growing problem of electronic waste, 80% of which is dumped in landfills.[72] The pollutants from these products poison land, water, and people, often the poorest amongst us.[73] Yet electronic waste contains valuable materials like copper and gold which should facilitate recycling.[74] It would be suicidal for a natural ecology to dispose of precious materials like this.

Companies like *Rapanui*, which sells clothes made from recycled materials,[75] show a way forward, as does the city of Burlington, Vermont. It sources all of its energy from renewable sources, using solar panels, wind turbines, hydro-electric and biomass energy (from locally managed forests). It seeks to be carbon neutral and has developed the agriculture of its local region to support the city.[76] It is not a panacea because of the embedded energy and materials in the built environment of the city and other requirements for nonlocal components for high tech, but it is a pathfinder to the future. In the end, just as wealthy people need to use less water, they also need to use less energy. A mutualistic system would not expand its demands for power beyond what is sustainable.

EARTH. In natural ecosystems life is limited by what is available in the environment. Plants, for example, use materials like iron made available through the weathering of rocks, both locally, through soil weathering, and weathered and transported over longer distances into the oceans. In contrast, urban ecologies use materials that are sourced

---

[72] EPA (Environmental Protection Agency) 2020. Cleaning Up Electronic Waste (E-Waste). www.epa.gov/international-cooperation/cleaning-electronic-waste-e-waste (accessed October 2021).

[73] Smith, A., Hall-Pogar, T. 2015. E-Waste: Hidden dangers of technology. Purdue University Global. www.purdueglobal.edu/blog/information-technology/ewaste-hidden-dangers/ (accessed October 2021).

[74] Fu, J., Zhang, H., Zhang, A., Jiang, G. 2018. E-waste recycling in China: a challenging field. *Environmental Science and Technology* 52, 6727–6728.

[75] https://rapanuiclothing.com/our-story/.

[76] www.politico.com/magazine/story/2016/11/burlington-what-works-green-energy-214463 (accessed October 2021).

globally, and the rate of consumption of these, like cement, is accelerating (Figure 12.2); perhaps 70% of this cement – scaled by energy consumption – is used to build urban structures each year. Much energy is expended in the excavation and processing of materials to make buildings and roads, and this means that new constructions have considerable "embedded energy" within them.

Cities have concentrated vast resources[77] that could be reused but often are disposed of. A mutualistic city seeks to enhance the lifespan of its structures and reduce embedded energy. Reuse can be good from a cultural perspective too, preserving old buildings gives people a sense of their history, and regenerates areas that are suffering urban decay. On the negative side, older buildings may be energy inefficient, and there may be technical problems in renovating them. But the positives of adaptive reuse can outweigh the negatives.[78]

A mutualistic city uses materials which store carbon[79] and reduces its reliance on cement.[80,81] The fabric of buildings can be recovered to make bricks out of waste material.[82] And plastics can be recovered to make materials for road surfaces.[83] But this is only part of the solution, because when the road surface wears out, it too will need to be recycled, whilst the surface leakage of plastics into the neighboring environment needs to be managed in a way that is not damaging. Systems of reuse

[77] J. Zalasiewicz, M. Williams, C. N. Waters, et al. 2016. Scale and diversity of the physical technosphere: a geological perspective. *The Anthropocene Review* 4, 9–22.

[78] Bullen, P.A., Love, P.E.D. 2010. The rhetoric of adaptive reuse or reality of demolition: views from the field. *Cities* 27, 215–224.

[79] www.urban-hub.com/cities/recyclable-architecture-changing-how-we-build-use-and-re-use-urban-structures/ (accessed October 2021).

[80] Aalto University. 2020. Building cities with wood would store half of cement industry's current carbon emissions. *ScienceDaily*. www.sciencedaily.com/releases/2020/11/201102110010.htm (accessed October 2021).

[81] International Living Future Institute supports the idea of regenerative buildings. https://living-future.org/ (accessed October 2021).

[82] Butler, L. 2016. Wastebasedbricks: laying the foundations for sustainable building. https://resource.co/article/wastebasedbricks-laying-foundations-sustainable-building-11520 (accessed October 2021).

[83] Santos, J., Pham, A., Stasinopoulos, P., Giustozzi, F. 2021. Recycling waste plastics in roads: a life-cycle assessment study using primary data. *Science of the Total Environment* 751, 141842.

must eventually evolve to resemble natural ecologies where decomposer organisms like fungi and bacteria break down existing redundant structures, like the body of a dead animal or plant, in this way releasing energy and nutrients for other life to grow. And whilst a tree is being decayed in this way, it continues to form a home for other plants and animals and can be reused for many years. Similarly derelict buildings and spaces could be allowed to decay, providing a habitat for plants and animals, and fostering biodiversity because of their inherently heterogeneous properties.[84] To facilitate this, a mutualistic city would foster a planning process that allows people and buildings to migrate across the landscape giving time for natural regeneration.

LIFE. The ability of ecosystems to adapt to environmental change relies on inter-relationships between species developed over thousands or millions of years. Humans have damaged these relationships, halving the mass of life over the past 10 millennia by cutting down trees[85] and significantly reducing the diversity of species.[86] This threatens the stability of many ecosystems from the Gulf of Mexico to the forests of Amazonia. Cities are implicated in these processes.[87] As much as 290,000 km^2 of habitat may be lost to city growth through the first three decades of the twenty-first century (Figure 12.2), an area equivalent to the combined landmass of Britain and Ireland. Despite these losses, all is not lost. Cities may be a refuge for pollinating insects such as bees,[88] which can be more abundant and diverse in urban areas due to the richness of plants in gardens and the increasing loss of bees in the

[84] Flyn, C. 2019. Life amid the ruins: abandoned places as islands of biodiversity. https://harcruins.wixsite.com/ruinationanddecay/post/life-amid-the-ruins-abandoned-places-as-islands-of-biodiversity (accessed October 2021).

[85] Bar-On, Y.M., Phillips, R., Milo, R. 2018. The biomass distribution on Earth. *PNAS* 115, 6506–6511.

[86] Ceballos, G., Ehrlich, P.R., Barnosky, A.D., et al. 2015. Accelerated modern human-induced species losses: Entering the sixth mass extinction. *Science Advances* 1, e1400253.

[87] McDonald, R.I., Mansur, A.V., Ascensão, F., et al. 2020. Research gaps in knowledge of the impact of urban growth on biodiversity. *Nature Sustainability*, 3, 16–24.

[88] Hall, D.M., Camilo, G.R., Tonietto, R.K., et al. 2017. The city as a refuge for insect pollinators. *Conservation Biology* 31(1), 24–29.

countryside due to the pesticides and herbicides of nonorganic farming and big agriculture's creation of vast, monoculture landscapes.[89] Fostering biodiversity in cities may help offset, at least slightly, these losses.

In natural ecosystems an oak tree may support over 2000 species.[90] And yet many of the structures we build, of glass, concrete, and steel, are poor surfaces for other organisms, and interfere with their existence. The introduction of street-lighting in cities, for example, disrupts the behavior of nocturnal seed dispersers and insect-feeders like bats, and may be implicated in reduced forest resilience.[91] A mutualistic city reverses these trends. It would make dark spaces at night that did not disrupt the diurnal rhythms of other creatures. It would create areas for other organisms to occupy by expanding green space, connecting habitats, and providing a greater range of environments.[92]

Bats have shared our homes for millennia,[93] but in recent decades the increasingly sealed nature of buildings may be reducing roosting availability for species that have adapted to live in cities.[94] A mutualistic city plans for co-habitation by purposefully incorporating features such as bat and bird bricks,[95] providing permanent artificial roosting space within the structure. It builds houses that shelter both humans and nonhumans.

---

[89] Baldock, K.C., Goddard, M.A., Hicks, D.M., et al. 2015. Where is the UK's pollinator biodiversity? The importance of urban areas for flower-visiting insects. *Proceedings of the Royal Society B: Biological Sciences*, 282(1803), 20142849; Goddard, M.A., Dougill, A.J., Benton, T.G. 2010. Scaling up from gardens: biodiversity conservation in urban environments. *Trends in Ecology and Evolution* 25(2), 90–98.

[90] Mitchell, R.J. 2019. Collapsing foundations: the ecology of the British oak, implications of its decline and mitigation options. *Biological Conservation* 233, 316–327.

[91] Gaston, K.J., Visser, M.E., Hölker, F. 2015 The biological impacts of artificial light at night: the research challenge. *Philosophical Transactions of the Royal Society B* 370, 20140133.

[92] Lepczyk, C.A., Aronson, M.F.J., Evans, K.L., et al. 2017. Biodiversity in the city: fundamental questions for understanding the ecology of urban green spaces for biodiversity conservation. *BioScience* 67, 799–807.

[93] Voigt C.C., Phelps, K.L., Aguirre, L.F., et al. 2016. Bats and buildings: the conservation of synanthropic bats. In: Voigt C., Kingston T. (eds.) *Bats in the Anthropocene: Conservation of Bats in a Changing World*. Springer, Cham, Switzerland.

[94] Russo, D., Ancillotto, L. 2015. Sensitivity of bats to urbanization: a review. *Mammalian Biology* 80(3), 205–212.

[95] These incorporate space for roosting.

Humans benefit from this relationship in the form of well-being, with a recent study indicating that 75% of occupants with roosting bricks felt positively towards them.[96] And a mutualistic city encourages green infrastructure such as flower-rich green roofs[97] and wildlife-friendly gardens which facilitate occupation by other species through bird feed, bird boxes, and wildflowers, with beneficial effects on human well-being and biodiversity.[98]

The urban landscape is of course a natural habitat for species that already co-habit with humans, but the reduced human activity as a result of the global Covid-19 pandemic released a specific disturbance pressure and showed that unexpected biodiversity, such as deer, could also occupy the urban space. Such patterns would be enhanced by a mutualistic city by reducing hard barriers such as walls and fences, that prevent movement across the landscape, whether it simply be access holes or wider corridors.[99] In a mutualistic city, the natural dynamics of predator and prey interactions – peregrines upon pigeons – will occur more readily.[100]

There are wider advantages to embedding biodiversity in cities. Trees, for example, have a positive benefit on local climate, reducing the heat island effect, and mitigating adverse weather effects such as flooding.[101] Although some studies have shown that a city's vegetation has a negligible impact on carbon capture,[102] others have shown that urban

[96] Roberts, S. 2017. The attitudes of housing occupants to integral bird and bat boxes. MSc thesis, University of Gloucestershire.

[97] Filazzola, A., Shrestha, N., MacIvor, J.S. 2019. The contribution of constructed green infrastructure to urban biodiversity: a synthesis and meta-analysis. *Journal of Applied Ecology* 56, 2131–2143.

[98] Davies, Z.G., Fuller, R.A., Loram, A., et al. 2009. A national scale inventory of resource provision for biodiversity within domestic gardens. *Biological Conservation* 142(4), 761–771.

[99] www.hedgehogstreet.org/ (accessed October 2021).

[100] Fleming, P.A., Bateman, P.W. 2018 Novel predation opportunities in anthropogenic landscapes. *Animal Behaviour* 138, 145–155.

[101] Livesley, S.J. McPherson, G.M., Calfapietra, C. 2016. The urban forest and ecosystem services: impacts on urban water, heat, and pollution cycles at the tree, street and city scale. *Journal of Environmental Quality* 45, 119–124.

[102] Velasco, E., Roth, M., Norford, L., Molina, L.T. 2016. Does urban vegetation enhance carbon sequestration. *Landscape and Urban Planning* 148, 99–107.

vegetation may capture a small – but significant – part of the CO_2 released by urban metabolism.[103] And in coastal settlements already subject to marine ingress as a result of rising sea level, vegetation is protective, for example the restoration of mangrove forests can help preserve coastlines, regenerate biodiversity, and enhance the livelihoods of human settlements at the coast.[104]

Richer biodiversity means more resilient ecosystems; healthier ecosystems mean healthier humans.[105] A mutualistic city's green space goes far beyond protecting the local environment. If carefully planned[106] it provides a huge range of settings for life to diversify into, and food, medicine, and general well-being for its human inhabitants.[107] In a mutualistic city there will be equal sharing and exposure to wildlife experiences, and this will reconnect people with the nonhuman part of nature.[108]

Blending into its immediate hinterlands, the mutualistic city's benefits spread well beyond its borders. Minimizing the materials – both biological and nonbiological – that it draws from distant places, it serves the global good.

AIR. People have caused rapid change to the air from industrial, construction, agricultural, and deforestation processes that release CO_2, most over the past 70 years (Figure 12.2).[109] Atmospheric CO_2 (above 410 parts per million), is at its highest level for 3 million years, compared to 280 ppm at

---

[103] Chen, W.Y. 2015. The role of urban green infrastructure in offsetting carbon emissions in 35 major Chinese cities: a nationwide estimate. *Cities* 44, 112–120.

[104] Building with Nature Indonesia www.ecoshape.org/en/projects/building-with-nature-indonesia/ (accessed October 2021).

[105] Tallavaara, M., Eronen, J.T., Luoto, M. 2018. Productivity, biodiversity, and pathogens influence the global hunter-gatherer population density. *PNAS* 115, 1232–1237.

[106] Hostetler, M., Allen, W., Meurk, C. 2011. Conserving urban biodiversity? Creating green infrastructure is only the first step. *Landscape and Urban Planning* 100, 369–71.

[107] You, Y., Pan, S. 2020. Urban vegetation slows down the spread of coronavirus (COVID-19) in the United States. *Geophysical Research Letters* 47(18), e89286.

[108] Soga, M., Gaston, K.J. 2016. Extinction of experience: the loss of human–nature interactions. *Frontiers in Ecology and the Environment* 14(2), 94–101.

[109] Syvitski, J., Waters, C. N., Day, J., et al. 2020. Extraordinary human energy consumption and resultant geological impacts beginning around 1950 CE initiated the proposed Anthropocene Epoch. *Communications Earth and Environment* 1, 32.

the beginning of the Industrial Revolution, causing global warming and the many issues that arise from this. Urbanization and industrialization produce significant pollutants like ozone, sulfur dioxide, volatile organic compounds, and tiny particulate matter (known as PM).[110] Exposure to PM, especially the finer particles, is acute in many developing countries and remains a significant health problem throughout the world.[111] This especially impacts the urban poor, who are more vulnerable due to poor housing and are disproportionately harmed by air pollutants.

A mutualistic city actively reduces or captures carbon by sourcing all of its energy from renewable sources, and uses materials that store carbon, like wood. Major cities like London, Los Angeles, and Delhi could reduce their greenhouse gas emissions by 87% and small airborne particles (PMs) by nearly 50%[112] through changes in transport infrastructure, industrial processes, and domestic energy use. This is a major task for London where air pollution has improved for a century, but a greater task for Delhi which is earlier in its evolution towards a more environmentally sustainable state.[113] In the interim, where pollutants will still be produced, the mutualistic city captures these from the atmosphere in a way that makes them useful.[114] Trees can scrub the atmosphere of pollution like PM which attach to leaves and then are washed away in rainwater.[115,116] And the mutualistic city captures the rainwater and its contained particles and recycles the leaf-fall.

---

[110] These are small airborne particles: $PM_{2.5}$, for example, is material less than 2.5 microns diameter.

[111] Ritchie, H., Roser, M. 2019. Outdoor air pollution. https://ourworldindata.org/outdoor-air-pollution (accessed October 2021).

[112] https://ccacoalition.org/en/news/35-cities-unite-clean-air-their-citizens-breathe-protecting-health-millions (accessed October 2021).

[113] Ritchie, H., Roser, M. 2019. Outdoor air pollution. https://ourworldindata.org/outdoor-air-pollution (accessed October 2021).

[114] e.g., Li, J., Han, X., Zhang, X., et al. 2019. Capture of nitrogen dioxide and conversion to nitric acid in a porous metal–organic framework. *Nature Chemistry* 11(12), 1085.

[115] www.bbc.com/future/article/20200504-which-trees-reduce-air-pollution-best (accessed October 2021).

[116] Maher, B.A., Ahmed, I.A.M., Davison, B., Karloukovski, V., Clarke, R. 2013. Impact of roadside tree lines on indoor concentrations of traffic-derived particulate matter. *Environmental Science and Technology* 47(23), 13737–13744.

CONCLUSIONS

Will Steffen's essay (Chapter 3) traces the birth of the Earth System concept through the sequence of images that helped scientists to understand our planet as a single integrated whole. From the perspective of Earth System scientists, organic life and nonorganic matter are ultimately inseparable, interacting constantly. The bounteous Holocene world we once inhabited was the happy result of a relatively stable Earth System. Now, the forces of the Anthropocene have destabilized the Earth System, pushing it along a dangerous trajectory. Cities today are a major engine of that destabilization, their dense and rapidly growing human populations, their needs for food, water, materials, energy, and all else are accelerating. Here, we've sketched out another kind of city, one which could help restabilize the Earth System. These mutualistic cities recreate beneficial, cyclical exchanges between humans and nonhuman nature and in so doing help slow the acceleration toward tipping points of no return. They would be made from materials that grow and decay, their buildings and their devices would not just conserve energy but capture and recycle it. Most especially they would emulate natural ecosystems, not exceeding the energy and nutrients of their environment, limiting human population and consumption. And they would give everyone a voice and a stake in making these urban areas flourish. Building such cities is a tremendous challenge. Critics – and we ourselves – can think of a thousand reasons why such cities are impossible. Our political and economic systems require nearly total transformation and, as Manuel Arias-Maldonado explains in Chapter 7, we still struggle to envision that change. But on the journey to a mutualistic city some steps could be achieved by careful zoning policies, by incentivizing builders to recycle materials and to adopt designs that are more attuned to local ecologies,[117] and by encouraging space for nonhuman life, ensuring, for example, that buildings allow for nesting and migration. What is the alternative? Captain Elon's spaceship in Clive Hamilton's story (Chapter 11) isn't an attractive option. Even if the boldest plan to escape

---

[117] Seyfang, G. 2009. Community action for sustainable housing: building a low carbon future. *Energy Policy* 38, 7624–7633.

our devastated planet succeeded, the vast majority of us would be left behind. Better to wisely confront our challenges here. In our rapidly changing world, recognizing that we will always live, for better or worse, within the Earth System is the first step. Learning to live mutualistically within that system is the second.

Afterword

Jürgen Renn and Christoph Rosol

Possibly the most important element in creating the Anthropocene is the evolution of knowledge, since it was knowledge that provided humanity with the tools to change the Earth System. As we have come to know more and more, we have gained powers that we are only now beginning to understand. As this book shows, many kinds of knowledge are also essential to understanding and confronting the Anthropocene, and this brief afterword takes up this central theme.

Historians of knowledge, if they were to approach the Anthropocene like any other problem, would be expected to ask a certain set of questions. They would ask when it was that science and technology began to drive the Anthropocene. They would explore the interaction of societal structures and knowledge systems under different historical and cultural circumstances to identify the historical processes that have amplified science's planetary impact. And they would interrogate how we have come to know about, and how we monitor, these grave changes. However, the challenge of the Anthropocene goes beyond the exploration of a new topic and the fine-tuning of a methodological approach.

There is knowledge *of* the Anthropocene: the varied ways in which we know about a fundamental shift in planetary-wide affairs in the more or less recent past. And there is also knowledge *in* the Anthropocene: the new modes of knowing and doing which in themselves will influence the direction of the Anthropocene. To catalyze action, we have to recast our understanding of the historical evolution and future possibilities of knowledge. In practice, this means that we need to build bridges among varied knowledge systems and many disciplines, so as to counter what has become an increasing fragmentation of knowledge. This involves overcoming the rift between the "soft" humanities and the "hard" natural sciences and engaging other, non-Western forms of knowledge.

The Anthropocene offers us an opportunity to do things differently. The production of knowledge in the future will need to proceed with greater direction and purpose. This means acting with greater responsibility and care, and learning to keep both local perspectives and the whole planetary system in mind, as well as broader historical contexts and solution-oriented applications. Extending our inquiries to the present and to the future, we need to identify the current analytical and interpretative approaches to studying the complex interactions and coevolutionary dynamics that have led the Earth onto an Anthropocene path. How do we combine and apply their insights to cope with its further unfolding and rapid intensification?

Science, technology, history, the humanities and social sciences, arts, and letters, as put together in this volume, are all essential to this new form of knowledge in action. The Anthropocene calls for opening up perspectives rather than reducing or collapsing them into one another. It calls for a plurality of knowledge, a "democracy of voices" as Julia Thomas calls it, that does not end up in a cacaphonic assemblage but is the harbinger for mutual understanding and collaboration about our shared predicament. The history of science and technology shows that it is in open spaces that critical work and disruptive innovation develops, as the example of the Humboldtian enlightenment shows. The outcome will not be a single unified type of knowledge, but instead a stimulus for new, Anthropocene-adequate forms of intellectual and scientific inquiry.

At the Max Planck Institute for the History of Science (MPIWG) in Berlin, where we both work, we have made reorienting knowledge our goal. Over the past decade and through a multitude of novel collaborations and joint programs with scientists, humanities scholars, artists, and activists, we came to realize how necessary – and how difficult – it is to overcome borders not only between the natural and the human sciences but between different forms of knowledge production and dissemination.

One focus of attention is the ongoing global energy transition, where historical analyses of technological and cultural path dependencies combine with policy-oriented frameworks. Transforming our energy systems is less about technological change than it is about fundamentally altering the way we live. As Amitav Ghosh's parable "The Ascent of the Anthropoi" (Chapter 6) indicates, almost all have been drawn into the assault on the living mountain, embracing industrialized modes of consumption, but a few continue to resist the allure of perpetual growth, and call for other visions of the good life.

Reorienting research to a systemic understanding of the interdependent and highly dynamic interplay between the human and the Earth is something we have come to label "geoanthropology." It merges Earth System research with cultural theories and histories of socio-material, political, and informational flows to form a new discipline. Cast into a multidisciplinary research framework that studies the complex coevolution of natural systems and human norms, geoanthropology aims to investigate the concrete human-created destabilization of the Earth System and the biosphere, the limits of socio-ecological carrying capacities, possible system thresholds, as well as necessary socio-economic and cultural reaction times. With its focus on specific temporalities and critical dynamics, geoanthropology presents another opportunity to expand current, highly specialized knowledge domains, whether these apply to the study of human history, atmospheric processes or extinction cascades, and put them in conversation with one another. This will allow for a more comprehensive understanding of the reciprocal logics between the changes in the bio-physical, socio-cultural, and technological worlds.

Clive Hamilton gives us searing vision of a doomed mission to Mars in the hope that we will turn away from hubris and towards the mutualism of Mark Williams' thriving cities of the near future. Human civilization clearly is on a dangerous path and there is only limited time for concerted action. Societies will have to make critical if not grave decisions over the next few years, and in as fair and globally just a way as possible.

Given the complexity and urgency of the problem, this is an ambitious task which, also at an intellectual level, must go beyond proposals directed at single facets of a problem. In the Anthropocene, there is a need for new forms of knowledge and knowledge production that take the connectedness and planetary feedbacks of all human activities as their objects of analysis. Such a combined framework will, we hope, allow a productive codevelopment of both diagnosis and treatment.

Biographies of Chapter Contributors

Manuel Arias-Maldonado is Full Professor in Political Science at the University of Málaga, Spain. Having being raised near the Mediterranean shores himself, he has witnessed throughout the years subtle changes in the local environment and thus felt the need to reflect upon them. He has written extensively on environmental political theory, but has also been drawn to topics such as political liberalism, political emotions, populism, and cinema. He is the author of *Real Green: Sustainability after the End of Nature* (Ashgate 2012 and Routledge 2016) and *Environment and Society: Socionatural Relations in the Anthropocene* (Springer 2015), as well as co-editor of *Rethinking the Environment for the Anthropocene: Political Theory and Socionatural Relations in the New Geological Epoch* (Routledge 2019). He has been a Fulbright scholar in Berkeley and a visiting researcher in the Rachel Carson Center of Munich. He wishes to make at least a modest contribution to a sustainable, more fair, and free society.

Dominic Boyer is a writer, media maker, and anthropologist. He has held teaching positions at the University of Chicago, Cornell University, and Rice University and been the recipient of grants and fellowships from the National Science Foundation, the Alexander von Humboldt Foundation, Fulbright, SSRC, and the Wenner-Gren Foundation. His work focuses on the energy and environmental challenges of our era, particularly the need to decarbonize society and to break the ecocidal trajectory of global capitalism. He has recently helped lead research projects on the contentious politics of wind power development in Mexico and on the emotional impact of catastrophic flooding in Houston. He is increasingly interested in electric futures across the world and on amphibious urbanism in coastal cities experiencing sea level rise. In the past decade, he has curated environmental art exhibitions, produced podcasts, made a documentary film, and, together with his partner in all things, Cymene Howe, installed the world's first memorial to a glacier fallen to climate change. Current creative projects include a television series about petroculture, a non-academic book about Iceland's disappearing glaciers and a game about sentient petroleum. During 2021 he held an artist residency at The Factory in Djúpavík, Iceland, and he will be a Berggruen Institute Fellow in Los Angeles during 2021–22.

Gavin Brown is a Visiting Professor in Geography at The University of Sheffield. Prior to that, he was Professor of Political Geography and Sexualities at the University of Leicester, where he worked from 2007 until 2021. Gavin has wide-ranging research interests, having written extensively about the geographies of sexualities and LGBTQ people's lives, as well as protest movements and solidarity, for more than two decades. Crossing both of these research areas is an interest in critical geopolitics and the importance of making visible diverse economic practices that exist alongside and within hegemonic forms of neoliberal capitalism. His attention to these diverse economic practices is always imbued with an ethical commitment to exploring how they might be expanded to meet human needs in ways that do less harm to the planet and other beings. He is the author or editor of five books, including *Youth Activism and Solidarity: The Non-stop Picket against Apartheid* (Routledge 2017), *Protest Camps in International Context* (Policy Press 2017), and *The Routledge Research Companion to Geographies of Sex and Sexualities* (Routledge 2016). He is currently working on two new projects: the first is a reconsideration of key South African anti-apartheid campaigners as geopolitical theorists; the second is a multi-sited ethnography of PrEP (pre-exposure prophylaxis against HIV infection).

Kate Brown is the Thomas M. Siebel Distinguished Professor in the History of Science at the Massachusetts Institute of Technology. She grew up in the de-industrializing Midwest and since has had an interest in modernist wastelands. She is the author of the prize-winning histories *Plutopia: Nuclear Families in Atomic Cities and the Great Soviet and American Plutonium Disasters* (Oxford 2013) and *A Biography of No Place: From Ethnic Borderland to Soviet Heartland* (Harvard 2004). Brown was a 2009 Guggenheim Fellow. Her work has also been supported by the Carnegie Foundation, the NEH, ACLS, IREX, and the American Academy of Berlin, among others. Her latest book, *Manual for Survival: A Chernobyl Guide to the Future* was published in 2019 by Norton (US), Penguin Lane (UK), Czarne

(Poland), Capitán Swing (Spanish). In 2020, it was translated into Ukrainian, Russian, Czech, Slovak, Lithuanian, French, Chinese, and Korean.

Moya Burns is an ecologist interested in understanding how humans have altered the environment, but more importantly, how we can co-exist with greater levels of biodiversity in the future. Her research has ranged from studying the impacts of fragmentation on sub-tropical rainforests in Australia, to investigating the role of climate change in altering ecosystems of the Peruvian Amazon. In recent years, Moya's work has increasingly focused on improving biodiversity in urban areas, including projects investigating the impacts of artificial lighting on mammals and improving roadside verges for pollinating insects. Moya has worked within the charitable, private, and governmental sectors, as well as academia, which means she brings to her work a holistic understanding of the viewpoints of the multiple stakeholders involved in creating biodiverse landscapes of the future. When not pondering ecology, Moya can be found walking, cycling, and running in the National Forest and the Peak District.

Dipesh Chakraberty is the Lawrence A. Kimpton Distinguished Service Professor of History and South Asian Languages and Civilizations at the University of Chicago. He was a founding member of the editorial collective of *Subaltern Studies*, a founding editor of *Postcolonial Studies*, and is a Consulting Editor of *Critical Inquiry*. Among his publications are *The Climate of History in a Planetary Age* (2021) and *Provincializing Europe: Postcolonial Thought and Historical Difference* (2000; 2008).

John Clarkson is a conservationist who has been lucky enough to experience the magnificence of wildlife – from the very first adult large blue butterfly to emerge at a reintroduction site in Somerset to a pod of killer whales marauding through the coastal waters off Victoria Island – and by contrast to run in the foothills of the Andes with Mapuche farmers and to share roti with Malay foresters. He has mainly worked for local voluntary conservation organizations across Britain but also spent time teaching and researching at a university in the East Midlands of England, all the while trying to save species (whether by influencing policy or undertaking management) and to encourage others to do so as well. Learning to live with alpacas and chickens more recently has only heightened his sense of a need for humans to be more respectful of the other organisms with which we share this one very special rock.

Amitav Ghosh was born in Calcutta and grew up in India, Bangladesh, and Sri Lanka. He is the author of two books of non-fiction, a collection of essays and ten novels. His books have won many prizes and he holds four honorary doctorates. His work has been translated into more than 30 languages and he has served on the Jury of the Locarno and Venice film festivals. In 2018 he became the first English-language writer to receive India's highest literary honor, the Jnanpith Award. His most recent publication is *Jungle Nama*, an adaptation of a legend from the Sundarban, with artwork by Salman Toor. His new book, *The Nutmeg's Curse; Parables for a Planet in Crisis*, a work of non-fiction, was published by the University of Chicago Press in October 2021. He lives in Brooklyn, New York, with his wife, the writer Deborah Baker.

Clive Hamilton lives on one of the songlines of the Ngunnawal people, the traditional owners of the Canberra region, where he was born and grew up and where the life-force of the country entered into him, unnoticed. He is therefore among the friends of the Earth, baffled by the technofixers and the masters of the universe. He has written several books about climate change and the Anthropocene, including the "trilogy" *Requiem for a Species: Why We Resist the Truth About Climate Change* (Earthscan, 2010), *Earthmasters: The Dawn of the Age of Climate Engineering* (Yale University Press, 2015), and *Defiant Earth: The Fate of Humans in the Anthropocene* (Polity, 2017). After many years running a think tank, he became professor of public ethics at Charles Sturt University in Canberra. He has held various visiting academic positions, including at the University of Oxford, Sciences Po, and Yale University, and his opinions have been published in the *New York Times, Foreign Affairs, Nature, Scientific American*, and the *Guardian*, all of which might look impressive, except that as each year passes he wonders whether it was all ephemeral and meaningless.

A proud native Oklahoman, **Kyle Harper** is the G.T. and Libby Blankenship Chair in the History of Liberty, Professor of Classics and Letters, Senior Advisor to the President, and Provost Emeritus at his *alma mater*, the University of Oklahoma. An economic and environmental historian who specializes in the ancient world, Harper is the author of four books. His first book, *Slavery in the Late Roman World*, was published in 2011 and awarded the James Henry Breasted Prize. His second book, *From Shame to Sin: The Christian Transformation of Sexual Morality*, appeared in 2013 and received the Award for Excellence in Historical Studies from the American Academy of Religion. His third book, *The Fate of Rome:*

Climate, Disease, and the End of an Empire, was first published in 2017 and subsequently translated into 12 languages. Harper's fourth book, *Plagues Upon the Earth: Disease and the Course of Human History*, is a global history of infectious disease spanning from human origins to COVID-19. It draws from a range of disciplines, including the natural sciences, to tell the story of humanity's long and distinctive struggle with pathogenic microbes. Harper's work as a scholar tries to integrate the natural sciences, social sciences, and humanities to deepen our understanding of human expansion as a planetary force.

Cymene Howe has a longstanding interest in how people and environments co-create each other – an inheritance from her eco-radical grandma. Doing field research in the Americas (Nicaragua, Mexico, United States) and now in the Arctic (Iceland, Greenland), she has been witnessing the imprints of the Anthropocene everywhere. Her current project focuses on how melting ice in the Arctic affects local populations and how that melted ice also impacts coastal communities "downstream" in both the USA and Southern Africa. As a Professor of Anthropology at Rice University, she regularly publishes in transdisciplinary journals, books, and other media forms. Her books *Intimate Activism* and *Ecologics: Wind and Power in the Anthropocene* were both published with Duke University Press. Two other collections *Anthropocene Unseen: A Lexicon* (Punctum 2020) and *The Johns Hopkins Guide to Critical and Cultural Theory* (Johns Hopkins University Press 2012) are co-edited projects meant to move discussions forward in both social theory and critical ecologies. Cymene is the co-host of the *Cultures of Energy* podcast – a series of conversations on environmental precarity and responses to it. She also co-produced the documentary film *Not OK: A Little Movie about a Small Glacier at the End of the World* (2018) and, with Dominic Boyer, created the world's first funeral for a glacier fallen to climate change. The Okjökull memorial event in Iceland served as a global call to action and in memory of a world rapidly melting away. Currently, she is working on a new glacial installation and a book about living with precarity at the end of the world.

Francine McCarthy is Professor of Earth Sciences, Associate Member of Biological Sciences, and Core Member of Environmental Sustainability at Brock University. Its campus lies in the Niagara Escarpment UNESCO World Biosphere Reserve, roughly an 80 km hike along the Bruce Trail from Crawford Lake whose unique sedimentary environment records annual environmental change over the past 1000 years. This is the site that she and more than 20 researchers from several Canadian universities have been studying over the past three years to assess its potential to define a new interval of geologic time defined by over-whelming anthropogenically driven changes to Earth systems – the Anthropocene Epoch. She has published more than 50 refereed journal articles on the use of microfossils in marine and freshwater sediments to reconstruct past environmental change. Like Julia Adeney Thomas, but coming at it from the opposite perspective, she seeks to bridge the divide between the humanities and the sciences to address our global environmental crisis.

Minal Patak works as a Senior Scientist in Working Group III of the Intergovernmental Panel on Climate Change (IPCC). Working Group III covers the mitigation of climate change, i.e. methods for reducing emissions of green-house gases and enhancing atmospheric sinks. She was an author on two recent IPCC Special Reports – "Global Warming of 1.5C" and "Climate Change and Land" and is the co-editor on the forthcoming Sixth Assessment Report of the IPCC in 2022. She heads the South Asia Hub of the global Urban Climate Change Research Network. Having lived and worked in Ahmedabad, a rapidly growing city in India and having been on the frontlines of global climate change assessments, she feels strongly about the urgency of implementing and upscaling solutions that address climate change, development, and equity. In an attempt to make science accessible for all, she regularly hosts talks for local government officials, industry, NGOs, and young students. She is a Visiting Researcher at Imperial College London and has held visiting scholar positions at the Department of Urban Studies and Planning, Massachusetts Institute of Technology and Universiti Teknologi Malaysia, Johor Bahru.

Jürgen Renn is a director at the Max Planck Institute for the History of Science (MPIWG). His research concerns long-term developments in knowledge, espe-cially the globalization processes and historical dynamics that led to the Anthropocene. On the basis of this research, he developed a theory of the evolution of knowledge, which considers cognitive dynamics as well as social contexts. Jürgen Renn has promoted the communication of scientific knowledge through exhibitions, newspaper articles, television broadcasts, and interviews. In addition, he has been involved in the sustainability debate at the interface between science and politics. His recent book, *The Evolution of Knowledge: Rethinking Science for the Anthropocene* (2020), examines the role of knowledge in global transformations going back to the dawn of civilization while providing vital perspectives on the complex challenges confronting us today.

Christoph Rosol is a historian of climate science and media technology committed to forging communities in which multidisciplinary and collaborative Anthropocene research can flourish. He has been a member of the curatorial team at the Haus der Kulturen der Welt (HKW) since the inception of its Anthropocene programs. He also established and now leads the research cluster *Anthropocene Formations* at the Max Planck Institute for the History of Science (MPIWG). When this work started in 2012, these double positions felt schizophrenic. Now, after 10 years, working both as a curator and as a researcher feels like an adjustment to the new necessity for more permeable institutional boundaries. Christoph also co-leads with curator Katrin Klingan the *Anthropocene Curriculum*, an international, collaborative platform for Anthropocene research, education, arts and activism which models cross-disciplinary work.

Bernd Scherer grew up in the hilly parts of the Saarland in South-West Germany. His small village was surrounded by forests and extended meadows. The childhood experiences of nature raised his awareness of environmental changes and inspired him to several projects, of which the "Anthropocene-Project" at HKW became the most important. He has served as Director of Haus der Kulturen der Welt (HKW) in Berlin since 2006 and has held an honorary professorship at the Institute for European Ethnology at Humboldt University in Berlin since 2011. The main areas of his work are philosophy, semiotics, aesthetics, and intercultural questions. He has initiated and headed a series of international cultural projects, including "Über Lebenskunst" (2010–2011), a project of the German Federal Cultural Foundation in cooperation with HKW. Since 2012, Scherer has headed "The Anthropocene Project" and, since 2014, the project "100 Years of Now," both at HKW. As part of the latter project he curated the "Dictionary of Now." In addition, he directs the conceptual development of HKW's third large-scale project, "The New Alphabet." During his tenure at HKW, Scherer has guided its conceptual development from an institution that presented non-European cultures into one dedicated to "curating ideas in the making" in a world that is changing not only globally, but also in planetary terms.

Will Steffen is an Earth System scientist whose career has focused on how our planet operates as a single, interconnected system and how humans are changing the trajectory of the Earth System. In his journey into the Anthropocene, Steffen has climbed to 7000 metres in the Himalaya, participated in Carnival dances in the depths of the Brazilian Amazon, accompanied the King of Sweden to the Greenland ice sheet, and witnessed a Mafia murder in Siberia. He has also found a bit of time to make some contributions to the Anthropocene literature. Steffen led the synthesis project of the International Geosphere-Biosphere Programme (IGBP) that produced the book *Global Change and the Earth System: A Planet Under Pressure* (2004). He has co-authored numerous articles on the Anthropocene, including an oft-cited paper "The Anthropocene: Are humans now overwhelming the great forces of Nature?," with Paul Crutzen, who introduced the term and concept of the Anthropocene, and eminent historian John McNeill. In 2020 Steffen and colleagues published a paper, "The emergence and evolution of Earth System science," that tracked the origins and development of this rather recent area of integrative science. He is a member of the Anthropocene Working Group and is an Emeritus Professor at the Australian National University in Canberra.

Julia Adeney Thomas spent her childhood in the coal country of southwest Virginia. Her heart remains in those Appalachian mountains even as she's come to love other places too. Japan is one such place, and, as an intellectual historian of Japan, she's written about concepts of nature, political thought, historiography, and photography as a political practice. But these days, the Anthropocene preoccupies her both as a terrifying reality and an intellectual conundrum. Working with Mark Williams and Jan Zalasiewicz on *The Anthropocene: A Multidisciplinary Approach* (Polity Press, 2020) proved to be a steep but joyous learning curve. Other publications include *Reconfiguring Modernity: Concepts of Nature in Japanese Political Ideology* (University of California Press, 2002, winner of the AHA John K. Fairbank Prize), *Japan at Nature's Edge: The Environmental Context of a Global Power* (University of Hawai'i Press, 2013), *Rethinking Historical Distance* (Palgrave Macmillan, 2013), *Visualizing Fascism: The Twentieth-Century Rise of the Global Right* (Duke University Press, 2020), and *Strata and Three Stories* (Rachel Carson Center, 2020) as well as many articles including "History and biology in the Anthropocene: problems of scale, problems of value" (*American Historical Review*, 2014). She is currently working on *The Historian's Task in the Anthropocene* (under contract, Princeton University Press). With colleagues around the world, Julia seeks to bring the humanities, social sciences, and sciences together to address our global environmental crisis. She teaches history at the University of Notre Dame.

Mark Williams is a palaeontologist at the University of Leicester. He grew up in the small town of Biddulph on the northern extremity of the Staffordshire coalfields in England and was lucky enough to be able to pick out the fossils of goniatites – ancient relatives of squid – from rocks cropping out just up the road from where he lived. That experience stayed with him through his life, and he has spent his career trying to explore the evolution of the biosphere over hundreds of millions of years, including in the Anthropocene. He has written several popular science books with his friend Jan Zalasiewicz and has been a member of the Anthropocene Working Group since its inception. He co-authored the book *The Anthropocene: A Multidisciplinary Approach.*

Jan Zalasiewicz is Emeritus Professor of Paleobiology at the University of Leicester. Growing up around the coal country of Lancashire, he is a generalist, with field geology, palaeontology, and stratigraphy somewhere in the mix, and longstanding enthusiasms for mud and mudrock, long-dead plankton, and the enigmas of ancient climates. Interest in human-made geology started by chance, then became inescapable. He has written books such as *The Earth After Us, The Planet in a Pebble,* and *Geology: A Very Short Introduction,* and (with Mark Williams) *Ocean Worlds* and *Skeletons.* With Julia Adeney Thomas and Mark Williams, he co-wrote *The Anthropocene: A Multidisciplinary Approach.* A member of the Anthropocene Working Group of the International Commission on Stratigraphy, he is a co-editor of its recent summary, *The Anthropocene as a Geological Time Unit: A Guide to the Scientific Evidence and Current Debate.*

Index

For EU product safety concerns, contact us at Calle de José Abascal, 56–1°,
28003 Madrid, Spain or eugpsr@cambridge.org.